Learn to Love Teaching Again

TIPS AND TOOLS FOR EVERY TEACHER

by Debbi Herrera, M. Ed.
with Brenda Cole, Ph. D.

Incentive Publications, Inc.
Nashville, Tennessee

Design and Illustrations by Kathleen Bullock
Cover by Robert Voigts
Edited by Marjorie Frank
Copyedited by Cary Grayson

ISBN 978-0-86530-050-7

1   2   3   4   5   6   7   8   9   10   14   13   12   11

Printed by Sheridan Books, Inc., Chelsea, Michigan • February 2011
www.incentivepublications.com

Contents

Introduction

To our readers,

A woman showed up at traffic court after receiving a ticket for speeding. "Your Honor," the woman said, "can we hurry this along? I am a school teacher and I have a classroom full of students waiting."

The judge leaned back in his seat. "A school teacher, eh?" he repeated, smiling broadly. "Well, I have been waiting for this day for a long time. You go sit down at that table in the corner and write 'I will not speed' five hundred times!"

It can be the best of jobs; it can be the worst of jobs.

You are an educator. I do not have to describe for you the thrilling anticipation of the first day of school, the feeling you get when you hold every student's attention while delivering a dynamic lesson, or the satisfaction of watching that struggling student when she or he finally achieves success. Who needs the ecstasy of reaching a mountain peak—when you can teach?

You are an educator. So, I don't need to present an argument for the idea that teachers (and administrators) are under tremendous stress. You know that well. You experience and observe it daily.

My colleague and co-writer, Dr. Brenda Cole, and I love teaching and teachers. But we are dismayed at the stress that chips away at our fellow educators—often resulting in fatigue, bitterness, physical ailments, despondency, and sometimes a change in careers. Here's how Brenda puts it:

As an assistant principal, I dealt with problems, issues, and complaints of veteran teachers for years. When I went back to school and researched for my dissertation on teachers' attitudes and stress levels, I realized that the majority of the complaints could be changed by the teachers themselves. They have to understand that they have control of their environments and their own attitudes toward those obstacles. When they do, the whole picture of the teacher-on-the-road-to-burnout can change.

It took only one semester of teaching prospective teachers for me to learn how excited and passionate they were. It made me recall the excitement I once had for teaching children—a profession that actually rejuvenated my spirit. I believe strongly that all veteran teachers can recapture their love for teaching and rekindle the kind of passion demonstrated by these fresh, eager, soon-to-be teachers.

We created a book with your rejuvenation as its primary goal.

Believing that the stress and discouragement can be reversed—and that the passion for teaching, though shaken, still lies dormant in most educators—the two of us looked for ways to help educators rekindle their love of the profession. We were disappointed to find few resources. So we set out to create a comprehensive source for educators, with input from those folks on the front lines—the teachers themselves, your colleagues.

I come to you with a background of classroom teacher, curriculum specialist, principal, educational author, and educational consultant. Dr. Cole is the kind of vibrant math and science teacher who can deliver a dynamic semester of physical science instruction with resources found at the grocery store. We both are so passionate about teaching that, even as administrators, we choose to continue working in classrooms. When she was a part of my administrative team for many years before going on to earn her doctorate degree, you could not wipe the silly grins off our faces as we passed each other in the school office—me dashing off to teach eighth grade language arts and Brenda running to the sixth grade science lab.

- We wanted to share workable, tested ideas from practicing teachers. So, for this book, we sought advice, comments, tips, and viewpoints from real teachers around the country. (You will find many of their names cited in the text, though some preferred to remain anonymous.) Examples in the book were taken from real settings in current classrooms. Chapters were constructed around issues that educators face on a daily basis.

- Laughter and joy must be a part of teaching. So, you will find jokes, anecdotes, and amusing stories interspersed with research, best practices, and plain old-fashioned common-sense solutions.

- Teachers need practical tools to do the kinds of things that make them more effective and their jobs more enjoyable. So we have ended each chapter with a hearty TOOLS section. These pages are full of ready-to-use tips and forms.

- Each chapter also contains one or more "Me Moments." These are suggestions for pampering yourself—strictly for the purpose of de-stressing and nurturing the human part of you that needs refreshing.

> **If you have lost your joy for teaching . . .**
> **If you can't quite remember why you entered the profession . . .**
> **If you have need of an injection of positive energy . . .**
> **Then this is the book for you.**

It can be the best of jobs; it can be the worst of jobs. But if you ask me, teachers are the luckiest people on earth; and we are all fortunate that there are those among us who answer the call to enter the teaching profession.

Debbi Herrera

Teacher Stress Is No Laughing Matter

You know you are a teacher under stress if you want to slap the next person who says, "Wow, it must be great to have your weekends and summers free!"

Julianna Dunn works hard to live up to everyone's standards. She wants the principal to be pleased with her work, the parents to say only nice things about her, and the third-graders to always remember her as their favorite teacher. She is the first to turn in lesson plans and volunteer for extra duties. Weekly, she writes personal notes home to each student's parents or guardians. On weekends, she spends hours creating enticing centers, projects, and treats for her students. **Ms. Dunn loves her job, but feels as if she is about to lose her mind.**

One thing Marita Russo likes about her job is the time she can spend with her own children. She often picks them up after school and brings them back to her classroom, where they finish their homework and help organize materials for her lessons the next day. School holidays and weekends give Marita time to comb through rummage sales and dollar stores for classroom items, her children in tow. **Mrs. Russo is pleased to have a profession that allows her to have this much time with her children; but why does she always feel so drained?**

Four years ago, Stephen Maas was delighted with his first group of middle-school students. This year, he has noticed a disturbing difference. Even after a full night's sleep, he feels tired in the mornings. He has begun to ignore the alarm clock and get to school late. Before classes start, Stephen lingers in the teachers' lounge over his coffee cup until the last possible moment. He is ashamed to admit that some mornings he assigns the first period students busy work to give himself time to drum up enthusiasm for the day. **Mr. Maas wonders: Where did all that excitement for teaching go?**

Do you see yourself in Ms. Dunn, who is trying to be all things to all people, or in Mrs. Russo, who has blurred the line between her personal and professional life, or in Mr. Maas, who has lost his excitement for teaching? Can you remember the day you became a teacher and the exciting promise the profession brought—how you thought you would change lives, how you looked forward to the gleam of students' faces as they looked up to you for guidance? Do you remember the thrill you felt when students walked out of your classroom knowing something new?

If those thoughts seem to be long-ago memories, if you find yourself exhausted and "run ragged" all of the time, or if you are considering a change of profession (to perhaps a master pumpkin grower), you could be overly stressed, headed toward teacher exhaustion, or smack dab in the middle of a full-blown teacher meltdown.

Losing the Love

Once you get that first job, a host of situations, programs, people, and processes turn into causes for disillusionment, disappointment, and distress. Just about all of these could fall into the category of "stressors." And too often, these realities build up an overload of true physical and mental stress—along with a gradual (or quick) slide away from the joys of teaching. Do you want a chance to hang onto or reclaim your passion for teaching? If so, you must pay attention to the stress in your life and gather some tools to help manage, diminish, or eliminate it.

How Did We Get On the Top Ten List?

Job stress and burnout are hot topics. All kinds of media and institutional sources research, analyze, and report the problem and its consequences. When researchers attempt to identify the highest-stress professions, educators are usually near the top of any list. These are just a few of many examples:

Top 10 Most Stressful Professions	Top 10 Most Stressful Jobs	Top 10 Most Stressful Fields
1. air traffic controller	1. **inner-city high school teacher**	1. information technology (IT)
2. police officer	2. police officer	2. medicine and other caring professions
3. **teacher**	3. miner	3. engineering
4. registered nurse	4. air traffic controller	4. sales and marketing
5. coal miner	5. medical intern	5. **education**
6. surgeon	6. stockbroker	6. finance
7. firefighter	7. journalist	7. human resources
8. correctional officer	8. customer service rep	8. operations
9. pilot	9. secretary	9. production
10. Marine	10. waiter	10. clerical
Carreercast.com, 2010	*Health Magazine, 2008*	*JobBank USA, 2010*

According to the report, "The Scale of Occupational Stress: further analysis of the impact of demographic factors and type of job" (2000), 41.5 percent of teachers reported themselves highly stressed. Without question, a teacher has one of the most important jobs in America today. As educators, we prepare our students for their futures, as well as our futures and the future of the society. However, today's teachers are faced with more complex challenges than at any other time in the history of education. The challenges that tax teachers every day can (and do) become overwhelming. Many teachers are stressed by the daily tasks of running their classrooms, because they have lost the belief that they can make a difference.

Why does the field of education consistently show up on these lists of most stressful professions? According to real teachers on the job, these are some of the factors that make the profession highly stressful:

- high expectations and low pay

- too much to do and too little time

- growing pressure from school administration and state education departments to show achievement results

- difficult relationships with parents

- the challenges of managing today's students

- increased emphasis on and importance of standardized tests

- seemingly endless, burdensome paperwork

- bureaucratic regulations, meetings, and requirements

- constant change in expectations and programs

- job insecurity and unexpected changes in assignments

- lack of career advancement opportunities

- loads of take-home work, making the balancing of home and work responsibilities exceptionally difficult

- lack of support

In addition, schools often lack the funds to support good instruction, so teachers end up using money from their own pockets for school supplies and instructional materials. This adds to their personal financial burden—which (since we know that the teaching profession doesn't pay all that well) adds fuel to personal stress. After years of buying supplies, many teachers feel resentful and angry at their school officials, school districts, and state legislators.

Learn To Love Teaching Again

Another trend disheartens teachers. For a long time, educators were admired and respected. Parents stood behind teachers, and children knew any disciplinary infraction at school would also be dealt with at home. But this is no longer the case. In recent decades, there has been a negative shift in the attitude of many Americans toward the teaching profession. So an already stressful situation is made worse by the lack of respect and appreciation.

On the Lookout for Stress

Stress is a reaction to an intimidating or threatening situation. A stressed reaction is a heightened physical reaction in which the body is prepared to take some sort of action to alleviate the pressure. That action may not be healthy (like reaching for a cigarette or a bag of potato chips), but a person is galvanized to do **something**. The education profession is loaded with stressors—situations, events, and feelings that induce the physical responses of stress. This fact has serious implications for the health and well-being of each educator, as well as for the students they teach and the families they touch.

Quick Teacher Stress Self-Check List

___ The school principal has your home, cell, and pager numbers on speed dial.

___ In order to live with you, your cat is on prescription anti-anxiety medication.

___ People have trouble understanding you, because you always talk through clenched teeth.

___ You don't have time to wait for a microwavable meal at lunchtime.

___ Your "To-Do" list includes weaning your four-year-old off decaf.

___ You need to consult your day-timer to see if you have time to take out the trash.

If you checked any of these items, you definitely need to explore some stress-reducing strategies.

Physical Changes Due to Stress

The body reacts to stress by a "fight-or-flight" response, sometimes called the *stress response*. So when a human perceives something as dangerous or as extremely stressful, physical changes occur immediately.

- The brain triggers the release of hormones that prepare the heart, lungs, skin, circulation, metabolism, and immune system to fight or flee approaching danger.

- Chemical messengers are activated, instigating an emotional response such as fear, anxiety, or anger.

- Chemicals suppress the area of the brain that controls short-term memory, concentration, inhibition, and rational thought—allowing the body's resources to concentrate on response to the danger.

- Heart rate and blood pressure increase instantly; the lungs take in more oxygen, causing breathing to quicken; the spleen releases more blood cells to help the blood transport more oxygen; and blood flow may increase from 300–400 percent.

- The fight-or-flight response system cuts off any body function not directly needed to repel the perceived threat. Instead of digesting your food in your stomach, growing fingernails or hair, or even fighting off cancer cells, the body focuses on getting out of the stress situation.

- The immune system is stimulated, redistributing white blood cells to fight off impending infection.

- Fluids are relocated from the throat and mouth. This causes the mouth to dry and makes it difficult to speak or make a sound (such as a scream). The throat spasms, making it hard to swallow.

- As blood is redirected from the skin to support the heart and muscle tissues, the skin can become cool and clammy. Sweat may break out.

- The scalp can tighten, which is why you see cartoons that show a person's hair standing up when they experience a stressful situation.

Menu for a Stress-Free Diet

I. BREAKFAST:
1/2 grapefruit
1 slice whole wheat toast
8 oz. skim milk

II. LUNCH:
4 oz. lean broiled chicken breast
1 cup steamed spinach
1 cup herb tea
1 Oreo cookie

III. MID-AFTERNOON SNACK:
The rest of Oreos in the package
2 pints Rocky Road ice cream, nuts, cherries, and whipped cream
1 jar hot fudge sauce

IV. DINNER:
2 loaves garlic bread
4 cans or 1 large pitcher Coke
1 large sausage, mushroom, and cheese pizza (extra cheese)
3 Snickers bars

V. LATE EVENING NEWS:
1 entire frozen Sara Lee cheesecake (eaten directly from the freezer)

Learn To Love Teaching Again

Effects of Ongoing Stress

The fight-or-flight response is a lifesaver in dangerous situations. But the body was not meant to live in that state. When this response is activated constantly (by continuous daily pressure of a stressful work environment), the option to fight or flee is minimized, if not eradicated. Chronic stress wreaks havoc on the body—leaving it less able to respond to a stressful situation appropriately and leading to a litany of health problems. When we function under chronic stress, we are then doing little that is healthy or helpful to our students, our families, and most importantly—ourselves.

A chronic release of stress hormones can destroy brain cells over time. This can also tax the immune system, cause depression, and interfere with mental processes. Living in a continuous fight-or-flight response mode with increased heart rate and blood pressure can harm the heart and cardiovascular system. Other serious health issues, such as diabetes and even cancer, are associated with the effects of stress (Brantley, 2003).

> ### Teacher-to-Teacher Tip
>
> "Before I became a teacher I wish I had known that it would be such a stressful job! So I suggest that you make a point of planning some 'down time' for yourself during the day— even if it is just for a few minutes. That time is just as important as creating lessons or preparing for assessments."
>
> – Classroom teacher with 21 years experience

Stress also has a strong correlation to weight gain, because it reduces the body's ability to absorb nutrients effectively, thereby affecting the body's metabolism. Research has shown that stress alters the body's level of coenzymes that help convert food to energy the cells can use. This is worsened by the reality that busy, stressed people don't have time to think about eating well, and frequently grab easy, accessible junk food such as hamburgers, fries, and doughnuts (Chichester and Garfinkel, 1997).

Many people reach for food in an attempt to soothe their stress, expecting that eating will make them feel better. Unfortunately, the food choices tend to be full of fats and sugars, have little nutritional value, and include excessive caffeine or alcohol. These foods do not reduce stress or address the bad feelings. What they often do is set up a roller-coaster sugar ride—along with feelings of heaviness, bloating, and guilt. When people make such food choices to relieve tension, they get the opposite result—increased tension, unstable moods, depression, and long-term health problems (Davidson, 2003).

Symptoms of Stress

Because of the effects of prolonged stress on the body, chronically stressed people will likely experience one (or probably several) of the following physical and emotional symptoms. Read this list carefully and honestly. Note the symptoms that you experience frequently. They are your body's way of letting you know something is wrong.

- short-term memory loss
- rapid weight gain
- jaw pain
- high blood pressure
- fatigue
- increase in respiratory infections
- upset stomach
- anxiety
- chest pain or heartburn
- insomnia
- mood swings
- immune deficiencies
- depression
- cold, sweaty hands
- constipation
- persistent headaches
- muscle tension

- dizziness
- ringing in the ears
- dry mouth
- night sweats
- sleeping too much
- emotional exhaustion
- emotional instability
- forgetfulness
- low threshold for anger
- problems with concentration
- suicidal feelings
- feelings of being trapped
- apathy
- disorganization
- loss of logical thinking
- self-doubt
- low self-esteem

Oh, my!

Learn To Love Teaching Again

On the Lookout for Burnout

Burnout is an exhaustion of physical or emotional strength that occurs usually as a result of prolonged stress or frustration. By the time a person is burned out, he or she may likely have sunk into a type of lethargy, marked by disinterest and utter exhaustion—and may not even be aware of the level of distress.

A high level of stress is often noticeable by those around you, but to you it may be hidden within normal daily activities. For example, you might go home and slam pots and pans around while making dinner, or walk an extra mile on the treadmill at a heightened pace. Burnout is a state that can easily creep up on you. Watch for warning signs (like deliberately touching the hand of a sick student in hopes of getting the flu so you can have a few days away from your job). Ask your friends to watch for warning signs and let you know. Do the same for your colleagues. Take note when they are over-doing, overwrought, or exhausted.

The causes of burnout are always cumulative. A continual draining of energy resources—unmanaged and unalleviated—builds into a physical, mental, and attitudinal state that is far worse than being "stressed out." A stressed person is usually functional enough to respond in some way to various stressors. A burned-out person often has given up.

Symptoms of Burnout

Burnout often manifests itself in

- physical fatigue
- emotional exhaustion
- cognitive weariness
- sleep disturbances
- depression
- anxiety
- withdrawal from (or lack of) energy, joy, enthusiasm, satisfaction, motivation, interest, future plans or dreams, new ideas, ambition, humor, concentration, hope, self-confidence

Feelings of aggravation, uneasiness, and anger might replace a teacher's positive energies. These negative feelings may initially be presented in small and seemingly innocuous ways, but they can grow silently and significantly as a teacher's belief in the profession begins to slip away.

The Fallout from Burnout

When a teacher is overwhelmed by exhaustion and descends into feelings of hopelessness or futility, the consequences are broad. Burned-out educators are:

. . . less observant of their students

. . . less responsive to their students

. . . less effective in all their obligations and duties

. . . less supportive of and less connected to their colleagues

. . . less connected in a positive way to students' parents

. . . more disillusioned with their professional lives

. . . more likely to function poorly in school and at home

. . . more susceptible to various illnesses

. . . more likely to have high absenteeism rates

. . . more likely to drop out of the profession

The phenomenon of teacher stress and burnout leads to increased absences from the job. Another consequence has profound implications for the profession and the society: teacher dropout. Franklin Schargel, working with the National Dropout Prevention Center at Clemson University, reports that the teacher dropout rate in America is higher than the student dropout rate (Schargel, 2010).

According to the National Center for Education Statistics, nearly half of all teachers quit in their first five years. Stricter-than-ever accountability laws, significantly more paperwork, lack of planning time, problematic student behavior, too heavy a workload, too little support, low pay, and lack of power or voice in policies are listed as common sources of dissatisfaction that lead to teacher attrition (Singleton-Rickman, 2009).

All the literature on teacher attrition mentions such factors as retirement and relocation, but on-the-job stress and burnout are constant themes in the reports about teacher dropout.

Learn To Love Teaching Again

So What to Do About It?

This might all sound like a lot of bad news. It can be. But you can become part of the good news—an educator that handles a challenging job and, without becoming one of the statistics, escapes burnout and the ill effects of stress. Start by taking these specific steps:

1. Be vigilant about your own stress level.

Many people do not even recognize that they are overly stressed until health or other problems begin to surface. Stop from time to time and check on your stress level. Pay attention to the symptoms of stress and indicators of burnout listed earlier in this chapter. Also, take the Personal Stress Quiz found in the Chapter 1 Tools. (See pages 26–27.) Some people find it helpful to actually keep a stress journal. (Identify each stressor; note how you felt physically and emotionally; record how you responded; and describe what you did or could have done to make yourself feel better.)

Whatever technique you use, try to identify the specific sources of stress in your life. Don't explain it away as temporary. Don't blame it on other people or outside forces. Carefully examine your own habits, attitudes, and excuses surrounding your stress.

Remember this: As a teacher, you are so busy and so conditioned to think of others first, that you can easily forget to think of one very important person in your classroom—YOU!

2. Adjust your attitude toward stress.

Most people experience some form of stress every day. Daily stressors can include unresolved conflicts, an overwhelming sense of responsibility, financial burdens, or the reality of a major life change such as the onset of a debilitating illness, a change in marital status, the birth of a child, or an unexpected change in employment.

Stress is unavoidable and educators aren't the only ones who experience stress. But stress is not always negative; nor does it need to be viewed as a negative force. Some level of stress is essential in our lives. It is what pushes us to solve pending problems, meet deadlines, or protect ourselves from danger. Positive stress can be the feeling you get during a strenuous workout or the encompassing satisfaction that follows the successful completion of a difficult task.

Example: I loved to visit Mrs. Follet's kindergarten class. Mrs. Follet was always smiling, yet always in control. I surprised her one morning with an extra break, and took over her kindergarten class for a little while. Within five minutes of being alone with those adorable little munchkins, I was ready to claw at the safety windows and scream for release. The students seemed to keep increasing in quantity, as though they were cloning themselves at the block center. They wanted something from me every minute, pulling on my skirt and tattling on the little boy who did not wash his hands after using the potty. I finally left the classroom looking for two aspirin and a heating pad. Yet, put me in a junior high classroom, where all the students have large clumsy feet and pointy ram-rod elbows, where acne is more important than the upcoming presidential election, and where the students can't walk down a row of desks without banging and bumping into each one—and I am a happy camper. For me, kindergarten equals stress. Eighth grade equals bliss.

For stress to be felt, the situation must be perceived as threatening or undesirable. The key word here is **perceived**. I perceived being the only adult in a kindergarten classroom as undesirable; therefore, my stress response was very real.

Example: Ms. Bancroft receives a sealed letter in her teacher's box from the principal. She rushes to a colleague's classroom in a panic. "I just know this is a termination notice!" Ms. Bancroft exclaims. "I heard rumors they were letting teachers go! Howard's mother must have complained about me to the superintendent; she had it in for me from day one! What will I do? My son needs braces and we were just about to get a new car. I need this job!"

As she panics, Ms. Bancroft's colleague slowly opens the envelope and finds a gift certificate inside from a local restaurant, a thank you from the principal for an extra project that the two teachers had taken on. A stressful reaction is triggered by what Ms. Bancroft perceives as a threat, even though the threat is not real. The stress response is authentic, although the danger is not.

Even when the stressor is real, the outlook of the person can often determine the effect of the stress on himself or herself. In the scenarios below, in which teachers are in potentially stressful situations, it is the reaction of each person that determines the personal stress level.

Scenario A

Band teacher Mr. McEwan finds a notice in his box stating that music classes will no longer be a part of the school's curriculum due to budget cuts.

Positive Attitude Tip

Usually, you have the power to determine whether a stress situation has a positive or negative effect—depending on your personal perception of the "danger," your reactions, and the extent of your coping skills. Keep in mind that one person's utopia is another person's purgatory. You can have a say in your stress level. So take charge.

High-stress reaction: Fear and anxiety immediately set in. Mr. McEwan panics, wondering what his next move will be. That night he goes home and sits in the living room with the lights off, watching exercise equipment infomercials on television. As the days pass, Mr. McEwan complains so often to friends that they begin to avoid his phone calls.

Lower-stress reaction: Mr. McEwan decides to pursue a long-time dream. He decides to form his own band with some friends, touring local clubs and playing at special events. Meanwhile, he offers private piano and guitar lessons from his home, and gets a part-time job directing the choir for his church.

Scenario B

Mrs. Potter, a fifth-grade teacher, has lesson plans to prepare for Monday, but her husband wants the family to go on an overnight camping trip—leaving Friday after work and returning late Saturday night.

High-stress reaction: It is a beautiful day at the mountain campground. The trees rustle with a gentle breeze, the birds sing sweetly, the afternoon is cloudless, and the evening will likely bring a striking star-filled sky. However, even before leaving home Mrs. Potter decides that she will hate this camping trip. She does not like dirt in her clothes, insects in her food, or being very far from her hairdryer. Mrs. Potter is also certain that all the peace and quiet will drive her crazy and she can't stop thinking of the lesson plans she needs to prepare just as soon as she gets back home.

Lower-stress reaction: It is a beautiful day at the mountain campground. The trees rustle with a gentle breeze, the birds sing sweetly, the afternoon is cloudless, and the evening will likely bring a striking star-filled sky. Although she doesn't like camping and hates the thought of being so far from her hair dryer, Mrs. Potter vows to rest and relax for the weekend, and enjoy some quality family time. She plans to do nothing but take long walks and let her husband cook. She knows she can get her lesson plans done when she returns home. In fact, the beauty of the campground might even serve as inspiration for her science lesson this week!

The reality is this: We all face potentially stressful situations several times each day. Sometimes a white-knuckle response may be unavoidable, but if you can work toward facing perceived or real pressure with a "glass half-full" mentality, you will likely live longer, remain healthier, and maintain your place in a wonderfully rewarding profession.

Consider the differences between these approaches:

Negative Perspective	Positive Perspective
Yikes! This is all so new to me.	I am ready to take on this challenge.
I just don't have the resources to tackle this!	Necessity is the mother of invention.
This is just too complicated!	There has got to be another way to approach this.
I don't like change; and this is a big change!	I am willing to try. What do I have to lose?
There is just no time to get this done!	Let's see if we can shift some priorities.

Adapted from the Mayo Clinic: "Positive Thinking: Practice This Stress Management Skill"

3. Take specific steps to reduce or eliminate stress.

It doesn't happen automatically. Just reading about it, or saying to yourself, "I've got to do something about all this stress" won't get you off the path to burnout. It takes an intentional plan to balance your work with time and energy for fun, relaxation, important relationships, and healthy habits. There are numerous good books and other sources that can help you find ways that work for you to diminish and cope with stress. Include strategies like these in your plan:

laughter	asking for help when you need it
making healthy food choices	being a cooperative, supportive colleague
consistent exercise	using emotions in positive ways
prioritizing tasks	reduced caffeine intake
music	learning to forgive
watching funny movies	biofeedback
deep breathing	cutting out procrastination
reading a good book	conscious relaxation
yoga	moderating your drinking
learning to say "no"	reduced commitments
long, relaxing baths	being willing to compromise
setting realistic expectations	improved time management
massage	drinking green tea
building a support system	anger management
journaling	being with friends and families
being a good friend	positive thinking
guided imagery	playing games
healthy eating	improved communication skills
gardening	learning self-advocacy
better organization	self-assertiveness training
expressing your feelings	confronting, not avoiding, problems

Don't leave these kinds of things to chance or squeeze them in now and then. Purposefully plan periods of stress relief. In order to stay healthy and effective in your job and life, you MUST have breaks from the relentless stress. Look at stressful situations and think about how you can change the situation (avoid it or alter it) or change your reaction or attitude (adapt to it or accept it).

Teacher-to-Teacher Tip

"Don't try to control what you can't control."
– Middle grades teacher

4. Look out for each other.

As I noted earlier, people that are chronically stressed often or burned out may be beyond identifying their own condition—at least until some major health issue or other crisis occurs. But don't let things get to such a severe state! Pay attention, not only to yourselves, but to your colleagues. Let each other know when you see signs of prolonged, repeated stress.

A strong support system is an important factor in reducing teacher stress and keeping teachers in education. Many school districts are adopting induction programs that help new teachers adjust to their new teaching positions. In 2004, a new teacher mentoring program established in the state of California decreased new teacher attrition rate to 9 percent compared to 37 percent five years earlier (Rotherman, 2004). And, some state education departments have begun to pay attention to the problem of teacher burnout. Many require higher competency levels to enter the teaching profession and many are raising teachers' pay. Of course, financial compensation isn't everything. (And even highly competent professionals burn out.)

Effective induction and retention programs can also help districts retain experienced teachers by providing opportunities for them to expand and grow in their careers. They become energized to take on additional leadership roles and responsibilities, which can boost pay, confidence, success, and enjoyment. For example, some states and school districts provide salary bonuses to master teachers who mentor new or struggling teachers in their schools.

Take an active role in your school to help create policies and procedures that protect teachers' mental and physical health. Paperwork reduction policies, school-wide (realistic) homework policies, programs that define and support home-school relationships, adequate professional development, good support services for teachers and students, adequate financial compensation for after-school duties, a strong volunteer program, better pay—all these are institution-wide programs that make life less stressful for teachers. Review your district's plans and programs for teacher induction and retention. If such plans and programs do not address ways to reduce teacher stress, make recommendations that the district do so.

Learn To Love Teaching Again

5. Steer Clear Of Burnout

If you see a hazard in the middle of road, you steer around it. You certainly wouldn't step on the gas and aim for the hazard. So, why would you not look for signs of burnout and steer clear? If you are under constant stress, you are likely headed for burnout. Most experts will tell you to stop doing what it is you are doing and do something different. This does not necessarily mean that you need to quit your job. You can "do something different" in the way you manage your life at school and outside of school.

First of all, be aware that situations and actions such as these will increase the likelihood that you will burn out:

- taking on too much and not knowing when to say "no"

- setting or accepting goals that are unrealistic

- working in an environment that has unreasonable and punitive rules

- doing things that are in direct opposition to your personal values

- being in a place where you feel you have no voice—you are powerless, you feel that what you do doesn't matter

- trying to be (or expected to be) all things to all people

- becoming bored because tasks aren't challenging or because you have not tried anything new or done any growing as a professional

- allowing yourself to feel trapped in a job and not taking action

Remember also that if you are you constantly feeling powerless, hopeless, emotionally exhausted, frustrated, isolated, irritable, trapped, in despair, cynical, or apathetic, you are exhibiting symptoms of burnout. Although every person and situation is unique (even among teachers), take stock of your situation and yourself. In addition to the advice about reducing and alleviating cumulative stress, follow these tips to ward off or recover from burnout:

- **Gather a support system.** Every teacher needs a strong support system of fellow teachers, administrators, and parents. Cooperative, competent colleagues and mentors will help you deal with the challenges of today's classroom. If such a system does not exist, pull some colleagues together and create one. Part of a good support system is a climate of challenge. Identify supportive colleagues who will provide you with honest feedback.

- **Continue your own professional development.** Seek out opportunities to develop professionally through workshops, seminars, Webinars, membership in professional organizations, education journals and books, online courses, or additional college training. Teachers who increase their knowledge or skills are less at risk for frustration and stress than those teachers who don't (Harry Wong, 1991), and are less likely to leave the profession (National Education Association, 2003).

- **Work on a positive attitude.** Your own attitude is the most powerful tool for positive action. With a positive attitude, you'll see stressful situations as challenges rather than impossibilities (Harrell, 2003). Distinguish between the things that are under your control and those that are not. Then you can focus on areas that are possible to change— and you'll have less stress and risk of burnout. You may not be able to change the district or school, but you can change your behavior, your attitude, and your classroom.

- **Be proactive.** When you deliberately change from a reactive stance to a proactive one, your stress will diminish, and you'll be more likely to escape burnout. Take steps to change things that are stressful. Keep lines of communication open. For example, you will diminish parents' frustrations or demands and spare yourself the surprises of their discontent when you keep them informed about schedules, school policies, class expectations, and their child's progress and needs.

- **Manage your time effectively.** Take a course or read some books on time management. Effective time management helps teachers negotiate the incredible daily demands. Davis, Eshelman and McKay (2000) suggest that you: Clarify values. Decide what is important. Evaluate how time is currently spent. Set goals. Develop an action plan. Combat procrastination. Organize your time.

- **Carve out time to relax.** Deliberately plan for this. "Teachers must incorporate in the daily planning ways to build a better relationship with themselves to safeguard their emotional health as it relates to their job" (Canter, 1994).

Falling in Love Again

Much of the advice about stress and burnout applies to life in general and to many different jobs. But education has its own specific set of stressors, such as excessive paperwork, struggles with classroom management, difficult relationships with parents, poor communication with administration or colleagues, burdensome bureaucratic requirements, a workday that rarely ends when the workday ends, extra duties, and so forth. Use resources such as this book to learn deliberate strategies that will help you alter these components in ways that make them less stressful. When you get better at doing this, you'll be able to experience the joys of your job—and you will be very likely to fall in love with teaching again.

Me Moments

- Take a brisk walk outside at lunch. Even if you only have time to grab a quick walk around the parking lot or open courtyard, the change of scenery and exercise will do you a world of good.

- Follow the Chinese proverb, "The palest ink is better than the best memory." Keep a journal with you (or in your desk) to get things off your chest and to help you remember important things. This may also help you to figure out your priorities, when something needs to move off your platter.

- Take 10 minutes when you come home from school and put your feet up. Place a cool towel over your eyes. Listen to your favorite song and light a candle, if you like. Rejuvenate yourself before you start taking care of personal business.

- Every day, find time to do something you love.

- The title of this chapter says that teacher stress is no laughing matter. Actually, that is not altogether correct. Stress IS a laughing matter—because laughing relieves stress! So be sure to laugh several times a day.

Chapter 1 **Tools**

Personal Stress Quiz

Try this short quiz as a way to self-reflect on the kinds of experiences and feelings that often indicate a rise in stress or a path to burnout. For each item, circle the response that best demonstrates how often you feel in agreement with the statement.

1. *Lately all those around me (administrators, parents, peer teachers) seem incompetent. Everything they say or do contradicts what I believe. Even my students are less on-the-ball this year.*
> **I feel this way**
> **a. all of the time**
> **b. some of the time**
> **c. never**

2. *I do not have time to do the simple things anymore, like taking a walk after dinner, browsing through a magazine, sneaking an afternoon nap, or watching a favorite television show—even on weekends.*
> **I feel this way**
> **a. all of the time**
> **b. some of the time**
> **c. never**

3. *I entered teaching with such high hopes, but many of my efforts seem pointless now. The parents don't back me, the kids are unmotivated and uncooperative, and my principal comes up with a new program every month that is supposed to make a difference (but nothing ever really changes).*
> **I feel this way**
> **a. all of the time**
> **b. some of the time**
> **c. never**

4. *I feel stagnated in my teaching strategies and content, but I can't get excited about trying any new approaches or material.*
> **I feel this way**
> **a. all of the time**
> **b. some of the time**
> **c. never**

5. *Co-workers keep asking what is wrong with me. There is nothing wrong with me! I wish they would just leave me alone.*
> **I feel this way**
> **a. all of the time**
> **b. some of the time**
> **c. never**

6. *My principal does not support me. She or he just sits in that office all day or takes those long executive lunches. The only time I hear from my principal is when she or he sends around those weekly memos, asking us to do something more or different.*
> **I feel this way**
> **a. all of the time**
> **b. some of the time**
> **c. never**

7. *I have not slept well in weeks. I wish I could stay in bed for the entire weekend, with my head buried under my pillow.*
> **I feel this way**
> **a. all of the time**
> **b. some of the time**
> **c. never**

8. *I no longer enjoy working with colleagues to improve processes or programs for students. I increasingly avoid interaction, involvement, or cooperation.*
> **I feel this way**
> > **a. all of the time**
> > **b. some of the time**
> > **c. never**

9. *I hardly get to spend time with my family. And when we do have time together, I'm cranky and find that they annoy me.*
> **I feel this way**
> > **a. all of the time**
> > **b. some of the time**
> > **c. never**

10. *When I close my eyes to rest a moment or try to fall asleep at night, I cannot avoid rehashing all the things I have yet to do for my students.*
> **I feel this way**
> > **a. all of the time**
> > **b. some of the time**
> > **c. never**

11. *I find it difficult to go to work some mornings and I look for excuses to take the day off.*
> **I feel this way**
> > **a. all of the time**
> > **b. some of the time**
> > **c. never**

12. *I feel physically ill and exhausted. I have ailments like sore throats, migraine headaches, and stomach upsets much more frequently than I used to.*
> **I feel this way**
> > **a. all of the time**
> > **b. some of the time**
> > **c. never**

Go back and review your responses. If you see that you have marked "a" or "b" often, take this as a serious sign that you are sliding toward burnout. Don't ignore the sign, but set some goals to take better care of yourself in ways that relieve your stress and help you learn to love teaching again! Choose tips from the following chapters to use as you work toward a lower-stress teaching life.

How Are You Breathing?

Breathing helps regulate blood pressure, heart rate, and circulation, as well as other functions. Pay attention to the way you are breathing, and you'll get some clues to your stress level.

Stress can cause tissues in the chest to tighten, reducing the range of motion of the muscles. This results in "chest breathing" (shallow breathing, as opposed to the more beneficial deep, abdomen breathing). The rapid, shallow pants of chest breathing impair transfer of oxygen and nutrients through the bloodstream. Find out if you are "chest breathing," and learn to breathe deeply to de-stress or lessen the adverse effects of stress on your well-being.

How can you tell if you breathe from your chest or your abdomen?

Place your right hand on your chest and your left hand on your abdomen. If your right hand rises higher with each breath, you are a chest breather. If your left hand rises higher, you are breathing from your abdomen.

Practice the following breathing techniques at least twice a day and when you feel your stress level escalating.

1.

Place one hand on your chest and one on your abdomen. Concentrate your breathing so that the hand on your abdomen rises higher.

2.

Exhale through your mouth. Then breathe in slowly through your nose, as though you are trying to inhale all the oxygen in the room, for a slow count of 7.

3.

Exhale through your mouth for a slow count of 8. Contract your abdomen muscles to ensure that all air is expelled. Keep in mind that deeper breathing comes through exhaling thoroughly.

4.

Repeat this 5 times. You will breathe once every 10 seconds, or 6 times a minute—a pace in which heart rate is affected positively.

What Image Do You Reflect?

What Image Do You Reflect?

Workers in inside sales or "call-in" customer service positions are familiar with the tip of placing a mirror in their cubicles, so that they can monitor their facial expressions when interacting with people. This practice is effective because it allows one to change one's attitude and behavior simply by being aware of what the face (and body) is reflecting.

Place mirrors on the walls in your classroom—at spots that you pass or linger often. Glance at yourself from time to time to see what reflects back. Decide if this is the image you really wish to reflect at this moment. Pay attention to how student behavior is related to the different images you reflect. Also, use the mirrors to give yourself a friendly smile frequently. Research shows that smiling reduces your stress level. It also presents a friendlier, more attractive image to your students.

Today's Reflections   Write notes about what you see in the mirror.

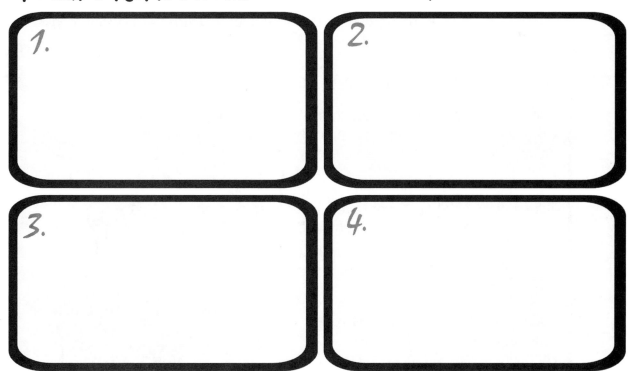

1.

2.

3.

4.

Write a sentence summarizing what you learned from checking your reflection today.

Music to Soothe the Savage Beast ♫

Music can induce calm and ameliorate stress. Not all your favorite tunes, however, will have a stress-reducing effect. So when you look for music to help calm you, choose carefully. There are some kinds and qualities of music that have been found to have the most beneficial effects on stressed human beings.

When choosing music to soothe the stress beast within you, build a collection of musical selections . . .

- that you like *(of course)*
- with drums or flutes
- from live performances
- created by sounds of nature *(such as ocean waves, rushing streams, wind, bird calls, and so on)*
- with repeating or cyclical patterns
- that can be played in the background while you work
- that have a rhythm slower than your heartbeat *(At about 72 beats per minute or less, this helps to reduce your heart rate and increases deep breathing.)*
- that create pleasant memories *(such as childhood songs or "oldies")*

Tips to Increase the Positive Effects of Music

Combine relaxation therapy, such as deep-breathing techniques, with music. Get in a comfortable position, lying flat on a couch or the floor—on in your favorite comfy chair.

Wear headphones to help you focus on the music. Take a walk with your favorite music. Concentrate on the silence between notes or runs in the music.

Take a 20-minute sound bath at the end of the day. (No water is necessary.)

Use soothing music in the classroom. Students need stress relief, too. (And when your students' stress level decreases, so does yours.)

Paper, Paper Everywhere!

A chilling wind blows against the woman moving oh-so-slowly forward, forging ahead with tired steps. She is bundled in an attractive denim-colored sweater set with little red apples for buttons. Fastened over her heart is a brooch made of dried pasta noodles. What catches and holds your eye is the bags. The woman seems weighted down with canvas bags in primary colors, some decorated with rows of red alphabet letters, and others displaying textbook company logos. Each bag overflows with papers—papers that snap in the strong breeze, papers that threaten to fly off with the next gust of air.

You know you are a teacher under stress if you find yourself tempted to mark all papers with an A+, because it would make your life so much easier.

Who is this woman? Is she without a home? Does she live on the streets? Does she search the back doors of kitchens for leftover food, or ask strangers for spare change? No, the woman is a teacher, bringing home the day's assignments to grade—along with reports and other paperwork to complete. How many times have you come home from school like this, carrying stacks of papers, projects, tests to grade, IEPs, and lesson plans? How many times has your workday turned into a ten-, eleven-, or twelve-hour marathon?

Losing the Love

Ask a group of teachers what is most burdensome about the job. Right up there at the top of the list, you will always find: "The paperwork!" So many of us feel buried by papers to grade, forms to fill out, records to keep, reports to submit, tests to create, or quizzes to score. Teachers cry out, "Please, just let us teach!"

The piles of paperwork can wear you out—literally. They can keep you from getting enough sleep, from taking any time to relax, and from nurturing relationships with family and friends. And that's just the paperwork you actually get done. Then there are all those unfinished paper tasks that keep hanging over your head. Those can truly burn you out. All together, this load is not good for your health. Nor does it contribute to effective, satisfying teaching.

There is hope! You can greatly reduce the hours and the stress of this responsibility. It takes a change of thinking, along with some very tangible practices. Together these strategies can give you release and help you get back to being the creative, caring, energetic teacher you really are.

Lots of Assignments ≠ a Good Teacher

Have you ever (even once) awakened in the wee hours of the morning with your face planted in an empty coffee cup while your dominant hand continued to write "good job" over and over again across students' essays on a topic such as "Three People, Living or Dead, That I Admire Most"? If so, be sure to read this section carefully—and twice.

Last year, I noticed that a young teacher in my school looked more frazzled each day. She went from perky Ms. Gidget-Meets-the-Sixth-Grade to Ms. Is-the-Day-Over-Yet? One morning I asked what was wrong. It was as if a dam broke. "Oh gosh," she gushed. "It's all these papers I'm taking home to grade! I stay up half the night. I feel that students need feedback right away on every assignment. I teach math, social studies, science, grammar, creative writing, and spelling, and if I give a class assignment in each of these subjects, plus homework, and multiply that number by my 26 students, that's HUNDREDS of papers I'm grading every night . . . ."

The teacher shook with frustration and fatigue. I gently took hold of her shoulders, forcing her to look into my eyes. "Listen to me." I spoke slowly but firmly in my most reverent principal voice:

"You. Do. NOT. Have. To. Grade. Every. Paper."

The relief and joy was immediate. It was as though I had told her that I would personally take over her class for the rest of the school year so she could take one long Rip Van Winkle nap in the teacher's lounge.

I'm sorry to tell you that my dog ate your homework.

I did not then and do not now suggest that students' written efforts should be routinely ignored. (You can use the excuse "my dog ate YOUR homework" with your class only so many times.) There has to be accountability to the students, the parents, and the school. What I suggest is that you find ways to teach, practice skills, and effectively assess—with less paperwork. In the past, teachers may have been judged by the amount of homework they assigned. (A big pile of paperwork meant a better teacher, so some thought.) But now that pile may seem to be more a sign of inefficiency and disorganization. Take some definite steps to free yourself (and your students) from this excess. Here are some ideas to get you started.

Rethink Your Paper Habit

Start the paperwork-reduction trail by paying attention to each piece of paper you personally create. (Maybe it will help you to think about the trees needed to make the papers, or the cramped hands your students will have completing them, or the headache you will get reading them. Or ask this question with each one: "Where will this paper end up after I grade it?" and face the truth of the answer: "more than likely crumpled at the bottom of a backpack.")

- Make sure that each assignment you give has a legitimate educational value.
- Don't use paper to practice something the students can practice in an active or hands-on way (without paper).
- Don't use paper to assess something you can judge without paper.
- Only give homework that practices what you have taught.
- Only give homework on skills or concepts you have evidence the student understands and can do.
- Don't give homework just to keep kids busy or to make parents think you are a competent teacher.

33

- Consider who's going to do the homework. If students are getting parents to do it, then it's a waste of paper and a waste of your time. Only give what the kids are actually able to do by themselves.

- When you give homework, keep it short and to the point. Five problems are better than fifteen. A paragraph summary is better than two pages.

- Mix up the kinds of assignments. Create far fewer tasks that require paper.

- Make sure you have mini-erase boards—one for each student. This way they can show what they know without turning in another piece of paper.

- Return all assignments quickly. If you can't get the papers graded promptly, then don't give the assignment.

- If you create assignments that are meaningful, you can give many fewer paper tasks. Try this: For one week, keep a record of the paper you generate. Include the things you create to give to students and the papers you collect from students to review or grade. Then consider what, of those pieces, you could have done without. What did each piece accomplish? Was it necessary or meaningful? Did it further students' understanding of a concept? Could you have accomplished the same purpose without paper to collect, process, and return?

Keep Moving

I spent a year in the homeroom and history class of Mr. Sherlock. By the time I moved on to seventh grade, I still had no idea how tall he was. You see, Mr. Sherlock never got up from his desk.

Today teachers are much more mobile. (You can tell by the shoes we wear to work.) And we can use that mobility to reduce the amount of grading we have to do.

Combine mobility with a clear sense of the goals for student work and you can find out what students know or can do at the same time you reduce your own paperwork.

Much of the homework you give can be quickly reviewed—without you taking the papers home or poring over them on your break. When you want to check homework, circulate quickly around the room with your notebook or grade book. Scan each student's work, making checkmarks or notes about the completion and quality of the work. This will not be hard to do—IF you have followed the above advice and given short, manageable homework assignments. It will be easy to see which students are struggling with an idea. The only homework papers you'll need to collect and review are those longer written works.

You can use the mobility trick to lessen paperwork on in-class assignments, too:

- In advance, decide your criteria or goal(s) for mastery of the skill or concept. (For example, will it be six correctly answered math problems in a row? . . . the pronouns properly identified in a short paragraph? . . . the appropriate use of the Spanish verb "ser" in three consecutive sentences?)

- As students begin to work on the assignment, walk among their desks, checking to see if they are on the right track and following directions. By visiting each student early in their work, you can catch problems before she or he gets mired in frustration.

- Move around the room again. This time, assist those students who are struggling with answers. You can quickly pinpoint any confusion without involving all students, and individual student time will be more productive.

- Keep in mind your mastery goal. Scroll down students' papers as you walk by. (For instance, do you see six correctly solved problems?) When a student has reached the goal, he or she can move on to some other predetermined activity.

- Keep whatever records you need as you make your "rounds." Do this in a notebook or grade book, giving a check mark or rating value. Some teachers carry a handheld electronic device to log entries into a grading database. Or, you can keep a pocketful of index cards for making notes about those students who will need more review.

> **New Teacher Tip**
>
> *Be very careful about falling into the trap of having students grade each others' work—even though it seems like an easy way to lessen your workload. This practice violates the privacy of students, often causes student embarrassment or shame, complicates social relationships in the classroom, and negatively impacts lower-achieving students in particular. Many districts even have written policies prohibiting this practice.*

When you use an on-the-go system such as this, your students will accomplish more and perform better. Your presence helps them to stay focused and assures them that they won't get lost in confusion or stray into off-task behaviors. With you there to encourage and make sure concepts are understood, students will take greater responsibility for completing quality work. They'll be motivated to show what they're doing, and will have greater satisfaction with their work. This is a different picture from a group of students plowing through an assignment without support.

Of course, this is good for the students—the keep-moving habit allows you to give quality instruction to individual pupils. At the same time, it eliminates your need to take home and grade that set of papers. (Chalk up another point for stress reduction!)

Learn To Love Teaching Again

Fall in Love with Rubrics

Determined to try some new, motivating teaching strategies, Ms. De los Santos used part of her summer to develop some new approaches. She made plans to include more small-group work, journaling, project-based assignments, and student presentations in her lessons. Yet, not far into the school year, grading those assignments had increased her paperwork load (as well as her stress level). Here's why: She found that a grade was not enough for such activities. She felt she needed to write comments for each student's project, group participation, or presentation—explaining in detail what was done well and what needed improvement. Imagine the hours this added to her workday!

Ms. De los Santos needs to know about the rubric—a knight in shining armor, ready to ride in and save the day! By creating some well-constructed rubrics, she could supply quality, useful feedback to her students while lowering her paper pile. There are benefits far beyond paper reduction. Rubrics offer clear and specific expectations for both students and parents.

A rubric generates a contract of sorts, outlining the grade that will be earned at each level of effort. Let me underscore that last point: When rubrics are used, students tend to understand that they earn their grades, as opposed to a teacher arbitrarily (arbitrarily, at least from a student's perspective) assigning grades. On a rubric, grading is objective and transparent, based on measurable and understandable criteria. The work of one student is not held up against the work of another student; each is challenged to meet impartial criteria. Students don't have to guess at the meaning of a grade.

Many studies show that feedback to students is a powerful strategy to improve achievement. Yet, one particular form of classroom feedback—interpretation of assessment results by a given set of criteria—enhances student achievement more than other forms of feedback. In their well-known 1986 review of 21 assessment studies, Fuchs and Fuchs (1986) found that students had a gain of 32 percentile points when they received (or participated in) evaluation based on specific expectations known to them ahead of time. Rubrics offer this kind of evaluation beautifully!

What Is a Rubric?

A rubric is a scoring tool—a set of criteria and standards linked to learning objectives. It can be used to assess a student's performance on many tasks and assignments. Although there is great flexibility in the form, content, and use of rubrics, the following components should always be included in some way:

1. **Stated objectives** to be measured. These might be written in the form of behavior, outcomes, tasks or task components, or performance. Ask yourself: What are the content objectives? What concepts are vital? What tasks should students be able to do? What do students need to understand and remember about the big idea of the topic?

2. **A range of scores** to rate the performance on the objectives. Assign values for each competency level of performance. The assignments of value for each criterion will vary depending on the age group of your students. Though students and parents are most accustomed to letter grades, number values are more specific and easier to compute. You may want to translate the numeric total into a letter grade to match your grading scale. For example, in the example shown below, the highest numeric score possible is 12 points. You might give an A for a score of 9 or greater.

3. **Specific performance characteristics or criteria** for the degree to which the objective is met. The criteria describe various levels of competency at which the student performs or meets the objective. Note that the criteria become progressively challenging and complete as the scores increase. Criteria must be stated clearly so there is no room for misinterpretation.

> ### Teacher-to-Teacher Tip
>
> *"If you intend to translate rubric scores into letter grades, give students an equivalency scale when you show them the rubric. This way they will know ahead of time what they have to do for a specific grade."*
>
> *– High-school teacher*

The following example combines these three components into a rubric. This particular rubric is designed to score student performance during a unit on dramatic poetry for grade 7.

Learn To Love Teaching Again

Dramatic Poetry, Grade 7

Objectives	Competency Level Criteria			
	Score 4	Score 3	Score 2	Score 1
Read and interpret dramatic poetry	Interpretation written on each of two poems— with personal response and at least three details from poem to support each interpretation	Interpretation written on each of two poems— with personal response and one or more details from poem to support each interpretation	Coherent interpretation written on each of two poems showing some personal response and one or no substantiating details	Attempt at interpretation written on one or two of the poems, little or no personal connection, little or no detail
Analyze the use of similes, metaphors, personification, and irony in dramatic poetry	Clear explanation of at least six examples of similes, metaphors, personification, and irony from the two selected poems	Clear explanation of at least five examples of similes, metaphors, personification, and irony from the two selected poems	Clear explanation of at least four examples of similes, metaphors, personification, and irony from the two selected poems	Clear explanation of at least three examples of similes, metaphors, personification, and irony from the two selected poems
Identify themes of dramatic poetry	Clear explanation of one theme from each poem, related to student's life, using multiple examples from the poem	Adequate explanation of one theme from each poem, related to student's life, using a few examples from the poem	Adequate explanation of one theme from each poem, with an attempt to relate to own life and to use examples	Adequate attempt at explanation of one theme from each poem

Teacher-to-Teacher Tip

"Avoid using vague criteria such as: 'shows an understanding of the material'; 'participates well'; 'good use of creativity'; 'interesting presentation'; or 'length is appropriate'. These are open for all kinds of interpretation for both the teacher and the student. Remember, one of the strengths of a rubric is objectivity."

— Fourth-grade teacher, fan of rubrics

Rubrics for Young Children

It's clear that rubrics offer many advantages for teachers and students at upper grade levels. But they are definitely useful for younger students as well. The rubric below was developed at Walter L. Parsley Elementary School in Washington D.C. for the purpose of assessing kindergarten writing skills.

Kindergarten Writing Goal

What Is the Student To Do?	How Well Was This Done?			
By the end of the school year, student will be able to:	Score 3 Proficient	Score 2 Developing	Score 1 Emerging	Score 0 Not Evident
write a few simple, decipherable words to accompany a drawing	*Uses initial and final consonants for most words; creates words to accompany a drawing— that are mostly decipherable by a reader.*	*Forms letters; uses some letter-sound relationships in attempts to form words; separates the "words" from the drawing.*	*Attempts to form letters; separates the "words" from the drawing.*	*Does not create "writing" of any sort.*

New Teacher Tip

Parents of very young students are apt to be extrasensitive to grading or to the classification of their children's skills. They may not completely understand that the development of children's physical and academic abilities progresses at varying speeds in the early primary years. When creating a rubric, don't use terms that can feel like judgment to anxious parents. For example, avoid a rubric like one I saw not long ago which used these categories (instead of numbers) to measure competencies for kindergarteners: "highly skilled, moderately skilled, poorly skilled, unskilled." Would you want to hear that your precious five-year old is "poorly skilled" or "unskilled"?

Learn To Love Teaching Again

Tips for Using Rubrics

- One rubric is not necessarily appropriate for all students. Yes, a benefit of rubrics is that they can standardize expectations for students. But any rubric can be adapted to different student needs or learning styles. Don't force any student into expectations that are not reasonable for him or her. Adapt a rubric, where needed, for individual students.

- Once you get familiar with the idea, you will find rubrics relatively simple to create. I find that when I generate a rubric individualized to a particular subject matter, style, and group of students, it is quite easy to make adaptations necessary for other assignments.

- The Internet is a plentiful source of rubric models and samples. Borrow ideas, but always make sure they are suited for or adapted to your students' specific needs.

- Before you use a rubric to judge a learning task or ability, share the rubric with your students. If they are able to read and understand the text of a rubric, give or show students a copy. Review and discuss it with them. If they are too young to read, tell them the criteria. Students deserve to know what constitutes a good performance before they attempt the performance. Their learning will increase significantly if they know the criteria.

- Create rubrics with the help of students. Give them chances to create their own. At the least, try to translate your rubrics into a student version that they can read or understand. (For little kids, this may need to be done with visual symbols.)

- With each rubric, decide what total score is appropriate for judging that the student has mastered the objective. Make sure to use the results of this scoring to inform your instruction. Students who score below the total number you've set will need further explanation, help, or practice.

- Develop a record-keeping system where you can keep track of scores from assignments, understandings, processes, or tasks you assess with a rubric. Make sure your record gives a full title for the rubric so you can remember months later what it was!

- Keep all rubric masters in a loose-leaf notebook organized by subject, strand, or theme. Keep a list of contents so you can find them easily and reuse them.

- Review the sample rubrics found in the Tools section at the end of this chapter.

Let Your Students Reflect on Work

Get students involved in the process of evaluating their own work. Even the very youngest students can reflect on a completed task or project. A self-reflection guide (or set of oral questions) leads them to think about what they've done, how well they did it, what difficulties or questions they encountered, and how they feel about it. This process reduces grading and paperwork for you (and that's great), but its benefits for the students are far more important. As they reflect on a completed assignment, students

- review what they've accomplished
- get another look at the whole of the task—and thus review the concept
- use higher-level thinking skills such as analysis and evaluation
- relate the assignment to their own lives
- take note of their personal responses to the work they've done
- grapple with what it means to do something well, meet the criteria, and feel satisfied or unsatisfied with a performance
- take a deeper personal interest in their work
- practice expressing their thoughts and evaluations

Tips for Student Reflections

Here are some bits of advice about the process of student reflections on their own work:

- Think about what you believe students should consider when they have finished their work.
- Design simple questions that will help spur student reflections.
- See the sample student reflections in the Tools section at the end of this chapter.
- Don't ask too many questions.
- You can ask different kinds of questions on different assignments.
- Interview younger students to gain their insights into their work. Or, have them draw faces to show their responses to questions.
- Keep the questions positive. (For instance, instead of asking, "What about your work does not feel good?" ask, "Is there anything you would do differently if you were to do this again?")
- View their self-reflections as you review the completed assignment. It is likely that their observations will give all you need to make an assessment about the work. Jot down notes in your grade book. Or, in some cases, keep their reflection as your "evidence" for a grade—and skip your grading altogether on that project.

Learn To Love Teaching Again

Understand Millennium Learners

Catherine, a college sophomore, called home to complain about the time she had just wasted registering online for next semester's classes. "This took way too long," she moaned. "It's an antiquated, cumbersome system!"

Remembering her own college registrations, the mother commiserated with her daughter. "How long did it take, sweetheart?" she asked with empathy.

Catherine sighed with exhaustion. "Twenty minutes!"

"Twenty minutes?" gasped the mother, remembering the long lines and the dozens of tables to navigate in her college gymnasium. Those registrations took all day!

Your students bring these attitudes and aptitudes with them to class each day:

- They expect immediate connection with people and information 24/7.
- They have zero tolerance for delays.
- They are at ease with and efficient at multi-tasking.
- They have a preference for images rather than written text.
- They live and breathe technology.

It is probably accurate to say that the majority of educators are far less at ease with today's technological gadgets, IT skills, and communications habits than their students. Unlike their students, many adults feel most comfortable in a pencil and paper world. These differences can create a gap between student and teacher expectations. Close that gap! Investigate strategies for instruction and assessment that connect with the way your students learn, gain and process information, and communicate. When you do so, you'll find that you reduce paperwork for yourself and your students.

How Do They Learn?

Consider these eight factors about your students and the world in which they operate. Caution: The ways **they** are learning (even outside school) will look very different from **your** primary, elementary, middle grades, high school (and maybe even college) life.

1. Even before they begin to read, today's students virtually build cities and save worlds. You may have been raised on the game "Candy Land," in which the biggest decision that had to be made was figuring out the number of dots on the dice. But toddlers today navigate computer screens with ease; many preschoolers know their way around YouTube and game apps on their parents' computers, PDAs, smart phones, or iPads.

2. Recent research sheds light on the difference between how adults and today's children peruse new material. An adult's eye movement follows the pattern shown below, which is based on how we were taught to read:

Because of their orientation to video games, the eyes of millennium learners may go to the center and bottom of the screen first. That is where the most important information is—the information that can assist them in achieving success. Looking at the center of the screen is the last action, because it contains the least relevant information.

3. Computers, hand-held devices, and the games and programs loved by students create worlds in which everything moves at "twitch" speed. Environments change and information is processed instantly by pushing a key, twisting a knob, nudging a stick, touching a screen, or pointing a wand.

4. Information today is available in seconds—most of it in small bites. Whereas we might have looked up information and found an article or a book or a complete encyclopedia entry, our students search and find sentences, phrases, short paragraphs, or brief facts. Assign students a topic and give one minute to search. They can note the short and fast pieces of "information" they find in that time. You'll be amazed what they find!

5. The flow of information is constant, but often much less formal. Think of the last few emails you have received. A person or two in my address book holds on to a "Dear Dr. Herrera" or a "Sincerely." But even most professional contacts that I have never met greet me with "Hi, Debbi!" instead of a formal greeting. And friends just start with a message or a "Hey." Language has changed with the quickened pace of communication.

One teacher asked students to write a brief reflection on their summer vacations. Here's a response that shows how language has responded to the quickened pace of communication:

"My smmr hols wr CWOT. B4, we used 2go2 NY 2C my bro, his GF & thr 3 :- kids FTF. ILNY, it's a gr8 plc. Bt we jst styd hom."

(Translation: "My summer holidays were a complete waste of time. Before, we used to go to New York to see my brother, his girlfriend, and their three screaming kids face to face. I love New York. It's a great place. But we just stayed home.")

6. Thanks to video games, students are now master negotiators who question the status quo. They think fast, make decisions fast, and take chances. They repeatedly find solutions through trial and error. They are used to gaining knowledge "just in time" to avoid disaster, ruination, or termination of the game.

7. Students' technology-connected lives have made it easy, and even necessary, to perform more than one task at a time. Today's 12-year old may be updating his MySpace page or FaceBook page (or both) while texting a friend on his cell phone and Skyping another friend while instant messaging and checking email. Oh, and he's also listening to an MP-3 player, watching TV, and doing homework.

8. According to Mark Prensky, today's "net generation" of students ". . . develop hypertext minds; they leap around." (2001) Prensky is the author of *Digital Game-Based Learning*, *Don't Bother Me Mom—I'm Learning*, and *Teaching Digital Natives*. Credited with inventing the terms "digital native" and "digital immigrant," he is a passionate advocate for changing teaching processes to ways that are more effective for the 21st century. This includes noticing how kids learn from video games. Prensky explains that these students learn by discovery and by assimilating information from multiple sources. They respond quickly, he says, and they expect others to respond quickly.

Chuckle!

You know it's going to be a stressful day when you give a test on ancient cultures in your first period history class and find this answer: "The Greeks were a highly sculptured people, and without them we wouldn't have history. The Greeks also had myths. A myth is a female moth."

So What IS a Teacher to Do?

The eight descriptors of millennium students have major implications for learning and teaching strategies (and attitudes) in the classroom.

- Open your mind. Perhaps (hopefully) the most obvious answer to the above question is: Give up the idea that your students will learn everything the way you did. Say goodbye to a classroom where all of the assignments are based on pencil-and-paper activity.

- Open your eyes. Pay attention to the way your students learn and operate. Present material in ways that fit their "hypertext minds." Don't expect students to approach everything in the linear way you would read a book.

- Get excited about their 21st-century skills. Take advantage of the skills kids develop with their technological games and devices: problem solving, negotiating, decision making, risk taking, and questioning. Build the use of these skills into your lessons.

- Switch activities around. Knowing that information flows fast, plan projects that allot less time for information finding, and more time for synthesizing, evaluating, and applying the facts. In "the old days," students may have needed weeks to gather information for a report or project. Now there's time to show them how to dig deeper and broaden their understandings.

- Don't fight their learning habits. Don't assume that the habits they bring from their digital worlds are detrimental to learning. The research in brain-compatible learning tells us that the brain holds onto concepts attached to visual images, physical movement, music, and social interaction. Incorporate images, sounds, music, action, and discussion into their assignments, practice activities, and assessments.

- Push them where they need to go. Because they are used to finding information in small bites, allow time for the questioning and discussion processes that push them to analyze the information they find, identify its limitations, and expand upon it.

- Believe that students can multi-task. Allow them to do this where it is fitting in the classroom. These students can work with music playing. Since music is "their language," it can actually relax them, make them feel at home in the classroom, break social barriers, prime their brains for a test, or wake them up and energize them for an upcoming task. Many sources recommend music for use in the classroom. Explore this idea, and . . . if you are not using it now, try it.

Learn To Love Teaching Again

- Get used to the fast pace. Acknowledge the lightning pace, the quick thinking, the "leaping around" of minds. Identify lessons and processes that benefit from those abilities and design activities that make use of them.

- Build socializing into your lessons. The world of kids today is full of interaction, back-and-forth talking or texting, and sharing of information. Make use of those interactive skills in your learning activities.

- Be prompt. Because they live in a world of quick responses, be sure to give them prompt feedback to their assignments, assessments, questions, and ideas.

- Get smart. Find out all you can about how today's students learn. To start, watch them play video games on their cell phones or the computer. Note how the games provide directed learning and immediate feedback! Ask students to tell you how they learn. Read some of Mark Prensky's books. You'll be amazed at what the world of digital gaming can teach you.

- Be wise. Be reasonable. None of the above advice means that you don't ask students to read longer passages, to write paragraphs or essays or papers, to slow down and focus on one thing in depth, or to be quiet once in a while. It does not mean that you turn the classroom into a high-speed, fast-action, non-stop Tony Hawk video game.

- Be attuned to what the students are missing. Students living in a constantly plugged-in, regularly on-screen, lightning-speed world do need to learn how and when to slow down. They need time to think. They need time to reflect on their learning. They need to learn when to get off the Internet, get away from a screen, and get the plugs out of their ears. They need to learn how to filter through the barrage of information bombarding them and how to discern what is reliable, useful, and relevant.

When you get away from some of the long written reports, you make more time for teaching the skills they need in this century. When you pay attention to who your learners are, you will appropriately incorporate the way they really do learn into your repertoire of instructional strategies.

How Does This Reduce Paperwork?

Knowing your learners and responding with behaviors such as those described above will lead to:

- a change in the kinds of classroom learning experiences. There will be more classroom discussion, talking, sharing, and use of technology by students to show work, interactive activities. Students will DO more—creating, performing, demonstrating—to show what they've learned. These are the kinds of classroom experiences that you can view, listen to, hear, monitor, and score or notate or grade without taking home a written product.

- a change in the kind of paperwork. You'll use notebooks, rubrics, checklists, student reflection sheets, and other responding or record-keeping or grading tools that track performance without YOU having to grade dozens of papers.

- more discernment about what you assign as paperwork. Instead of thinking of just about everything as a written task, you will choose carefully those assignments that will take your time to grade. This way, when you DO read a written paper, you will do a better job and respond more thoroughly—because you have fewer papers to grade.

- a new awareness that the "millennium learner" needs plenty of experiences that are nonpaper in addition to some very valuable ones that do involve paperwork.

Make Friends with Technology

Chuckle!

A computer business teacher asked her students to retype a formal business letter—a skill she thought they would need in the world outside school. The teacher saw Sherwood becoming impatient as he searched up and down his keyboard. "Sherwood, what is the problem?" asked the teacher. "I can't find the key to make this mark; you know, the line with the dot, the one that looks like an upside down exclamation mark!"

"Sherwood," the teacher said, after peering at the student's paper, "that mark is the letter 'i'."

Today's technology greatly impacts the way our students learn—even before they come to school. IN school, technology offers a world of approaches for improved instruction, increased academic achievement, better student motivation, and greater student involvement in learning. Here are just a few examples:

- My colleague Brenda's oldest daughter was required to purchase a handheld "clicker" for her journalism class. Students respond to the professor's questions by pressing a button, and the results appear instantly on the computer, promoting further discussion. What a great tool for instant feedback!

Learn To Love Teaching Again

- Seventh- and eighth-graders at Eminence Middle School in rural Kentucky were given personal digital assistants (PDAs), enabling them to receive homework and assessments via infrared beam from the teacher's PDA. Like many states, Kentucky has a standards-based curriculum that must be taught to all students. A conscientious teacher, concerned about the language barrier, pursued other resources to teach her ESL students. A partnership was developed with the Kentucky Migrant Technology Project that soon benefited all students. The use of the PDAs quickly grew to include:
  - downloading lessons in Spanish for ESL students,
  - organizing student time through the use of the PDA calendar,
  - the use of the calculator for math problems, and
  - a door to the Internet for all students, allowing the teacher to download onto the PDAs books and plays such as *Romeo and Juliet*.

The district saved money, as there were fewer textbooks to purchase and replace. The teachers saved time by avoiding the copy machine for assignments and tests.

- At a middle school in Oak Ridge, Tennessee, an eighth-grade physical science teacher saves time grading and posting grades by using a software program called Examview. Students take their tests on computers, after which the teacher records their grades on the network and places them in an electronic grade book.

- Many schools have used electronic grade books for some years. Parents reap the benefit of access to accurate and up-to-the-minute grades, which teachers can provide with little time investment.

Positive Attitude Tip

If you do not feel comfortable integrating technology into your instruction, you owe it to your students to find engaging ways to update your lessons. To avoid becoming overwhelmed with the move to technology, start small and select a topic that is comfortable for you.

Low-Cost Strategies

The preceding examples are just a few of thousands of projects in which schools, districts, or college programs made major changes in instructional, record-keeping, or grading processes with technological solutions. An increasing number of schools are moving toward more and more technology with less and less paperwork. But these examples, important as they are, are costly and take large-scale decisions and efforts. You can increase the use of technology in your classroom in simpler ways. Here are a few ideas—all of which reduce paperwork.

- Students can email you short summaries or answers to a single challenging problem.

- One teacher recently told me that when she discovered that all the students in one of her seventh-grade classes had cell phones, she decided to use them occasionally for an activity to wrap up a unit, lesson, or day. So she gives each student a question, problem, or topic—along with a directive. They text back to her with the answer or a short summary of what they learned.

- Many computers have software that will allow students to make short movies. Use this technology to demonstrate a concept learned.

- With a digital camera, students can make and share photo journals that convey key ideas learned in a lesson, or that share an investigation they have done. Combined with other images and text, students can create short presentations with programs such as PowerPoint.

- Blogs reduce paperwork and make good use of students' digital intelligence. A blog (or web log) is an online journal, with entries in reverse chronological order. Students dialogue about what they are learning, pose questions, ask questions, or any other learning activity you prescribe. If your students have Internet access in the school, you can reduce paper use by turning assignments into blogging activities. You can keep tabs on their work by looking at the blogs.

   To learn more about blogging in the classroom, visit the Internet. There are many sites that teach you how to create and maintain a blog and how to use blogs for valuable learning experiences.

- Instead of assigning your students a long written report on a topic, ask them to design a website, start a group or page to share on MySpace or Facebook, or create material for a podcast. For instance, during Black History Month, one teacher assigned the task of creating one of the above about Martin Luther

King, Jr. to give an accurate portrayal of the man and what he stood for. To do the task, students started with the easy-to-find facts. But instead of regurgitating them (as in the old days of "copying" stuff out of the classroom encyclopedia), students had to use higher-level thinking skills plus a host of organizational and practical skills to assimilate the information into a coherent presentation. To evaluate the assignment, the teacher had only to view the final product, along with her specially created grading rubric. No huge piles of paper were used either by students or teacher.

> *To learn more about podcasting in the classroom, visit the Internet. There are many sites that teach you how to podcast and how to use podcasts for valuable learning experiences.*

- Even if technology is not available in the classroom, students can apply content they have learned to design what a web page might look like on a particular topic, or to map out plans for a podcast, or to storyboard frames for a short movie, or to write and orally share a contribution to a blog they design off-line.

Good News!

When you learn more about the digital tools that your students use (and get better at using them yourself, incorporate their use into the classroom, and make use of the skills these "millennium learners" bring to school), you will get benefits you never imagined! Part of escaping burnout is growing, learning, risking, and succeeding at new things in your profession. Get jazzed about technology in your classroom, and you'll be moving in the opposite direction from burnout!

One Sixth-Grader's Recommended Homework Schedule

✔ Students should not spend more than 90 minutes per night on homework. To get good grades in all classes, use your time this way:

✔ 11 minutes looking for the assignments

✔ 15 minutes calling a friend for the assignments

✔ 20 minutes texting friends, which of course includes a few minutes naming the latest tunes you have downloaded for homework listening

✔ 5 minutes instant messaging friends to complain about the homework

✔ 5 minutes emailing a complaint to parents (in the next room) about how mean the teacher is and how dumb the assignment is

✔ 8 minutes in the bathroom

✔ 10 minutes getting a snack

✔ 6 minutes explaining to parents that the teacher never clearly explained the assignment

✔ 10 minutes sitting at the kitchen table waiting while Mom and Dad do the assignments

Shorten the Paper Trail

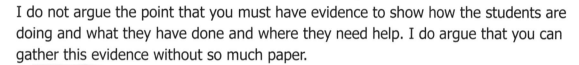

"What about accountability????"

"But, I have to keep papers to show to parents!"

"Students need to save work samples to show how they've improved!"

"I need evidence to support grades!"

Ahhhhh, yes . . . the paper trail . . . the evidence . . . the accountability!

I do not argue the point that you must have evidence to show how the students are doing and what they have done and where they need help. I do argue that you can gather this evidence without so much paper.

- Create, grade, and keep what you need to back up any assessments or grades.

- Keep what students need in order to have a good view of their progress.

- For each student, keep a portfolio of significant pieces of paper, computer files, or samples of work that show progress or demonstrate specific needs.

- Or, let students design and develop portfiolios. These can hold samples to show their accomplishments and progress, along with self-reflections on their work. Be sure to let students keep key pieces that are important to them.

- For your records: Keep a good notebook with notes about various assignments. This might be your grade book with extra pages, or might be in addition to your grade book. Keep notes for each student. Instead of 20 pieces of paper, interview students and jot down dates and comments in this notebook.

- When possible, store records and grades electronically if it is appropriate and student records are secure.

- But do not keep anything that does not have a specific purpose to show student progress or to show a specific ability or need.

Teacher-to-Teacher Tip

"Take fewer grades. Eliminate 'fluff.' It eases your workload and forces the students to see every assignment as meaningful!"
– High-school teacher, Texas

Face It! Manage It! Prioritize!

There's been a lot of advice about the paperwork you generate for yourself and your students. But then, there is everything else—such as . . .

permission slips

absentee notes

memos from the principal

memos from the department chair

memos from the curriculum director

notebooks of standards

lunch menus

requisition forms

emergency forms

attendance counts

lesson plans

lunch counts

printed-out emails

Sometimes it is just the size of the pile and the thought of it growing and burying us that immobilizes teachers. The sheer volume turns it into a monster with a physical form—bestial, really—with mocking eyes, foaming mouth, sneering taunts and jeers. It's a natural thing to want to just run away (avoid, hide, procrastinate) from the growing mound. But, that option will leave you with far more stress. So . . .

Face It!

Tackle the stuff head on. The pile may not be as bad as you think. Odds are, much of it will end up in the trash anyway once you sift out the essentials.

Manage It!

Do a quick sorting of paperwork as soon as you find it in your teacher box or you get to your classroom. Immediately dispose of anything that is not needed. Toss that invitation to a dog show if you are allergic to dogs. Take that memo about an upcoming meeting and dump it as soon as you write the date and details on your calendar. If looking at a bank of papers waiting on your desk makes your head spin, make sure to avoid careless deposits!

If something just needs a quick response, take care of it right away. If there is a birthday card in your box that needs signing, add your best wishes and pass it on. If you find a form that you forgot to complete, fill in the blanks right there and drop it off at the office on your way back to the classroom.

Use the computer as much as possible. Many school forms are now online or can be e-mailed as attachments. Take advantage of this. Not only do you reduce the menacing pile of paperwork, but since the information is saved on the computer, you save time. The next time that form needs to be filled out, much of it is already completed.

Establish a file system before school begins. A simple system can help even the folder-challenged and the manila-phobic. Create a file for extra assignment sheets to give to students who are absent (or absent-minded!). Use another file for extra student forms and one for parent communications. When you organize those forms and spare copies, you reduce the pile. You also avoid the stress of frantically digging around on your desk when you need something. Don't leave for the day until you've filed stuff lying on your desk.

Prioritize!

Use the Top Drawer System—a good plan that works for getting paperwork done!

Make a list of the things you consider "must-get-dones" for the day. This list might be written at home before your morning drive, as soon as you get to school, or even as the last thing you do every afternoon, leaving the list for your next day's arrival.

As you write the items on the list, divide those tasks into top-drawer, middle-drawer and bottom-drawer priorities. You can use actual drawers, such as one of those small plastic sets of drawers from a discount store. Write items in pencil so you can move them around on the list as needed.

Top drawer: Jobs that must be done today. There is no flexibility on the deadline.

Middle drawer: Tasks that have to be completed by late today or tomorrow.

Bottom drawer: Items that need to be taken care of by the end of the week. Sometimes these jobs will take care of themselves or will just go away. This is even more reason to place them in the "bottom drawer." Why waste today's valuable time on issues that may not even exist in a few days?

As things change during the day, simply adjust the items into different "drawers."

Learn To Love Teaching Again

Let's look at an example. Middle-grades history teacher Mr. Hamill has his "need-to-do" list ready for Monday morning:

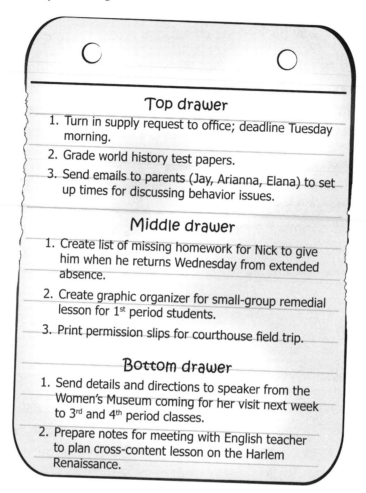

Top drawer

1. Turn in supply request to office; deadline Tuesday morning.
2. Grade world history test papers.
3. Send emails to parents (Jay, Arianna, Elana) to set up times for discussing behavior issues.

Middle drawer

1. Create list of missing homework for Nick to give him when he returns Wednesday from extended absence.
2. Create graphic organizer for small-group remedial lesson for 1st period students.
3. Print permission slips for courthouse field trip.

Bottom drawer

1. Send details and directions to speaker from the Women's Museum coming for her visit next week to 3rd and 4th period classes.
2. Prepare notes for meeting with English teacher to plan cross-content lesson on the Harlem Renaissance.

Mr. Hamill has stared down the paperwork monster. He feels a lot better now that he has a doable plan for getting the tasks done. And when the curriculum director requests a list of units he intends to teach this semester (due at the end of the week), or one of the students suddenly needs to leave for an out-of-town funeral and needs homework to take along (today)—he can rearrange tasks in the drawers.

Shred It or Recycle It!

Whatever paper you use—make it reusable. Unless papers are of personal, confidential manner (and be oh-so-careful about disposal of these), don't toss them thoughtlessly. Shred whatever it is that should not be seen again. Everything else that is recyclable should be recycled. Reuse papers right in the classroom—for problem solving, drawing, or doodling. If your school does not have a recycling program, start one.

Spread the Less-Paperwork Spirit

"Paperwork is endless. I can feel totally caught up one day and swamped the next. I take home papers to grade every night. It's a challenge to keep up with it, but it pays off. It's not just the papers to grade—it's the forms to fill out, lesson plans to prepare, committee duties to fulfill, orders to place, and on and on. Except for grading papers, I try to complete everything else at school. Unfortunately, that requires me to stay many long hours beyond the school day. A ten- or eleven-hour school day is typical for me."
– Teacher of over 16 years in the classroom

"Just let me teach! I know that we need to document our efforts more than ever before, but it takes so much valuable time away from actually teaching!"
– Elementary school teacher with over 21 years experience

"Employers are frustrated because there is so much paperwork and oftentimes you don't know if things are real or not."
– John Gay, English poet and dramatist, 1685–1732

Reading complaints like these may not make you feel any better, but at least you know you are not alone. Some paperwork requirements are out of your control. More student accountability and more legal liability means more documentation. Very little of this paperwork seems to have anything to do with why you became an educator. As Texas high-school teacher Audrey Myrosh laments, "There is a lot [of paperwork]. I'm not sure most of it is needed."

Teachers who may be willing to give up family or recreation time to prepare instruction just do not feel the same level of buy-in for filling out forms in triplicate that have no obvious and direct link to whether little Elliot, Keisia, and Marlene understand how to multiply fractions.

Many state education departments and school districts are making efforts to address this problem of too much paperwork eating into too little instructional time. Some districts are turning to online or web-based systems to help manage special education documentation. Everywhere, schools are rethinking paperwork requirements. If your school or district doesn't have a paperwork-reduction plan in place, push for a task force on the topic. This kind of participation gives you an opportunity to weigh in on practices and processes that directly affect teachers. You are in the trenches—who knows better than you just where the heaviest paperwork demands are and what is needed to lighten the load?

Even if you must start small, such as within your own grade level, department, or team, be part of some action to bring this to the attention of a wider group of your colleagues.

Falling in Love Again

Get creative! There are so many ways to cut down on burdensome paperwork! You just have to take bold steps to try them out. Join forces with colleagues, brainstorm ideas, and collect ideas from other places. When you succeed in personal paperwork reduction, or even better—a school-wide paper reduction, students with less paperwork busywork will be more engaged in the learning process, there will be faster feedback to students on their work, and the school will be less wasteful of the planet's resources.

And, as a teacher, there will be more time for you to do what you love. These are the things that led you to the profession in the first place: motivating, teaching, relating to, inspiring, nurturing, and guiding your students.

Me Moments

- Keep a good book of humor or cartoons, or a magazine article in your bag or desk drawer for those moments in which you just need a little break. If the book provokes a laugh, you get a shot of endorphins as an added bonus!

- Put yourself on a reward system for completed paperwork. Set small goals. Give yourself small rewards. For instance, create four piles of students' science reports. After grading one stack, get up and move around. Get yourself a small treat. Take a trip to the sink or water fountain for a cold drink of water. (I play one game of spider solitaire after every 45 minutes of paperwork). By rewarding yourself, you recognize your forward movement. (This is a stress reliever because thinking that we are getting nowhere puts us in a tizzy!) It's also a small celebration of your accomplishment.

Chapter 2 **Tools**

Guide to Creating Your Own Rubric

STEP 1 Topic
Identify the topic, assignment, skill, or major task to be evaluated.

STEP 2 Components
Identify components, such as outcomes, traits, individual skills, or tasks—the areas of performance that you will examine and assess. For example, ask yourself: If I am going to find out how well a fifth-grader is able to construct an argumentative paragraph, what are the components that make a successful argumentative paragraph?

STEP 3 Score
Decide on a scoring scale—such as 1 to 5 or 1 to 3. Keep the score range at 6 or below, with a smaller range for younger students. These numbers will constitute the span of performance levels related to the components.

STEP 4 Criteria
Identify the criteria for each level of performance. Start by writing a description of the top-score performance for each component. Ask yourself: What constitutes an excellent job on this? Then describe what a student product would look like at other levels (such as strong, adequate, satisfactory, developing, needs a lot of work, and so on). Write phrases or complete sentences. Describe performance for each score.

STEP 5 The Grid
Create a rubric grid with enough rows to list components and enough columns to describe criteria for all scores. Fill in the title for the rubric (topic or assignment), fill in the column titles, list the components, and put the descriptors into the rubric.

STEP 6 Share the Rubric
Be sure to share the criteria with students ahead of time, explained in language they understand. Students need to know what constitutes a good performance. Before they start the task, the rubric will show them how they will be evaluated.

Rating Home-made Chocolate Chip Cookies

Required Characteristics	Score 5	Score 3	Score 1
Appearance	Perfectly round with mounded middle, loaded with chips	Mostly round, somewhat flat, chips not plentiful	Flat, odd-shaped, few visible chips, or charred
Smell	Irresistible	Slightly inviting	Burned
Texture	Soft, moist, creamy	Overly chewey or crisp	Tough as nails
Taste	Fresh, warm, heavy chocolate, and very sweet	Slightly sweet, day-old taste	Stale, bland, not chocolatey

Rubric

Topic or **Skill**

What is the objective?	How Well Can I Do It? or How Well Do I Know It?			
score	4	3	2	1

Rubric

**Topic,
Assignment,
or Skill** _____

Components	Competency Level			
score	**4**	**3**	**2**	**1**

Rubric

Assignment _____

Competency Level

Assignment Components	Score of 4	Score of 3	Score of 2	Score of 1

Rubric

Topic or Assignment _____

Competency Level Criteria

Expectations	score of 4	score of 3	score of 2	score of 1

62

Rubric

Assignment _____

Performance Level

Trait, Skill, or Task	score of 5	score of 3	score of 1

Rubric Samples

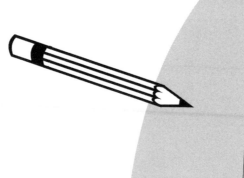

Rubric

Topic or Assignment _Dramatic Poetry_

Competency Level Criteria

Objectives	score of 4	score of 3	score of 2	score of 1
Read and interpret dramatic poetry	Interpretation written on each of two poems-with personal response and at least three details from poem to support each interpretation	Interpretation written on each of two poems-with personal response and one or more details from poem to support each interpretation	Coherent interpretation written on each of two poems showing some personal response and one or no substantiating details	1-page sensible attempt at interpretation written on one or two of the poems, little or no personal connection, little or no detail
Analyze the use of similes, metaphors, personification, and irony in dramatic poetry	Clear explanation of at least six examples of similes, metaphors, personification, and irony from the two selected poems	Clear explanation of at least five examples of similes, metaphors, personification, and irony from the two selected poems	Clear explanation of at least four examples of similes, metaphors, personification, and irony from the two selected poems	Clear explanation of at least three examples of similes, metaphors, personification, and irony from the two selected poems
Identify themes of dramatic poetry	Clear explanation of one theme from each poem, related to student's life, using multiple examples from the poem	Adequate explanation of one theme from each poem, related to student's life, using a few examples from the poem	Adequate explanation of one theme from each poem, with an attempt to relate to own life and to use examples	Adequate attempt at explanation of one theme from each poem

A score of 4 may be given for work that falls between 3 and 5 on a trait.
A score of 2 may be given for work that falls between 1 and 3.

Rubric

Problem-Solving Process

Assignment

Performance Level

Trait, Skill, or Task	score of 5	score of 3	score of 1
Conceptual Understanding	• Work shows that the problem is clearly identified and understood • Work clearly translates written problem into a mathematical idea	• Work shows the problem is adequately identified and understood • Adequate job of translating the written problem into a mathematical idea	• Work does not show clear identification or understanding of the problem • Partial or incorrect job of translating written problem into a mathematical idea
Strategies & Processes	• Appropriate strategies chosen for solving the problem • Strategies used in complete, clear, complex manner to move toward a solution • Use of clear and complete equations, symbols, models, pictures, diagrams	• Appropriate strategies chosen for solving the problem • Strategies used in somewhat complete, clear, complex manner to move toward a solution • Use of relatively clear and complete equations, symbols, models, pictures, diagrams	• Appropriate strategies not chosen or not used correctly • Strategies not used effectively to move toward a solution • Incomplete equations, symbols, models, pictures, diagrams, or these tools do not lead to a correct solution
Communication	• Words, pictures, symbols, and/or graphics that clearly and expertly show steps to a solution • Clear and sensible explanation of the use of the strategies and of the path taken to solution is clear and sensible	• Words, pictures, symbols, and/or graphics that adequately show steps to a solution • Adequate explanation of the use of the strategies and of the path taken to solution	• Words, pictures, symbols, and/or graphics do not clearly show steps to a solution • Skimpy or nonexistent communication of student's processes
Accuracy of Answer	• Correct answer • Student answer supported by student's work	• Mostly correct answer • Student answer supported by student's work	• Incorrect or incomplete answer AND/OR • Student answer not supported by student's work
Verification	• Work shows a review of problem-solving process and effective attempt to justify the answer or arrive at it in different way • Student's review supports student's answer	• Work shows a review of problem-solving process and an attempt to justify the answer or arrive at it in different way • Student's review supports student's answer	• Work does not show an effective or complete review of the process or a defense of the solution

A score of 2 may be given for work that falls between 1 and 3.

"To be, or not to be..."

Sample Grade K

Rubric

Topic or **Skill** _Assessment of Fine Motor Skills—Using Scissors_

What is the objective?	How Well Can I Do It? or How Well Do I Know it?			
score	4	3	2	1
Holds scissors appropriately	Cuts with proper placement of fingers on scissors	Cuts with scissors upside down, with thumb in the bottom position	Needs assistance to place scissors correctly in hand before cutting	Needs assistance to place scissors in hand, but cannot hold it correctly long enough to cut
Makes a cut repeatedly	Cuts with long snips	Cuts with a series of short snips	Needs assistance to manipulate scissors in appropriate motion	Cannot coordinate the appropriate seesaw motion of the scissors
Cuts lines and shapes	Accurately cuts out a preprinted shape, such as a square, circle, or triangle	Accurately cuts along jagged or wavy lines	Accurately cuts along a straight line	Needs assistance to cut along a straight line

This really helps!

Rubric

Topic, Assignment, or Skill _PowerPoint Presentation_

Components	Competency Level			
score	4	3	2	1
Content	Almost all of the content answered the question or directive of the assignment.	About three-quarters of the content answered the question of the assignment.	Content attempted to answer the question, but information was confusing and strayed off topic.	Content had little relevance to the assignment.
Language and mechanics	Words were spelled correctly, and appropriate grammar and punctuation were used.	There were few errors in grammar, usage, or mechanics.	There were many errors in language and/or mechanics.	There was little evidence of any attempt made to proofread or correct errors. Multiple errors interfered with presentation of the topic.
Purpose of assignment	The purpose of the assignment was clearly evident.	The purpose of the assignment was evident yet was not clearly presented.	Some attempt was made to convey the purpose of the assignment.	The purpose of the assignment was not clear.
Graphics, photos, and art	Graphics, photos, and clip art supported content effectively.	Graphics, photos, and clip art were used and mostly supported the content.	Some graphics, photos, and clip art were used, although not always effectively.	Very few graphics, photos, and clip art were used to support the content.
Slides	Presentation of content on slides was visually pleasing. Slide transitions were appropriate.	Slide transition or content presentation needed improvement on one or two slides.	Major errors were present in slide transition or content presentation.	No care was taken when placing content on slides. Transitions did not flow smoothly and detracted from the presentation.

My Thoughts About My Project

Student Name _____

Project Name _____

♣ What was your project about? _____

_____

_____

♣ What did you do first, second, (and so on)? _____

_____

_____

_____

♣ What did you do very well? _____

_____

_____

♣ What was the hardest part for you? _____

_____

_____

♣ What did you learn? _____

_____

♣ How could you show someone else what you learned? ____

_____

_____

Note: An adult or older student interviews the young student and records the answers on this sheet or in another record-keeping location.

66

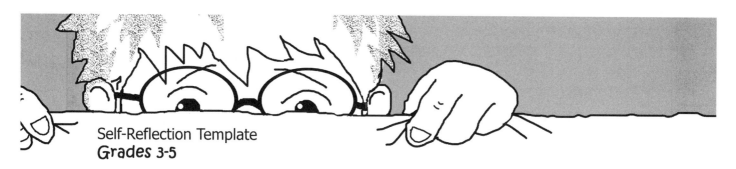

My Reflection on My Work

Student _____

Activity or Project _____

★ The purpose of this activity was

_____

_____

★ Three steps I took to complete this activity included

1. _____

2. _____

3. _____

★ One new thing I learned is _____

_____

★ Something that was hard about the activity was _____

_____

★ *Directions: Put a check in the boxes below that match your effort on this assignment.*

Tasks for this Activity	I did this very well.	I tried but did not always succeed.	I was not able to accomplish this for this project.
I made a plan for this assignment and was able to stick to it.			
I was able to concentrate and stay focused on my work.			
I understood the assignment and asked for help when I needed it.			
I spent time researching and used several resources to gather information.			

Self-Evaluation of My Work

Name: _____

Project: _____

For each heading, rate your effort by circling **low, medium,** or **high.**

1
My focus on the project:

low   medium   high

I chose this rating because
_____
_____
_____

2
My responsibility in getting the work done:

low   medium   high

I chose this rating because
_____
_____
_____

3
My participation in the small group:

low   medium   high

I chose this rating because
_____
_____
_____

4
My role as a positive team member:

low   medium   high

I chose this rating because
_____
_____
_____

5
My ability to solve problems that came up:

low   medium   high

I chose this rating because
_____
_____
_____

6
My satisfaction with the final product:

low   medium   high

I chose this rating because
_____
_____
_____

7
My satisfaction with the group process:

low   medium   high

I chose this rating because
_____
_____
_____

Yikes! The Parents Are Coming!

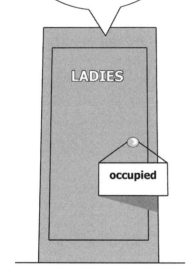

You know you are a teacher under stress when you hide in the bathroom every time you see a parent coming around the corner.

Years ago, Dr. Cole and I enrolled our three-year-old daughters in a new program at the school where we were teaching. This 3K program promised awesome benefits for our children, and the teacher seemed terrific. During the first week, my daughter was sent to the time-out chair. I took the news in stride and Brenda empathized. The next day Brenda's daughter went to time out. We were supportive of the teacher—knowing that our girls had to adapt to the social rules of the classroom. But a pattern developed; each day one of the girls warmed the chair. And each afternoon the 3K teacher looked for one of us to report the latest "misdemeanor" perpetrated by the child. We developed inner alarm clocks at dismissal time, and learned to make ourselves scarce.

In reality, the preschoolers' infractions were small (getting out of line or taking a block from another student) and were easily resolved by the teacher within the classroom setting. The girls sat in time-out for just a few moments. But being accosted daily with such a negative laundry list had us anxious and annoyed. In a few weeks, the constant barrage of reports had numbed us to the teacher's comments, even when the infractions were more serious. Brenda and I were not part of a team with the 3K teacher. We were forced into defensive positions.

When parents are driven to act like mother (or father) tigers protecting their young, there is little chance for educational teamwork. Such an oppositional relationship causes great (and unnecessary) stress for both the teacher and the parents.

Note: The word "parent" identifies any adult who has primary responsibility for a student.

Losing the Love

Pushy parents, hostile parents, skeptical parents, unsupportive parents, hovering parents, critical parents—some complaint about parents is usually on any teacher's list of things that make the job stressful. There's nothing that drains you, bugs you, keeps you on edge, or shakes your confidence quite like conflict with a parent. It doesn't even have to be an outright battle. Any tension with a parent or suspicion that a parent is dissatisfied with you can leave a knot in your stomach and tear your mind away from your teaching. And what about that feeling that parents are gossiping with other parents about you? That can shake the love of teaching right out of you. Even worse, troubles with parents (or just no connection with the parents) keep your students from having the supportive team that they need for success in school.

The idea in the cartoon on page 69 is no joke. Many teachers spend a lot of time avoiding parents. You **can't** hide in the bathroom forever. You **can** come out of the shadows and build bridges to families and parents. When you do this effectively, you'll have gained a major weapon in the fight against stress and burnout. And your students will flourish.

The Bridge to Parents

Effective teachers know that parental support increases the likelihood of student success. Teachers who run for cover as soon as the last school bell rings only think they are avoiding stress. Parents are the most important and influential people in the arena of a child's life (yes, even for teenagers!). On a school day, your students may actually spend more waking hours with you than with their parents; and you certainly have an impact on the students. But parents or guardians are the grounding force in your students' lives. Keep that in mind. If you want the best for your students, you must find a way to forge respectful, working partnerships with parents. What does a teacher-parent partnership look like? Together, all partners:

- act as affirming advocates for students.
- provide support for one another.
- join in learning activities for the student.
- create a decision-making and problem-solving team.
- engage in curriculum-based classroom projects.

Follow these steps on your way to building relationships with parents that boost student success and build the support you need:

1. Let parents know you care about their children.

Show your care and concern from Day One. When school starts (or even before school starts), begin a relationship with every parent or guardian.

- Send an email or "snail mail" telling a bit about yourself, your goals for the year, and your passion for teaching their children. (A written letter gives a more personal touch. Also, you may not have access to all parents' email addresses, or some parents may not have email access.)

- Establish an open-classroom-door policy for parents who need to drop in with an immediate worry.

- Let parents know how and when they can talk to you—in person, on the phone, or by email or written notes. Publish your school email address, and be sure to check and respond as soon as possible to any parental issues.

- Make it clear to parents that your goal is to help their child have a safe, comfortable, and academically successful experience in your classroom.

2. Let parents know that you respect them.

It may take a while to establish a partnership with some of your parents. They may come with anxieties about their own difficult school experiences. Some might feel intimidated if there is a language difference or if they themselves were not successful academically. Imagine the trepidation of a parent who barely made it through high school because of an undiagnosed learning disability now hearing similar concerns about his child! Know that parents who are belligerent may actually be so because they feel insecure or intellectually inferior around teachers. (They may have had teachers they

Learn To Love Teaching Again

didn't trust or teachers that terrified them when they were children.)

As the teacher, be caring and patient, and tread lightly where needed. Keep in mind the parents' fears, anxieties, and deep desires for their children to be loved and to be successful. From the very beginning, treat them as the primary adults in their childrens' lives. Respect their ideas, their excuses, their schedules, their worries, and their questions.

As my daughter grew older and more independent, I was deeply grateful to the teachers who answered my queries about assignments and other classroom issues within hours of my frantic emails. As a parent, this kind of support—showing care for my child and respect for me—was invaluable.

3. Communicate clearly and proactively.

Too often, communication to parents is poorly planned (or not planned at all). When a problem arises—a note gets sent, a quick email is dashed off, or a spur-of-the-moment phone call is made. Haphazard communication does not build solid relationships with parents. Instead, it leads to confusion for them, you, and eventually the students. Often it intimidates or angers parents—harming the relationship.

Chuckle!

After Jeff left the lights on in his Subaru overnight, the battery was dead. He had to get to work! He ran into the house and shouted to his wife to get in her car and push the Subaru fast enough to get it started. He explained that she needed to push him at about 30 mph for the car to start. When he saw her drive away, he was perplexed. While he sat fumbling for his cell phone to call her, he looked in his rearview mirror. Her car was barreling toward him from behind at about 40 mph. Jeff realized that his communication to her was unclear.

Think ahead about how you will make connections with the parents of your students. Have a plan. Start before school begins. For each individual contact you make with a parent, consider (**before** the call, note, or email) how you will make the message as clear as possible. Think about how you will eliminate the barriers that might leave the parent baffled or upset— because these things **will** get in the way of the message. Make sure that most of your communications are positive (not about problems). Long before a problem arises with a student, you should have set in place the trusting relationship with the parents that will make it easier to solve the problem as partners.

Positive Attitude Tip

Take a minute to picture the words you are about to say before they leave your mouth. If the sentence ends in an exclamation mark (and is not strongly positive), it is best to rephrase. If the sentence ends in two or more exclamation points, it's time to check your medication.

Clear communication:

- uses language parents can understand,
- states concisely the purpose of the communication,
- states concisely what you need from the parent(s),
- states concisely what you will do next,
- is done in a calm, warm tone (not a tone that could frighten, intimidate, or confuse them),
- summarizes the conclusions, consensus, decisions, or planned action, and
- lessens the stress level of teachers and parents when done well.

Proactive communication . . .

- fosters greater understanding and trust between parents and teachers,
- increases the intensity of the parent-teacher partnership, as parents have a better idea of what is happening and what is planned for the future,
- heads off problems based on misunderstandings before they have a chance to grow, and
- lessens the stress level of teachers and parents.

Proactive communication is the opposite from what is often (unfortunately) the nature of many parent-teacher contacts. This phrase describes a whole host of strategies and processes the teacher uses to actively establish and nurture a relationship with the parents throughout the year. Its purposes are to acknowledge parents as an important part of their child's learning community, to make use of the wisdom parents have to offer, to keep parents informed about what's going on at school, and to help them understand the expectations for their children. This kind of communication has some beneficial side effects: Parents feel more comfortable with and respected by the teacher. And with parents more aware of the academic activities and expectations for their children, there is likely to be the kind of home support that helps students do their best in school.

Every teacher has to settle on just the right approaches for communicating with parents. Consider these kinds of tools or practices for clear, proactive communication:

Believe me, these postcards to parents are worth the cost.

- a regular newsletter—the kind that can be posted on the refrigerator
- an electronic newsletter—as a supplement or option to the above
- before-school-begins phone calls, notes, or postcards
- ongoing email communication
- clear ways for parents to contact you
- periodic "good news" phone calls to individual families
- periodic "good news" notes or postcards to individual families
- invitations to parents to drop by during a particular time period
- special family events in the classroom (during school or evening)

Use the "Teacher's Checklist for Parent Communications" to guide your communication in all parent contacts. This is found in the Tools section at the end of this chapter.

4. Make newsletters a habit.

As a school administrator I became so convinced of the value of classroom newsletters that I required all my teachers to send them home twice a month. Teachers were free to design their own, customizing them to the age of their students and to the teacher personalities. I decided to follow my own directive by producing a school newsletter in the same time frame. Throughout our school community, staff, parents, and students reaped the benefits all year from this consistent proactive communication.

A regular newsletter is a sure way to keep open the bridge to families. Newsletters are also great ways to . . .

- promote student or class success,
- build awareness for parents of the curriculum topics and activities their children are pursuing,
- keep parents informed about upcoming tests, projects, or field trips,
- remind parents of schoolwide events,
- ask for donations of time or materials, and
- advertise needs for classroom speakers or other help.

We found that when teachers informed parents about upcoming content-area units of study, the parents often offered help or materials, or suggested potential speakers (or offered to be the speaker). This saved the teachers time and strengthened parent-teacher partnerships.

Problems between parents and teachers often arise because of misunderstandings about classroom expectations. For example, one fifth-grade teacher assigned a big geography project for his social studies class. He reviewed the project expectations repeatedly over an entire week, showing many examples and restating the deadline that was six weeks away. The day before the projects were due, three parents came looking for the fifth-grade teacher. They had just heard about the project from their children and were upset that the teacher actually expected all that work in just two nights. Now, if the assignment had been described in the two or three newsletters preceding its completion date, the parents would have had plenty of warning. And the teacher would not have had to wear that Groucho Marx disguise to school!

Teacher-to-Teacher Tip

"Be sure that all students get a chance to shine in print. Add a column in your student roll book and look for things to recognize in the newsletter. Check off names as they are included. Find something to celebrate about every child. "

– First-year teacher

"But I don't have time to do a newsletter every two weeks!" you might be protesting. Relax! This does not have to take hours of your time. And, believe me, it will take less time than you will spend on miscommunications and re-communications if you don't do this. Here are some tips to make it easy:

- Create a template to use all year long. Use column headings that will be standard for each newsletter—such as **Classroom News**, **School Events**, **The Brag Box**, **Homework Hints**, and **Monthly Calendar**. By including consistent features, parents will know where to look for information. (See sample newsletters in the Tools section at the end of this chapter.) Most of my staff developed templates with their favorite software programs, but one teacher knew that her discomfort with technology would add too much stress to her life. She chose to design a hand-drawn template, which suited her class and her personality and was just as effective a communication form.

- Add inviting touches with a family problem to solve, favorite jokes, student-created drawings or poems, or photographs of students involved in favorite activities.

- If you teach older students, assign some of the newsletter-writing tasks to them. This is a wonderful chance to work on writing, editing, organization, formatting, drawing, and computer skills. Pairs of students or small groups can be responsible for individual features. The computer allows for ease of putting elements together.

- Add information to the newsletter as it occurs, as opposed to writing it all at once on the same night the dishwasher dies or your daughter has a championship soccer game. As parents are reading the current newsletter, you can already have the standard columns (such as birthdays and scheduled events on the calendar) filled in for the next newsletter.

- Don't labor over every word. A classroom newsletter never needs to be in competition for a Pulitzer Prize. Parents are looking for straightforward, basic information—something they can glance over, get the news they need, and put on the fridge for future reference. (On the other hand, be absolutely sure that you do not send home a newsletter with spelling, grammar, or structural errors.)

Also, include these in your newsletter plans:

→ If you consider an electronic newsletter, be sure to give each parent the option to receive a hard paper copy. Do not assume that all families will have a computer available. Even if they do, they may not all have a printer.

→ If any of the parents are non-English speaking, find a way to provide a substitute communication that they can read. At the very least, try to provide a paper calendar in the native language.

5. Be confident in your professional ability.

Be professional and confident in your expertise as an educator. Remember that you have training to do what you are doing. Parents will feel safer and more cooperative if they believe their child is in capable hands.

- Do not be intimidated when a parent offers help or advice or asks questions. If you start a positive relationship with parents at the beginning of the year, parent questions or even criticisms will not unnerve you so readily.

- Welcome the support and involvement of parents. If you plan ahead for parent involvement, you'll feel more comfortable and less defensive when parents show up.

- Let your confidence also allow you to be humble and compassionate. Know that the parents have much to offer you in understanding their child. Use your position to offer help, hope, and security to them. Know also, there are often family circumstances of which you are not aware. A family that is just surviving due to economic disadvantages, abuse, or physical or mental illness may not be able to help a child complete a project. In that situation, look for ways to be inclusive of the child's caregivers, and use your expertise to find other ways to help the student be successful at meeting academic expectations.

New Teacher Tip

It's a challenge for a new teacher to win the confidence of students' parents. Be honest. Do not pretend that you have more experience than you really have. When you are not sure of something, say so. But assure parents that you will find out. Do your research and get back to them. What you lack in years of experience, you can make up for in diligence and reliability.

6. Welcome parents into the learning community.

It is far too easy (and common) for parents to feel uneasy when contacting a teacher, entering the classroom, or even setting foot in the school. The discomfort might have to do with their own past experiences as a student, or their experiences with former school personnel, or their embarrassment about what their children might or might not be doing, or their feelings about how their children are treated. Make sure the discomfort is not about the way

Learn To Love Teaching Again

you presently treat them or their children. Instead, take purposeful measures that show a welcoming spirit.

- Examine your own attitudes toward parents. If you are not keenly aware of your own fears, values, biases, and goals for parent relationships, you will be caught off guard with your responses to parents. Do your best to put your anxieties, suspicions, or reservations aside when you have any contact with parents. Use the "Teacher Self-Reflection on Parent Relationships" tool to help you examine your attitudes and style, found in the Tools section at the end of this chapter.

- See every parent as an advocate for his or her child and as a cheerleader for you—the person they trust to help their child have a happy and successful school year.

- Be accessible to parents. Let them know how to reach you. Make every effort to be hospitable, warm, and available when they need you.

- Invite them to the classroom. Even if you do not have time, take at least a few minutes to find out what they need. ALWAYS thank them for coming. ALWAYS ask for and honor their ideas.

- Plan ahead for reasonable ways parents can be involved in the learning processes of their children. Make sure you create options varied enough for all your parents' different schedules, talents, and ability to take part. Put these possibilities in writing. See ideas for using parents as volunteers later in this chapter.

Effective Conferences

Though Mr. Cameron had a full year of teaching under his belt, he was a bit flustered when Mrs. McGraw showed up for her parent-teacher conference. Taking a deep breath, he explained that her daughter Samantha did not always pay attention in class, and many times seemed a little flighty. To illustrate the point he explained how Samantha would do the wrong page in a workbook, or even sit in someone else's desk by mistake. Mrs. McGraw immediately became defensive. "I just do not understand. Where could she have gotten behavior like that?" Mr. Cameron quickly reassured Mrs. McGraw that Samantha was sweet and likeable and had many friends in class. The teacher then paused and quietly told Mrs. McGraw her appointment with him was actually for the next day.

How many teachers do you know who look forward to parent-teacher conferences? (Be honest!) In many schools, it's almost a tradition to face the biannual parent-teacher conferences with dread and groans. First, there's the preparation time. Then there's the stress of the conference itself—the relentless schedule, the vague suspicions or fears about what might happen or not happen, the worries about parent judgment, and on and on.

Are "parent-teacher conferences" on your list of personal stressors? If so, you definitely can cross this one off. The truth is that teachers **do** need to meet with parents a few times a year, whether through formal parent-teacher conferences at the end of grading periods or on an individual basis, engaging with parents before or after school. Parents need to hear about the progress of their children. Face-to-face meetings create trust, build better communication roadways, and help form a bond necessary for an optimal learning environment. Parent conferences **can truly be something you like**—if you have the attitude that they are good for the students, the parents, and you; if you are well prepared; and if you take specific measures to comfortably and meaningfully engage the parents. Follow these tips to make parent-teacher conferences productive:

1. Create a welcoming environment.

- Create a neat, uncluttered space. If the meeting is more impromptu and you don't have time to ready the whole room, find one spot you can clean up quickly. (Think of the stuff you jam in your hall closet at home when meticulous Aunt Sylvia calls to say she is in the neighborhood and wants to stop by just for a minute.)

- Avoid sitting behind your desk and having the parent sit across from you. That physical barrier can cause a feeling of distance or superiority. **Never** have parents sit in chairs meant for young children. Even if you feel comfortable perched on a first-grade stool, remember that most adults do not spend the day balanced on chairs meant for small bottoms. If you need to, meet the parents in another place with "grown-up seating"— such as the library, cafeteria, or on an outside bench.

"Actually, Mr. and Mrs. Lark, you're a bit late for the conference. Jeffrey was in my class last year."

- If you are scheduled for several conferences in a row, create a warm environment. Consider soft background music and a bowl of snacks. Offer water, tea, or coffee to the parents. Hand them a welcome note or picture from their child as they sit down. Simple gestures like these instantly set a friendly mood and de-stress anxious parents.

Learn To Love Teaching Again

- Think about how you present yourself. What kind of energy greets your visitors? Do you remain in your seat and wave them in? Do you give the impression that you're anxious to get this over with? **Do** be conscious of the attitude you project. Walk toward the parent(s) energetically, extend your hand, thank them for coming. Make sure the parents get the message that you are glad they came. Keep in mind that the first few minutes of your interaction with the parent sets the tone for the entire meeting.

2. Use effective listening techniques.

As parents speak, you must do more than simply hear them. You must do more than prepare what you are going to say next. **You must listen.** Listen not only to what the parent is saying. Hearing what the parent is **not** saying can be just as important. Follow these tips to practice effective listening:

- Give the parent your full attention. Make sure your posture shows engagement and interest. Tune out distracting thoughts.

- Try not to interrupt, but be ready to help if a parent is struggling with the language. Repeat what the parent states to affirm that you understand.

- Be supportive, not only of what the parent is saying, but of her right to her viewpoint. Even if you do not agree, make it clear that you respect her perspective and will consider it. Avoid getting caught up in stereotypes. (For example: "Ben behaves that way because he comes from a single-parent home," or "Lydia does not get the help she needs because her parents are immigrants.")

- Take notes, especially if you have several conferences in one day. Note-taking shows your interest, and leaves you with reminders of parents' ideas and joint decisions.

- Be patient and comfortable with silence. When you ask a question—especially one that is sensitive, simply wait. Give the parents a few moments to gather thoughts, and perhaps courage. If you get nervous and fill every thoughtful second with chatter, parents will get frustrated, and you'll reduce chances for real breakthroughs.

- Minimize distractions. Arrange a way to alert yourself a few minutes before the meeting's end so that you are not constantly looking at your watch instead of focusing on the conversation.

Positive Attitude Tip

Never surprise a parent with a conference. When you request a meeting, summarize its purpose. Too many near-accidents and anxiety attacks are caused when a parent gets this kind of phone call: "Mr. Axle, I need you to stop by this afternoon to talk about Patricia."

3. Make a student sandwich.

Before every conference, remember this axiom about parenthood: *Having a child is like living for the rest of your life with your heart outside your body.* When parents walk through your classroom door, emotions will be strong, many times centered on fear or anxiety. (I have led hundreds of conferences with parents. Yet, when my child's teacher asks to meet with me, I shake like a puppy in a thunderstorm.) Even if a parent is aware of what you are going to say, the process is intimidating. To build a parent-teacher partnership and to initiate effective change, select one issue for your focus. Sandwich that focus between compliments.

Example: *Ms. MacKenzie showed Tomas's parents three papers to illustrate the good progress he was making in math. Next, the teacher voiced her concern about Tomas's increasing difficulty getting along with others at recess. Once the parents understood the issue, teacher and parents moved on to make a plan to help Tomas improve his behavior. The teacher didn't dwell on the negative. She spent more time working with the parents on a solution. Ms. MacKenzie wrapped up the conference by passing on a compliment from her aide who had reported how well Tomas has cooperated in transitions to other classes such as music, art, and P.E.*

4. State any problem in clear, concise, observable terms.

You might approach a conference just itching to let the parents know how patient you have been to put up with their child. Inside, you might be screaming, "You have the rudest, most incorrigible child. Haven't you taught him any respect?" But, of course, such a statement would destroy any hope of a productive parent-teacher relationship.

If you feel really worked up about a student, take a walk before meeting with the parent. Or do whatever else needed to dissipate your anger and get hold of your emotions. Then, practice what you will say. Write it down if necessary. Make sure that any problem you raise is stated in observable, objective terms. Otherwise it will sound accusatory and judgmental—and this will put any parent on the defensive.

Instead of this . . .	Say something like this . . .
"Charlie doesn't seem to care about anything."	"The issue seems to be motivation. To reach his goal of a report card with As and Bs Charlie needs to get all his assignments in on time."
"Janai just wants to do things her own way. Nothing I say seems to get through."	"You can see from this spelling assignment that Janai needs to read and follow directions if she is going to successfully complete her work."
"Rick just never sits still."	"Rick has a lot of energy. Let's talk about some ways to channel that energy into productive activities in the classroom that will help him learn what he needs to learn."

5. Bring documentation to the meeting.

Do a "show and tell" of the points you wish to make to parents. Any meeting with a teacher puts a parent in a vulnerable position. Bring clear and appropriate examples to document any progress, lack of progress, compliments, or problems that you discuss. In particular, if you want parents to understand why grades are declining, or that you believe the student is not working to her potential, or that behavior issues are increasing—have precise, written information and examples to show.

However, don't overwhelm the parent! You don't need a wheelbarrow full of papers to show parents that Junior's handwriting is sloppy. Piles of "bad" examples will send parents running for the exit. Choose your documentation carefully. A few clear examples will make the point.

6. Leave them with a plan.

You can have a great welcoming attitude, be empathetic to the parent's problems, and state any issue clearly and concisely—then blow it all by leaving parents with the impression that you don't have any idea what to do. If you want to see results emerge from the conference, you **must** be prepared with a few alternatives for working on any problem. If you expect a parent to make a commitment to help facilitate a change in a child, you must also provide a promise of what **you** will do. Make sure parents leave the conference with a plan that states the problem and outlines what the parent will do and what you will do. Here are some examples:

Student behavior . . .	Teacher agrees to . . .	Parent commits to . .
Incomplete homework	look at student's assignment book each night and initial to show teacher believes the student understands what is to be done.	check assignments each night and initial the assignments when complete.
Calls out in class, disrupting the work of other students	start a behavior modification program.	support the behavior modification program at home, supplying rewards when appropriate.
Repeated tardies to school	be aware when the child comes in on time and give a positive greeting.	drop the children off first from the car pool.
Performing poorly in history	provide extra help in history two mornings a week.	bring the student to school two mornings a week for extra help.

7. Send home a reminder of key points.

When I attended my first conference with my daughter's high-school teachers, here is what I heard: "Late to class . . . " *sound of rushing water* . . . "first period . . . " *sound of screaming jet fighters* . . . "take more time . . . " *sound of an Amtrak train speeding past* . . . "very sweet . . . " *sound of the wings of a hundred hungry vultures* . . . . Because of my anxiety level, I heard and retained very little of what was said.

Give each parent a written record of key points made or decided at the conference. Base it on the "student sandwich." At our school we used a simple form entitled "Two Stars and a Wish," found in the Tools section at the end of this chapter. Before a conference, the teacher jotted a sentence or two under each heading. A final heading was left for the plan agreed upon by parent(s) and teacher. The form can be mailed or emailed, or given to the parent at the end of the conference.

Positive Attitude Tip

Respect the need of both parents to have information about their child's school life. In situations where there is a divorce or contentious divisions between parents (and/or guardians), be sure to have conferences with both sides—at the same time or at separate times. Make two copies of all written documentation and plans. If only one parent comes to the conference, send a copy of the materials to the absent parent or guardian.

ONE Very Good Habit

There's one technique that is a particularly effective tool to promote understanding between the parent and the teacher. It has been so helpful to me in so many situations, that I want to single it out in this chapter. It is the use of paraphrase to validate a parent's concerns. In any conversation, when you echo back what was just said, you let the other person know that you were indeed listening. At the same time you can check your understanding of the other person's communication to find out if you got what was intended. In a dialogue between parent and teacher, restating can meet the goals of:

- greater understanding between parent and teacher
- a spirit of cooperation from the parent
- increased chance of success for the student
- enhanced feelings of well-being and less stress for parents and teachers

"Listen in" on these conversations between teacher Mr. Dempsey and the parents of some students. In each scenario, the teacher has chosen to try this strategy: to listen to and, in order to show his understanding of what the parent said, to restate.

Scenario 1

Mr. Dempsey called Alberto's mother regarding a homework problem. He had barely introduced himself when Alberto's mother broke in and said, "You know, I come home so tired at night. The last thing in the world I can do is battle with Alberto over homework. I just do not have the time or energy to fight."

Mr. Dempsey's Response: "I hear how difficult it is for you right now, and how time is such a factor in your family life. I also hear you saying that you are concerned about how your son performs in school. We both want success for Alberto. I am here to work with you toward that goal. I am going to give you some suggestions that will help you check on his homework each night fairly quickly. As soon as we get off the phone, I will write you a note outlining those suggestions, so don't worry about writing them down as I explain them."

Scenario 2

Mr. Dempsey had a meeting with Fern's parents about a classroom behavior problem she was exhibiting. Fern's father responded, "Believe me—I'd do something if I could. I know that Fern's behavior at school is unacceptable. We see much of the same at home. Her mother and I just do not have any idea what to do to make Fern behave. It is so difficult; she just doesn't listen to a thing we say."

Mr. Dempsey's Response: "I hear you saying that you really want to help Fern learn to behave at school. And I recognize that it is not always easy to figure out how to do that. Kids are complicated. If you would like, we can work together to brainstorm some solutions. You know, I have worked with lots of kids like Fern. The situation is by no means hopeless. I can promise you that if we put our heads together, we can come up with a plan that will get Fern back on track."

Scenario 3

Reagan's father called Mr. Dempsey about a low grade that Reagan had earned in social studies. "I don't know if you recognize that my child is a very special child," said the father. "She has some learning difficulties, and I don't think you are giving her enough of a chance."

Mr. Dempsey's Response: "You are right to want the best for Reagan. That's why I want to work with you to see that she is successful in my class. I think I hear you saying that she has special qualities that I may not see. Tell me what I need to know about Reagan, and together we will come up with a plan that will meet her needs."

Get into this habit of restating what parents say to you. It will lead to better interventions and relationships that benefit the students, the parents, and you. Of course, to do this, you'll have to develop three other good habits:

1. Ask parents for their ideas, opinions, or feedback. (Or at least stop talking long enough for them to get a word in edgewise.)

2. Listen to what parents say. If you are going to paraphrase, you have to tune in to their voices, needs, and messages.

3. Examine your attitude about parents. You must recognize that they **do** know their child better than you do, and that they **do** have something valuable to say. Once you adopt that belief, you will do a better job of listening and reflecting back your understanding in a paraphrased statement.

Take a few minutes to practice this strategy. Think about how you would restate each of these parent concerns if they were directed to you:

- "My daughter says you pick on her all the time."

- "I never learned this kind of math when I was in school. How am I supposed to help with homework?"

- "Please stop calling me about my child. Her father left us years ago, and I am doing what I can. So she acts up a little in class. Kids will be kids, right? You're the teacher. Can't you handle it?"

Conference NO-NO'S

Don't come to the conference unprepared.

Don't assume body positions or use body language that intimidates or shows disinterest.

Don't seat a parent across the desk from you or in small student-size chairs.

Don't bring up past incidents.

Don't fall into gossip about former teachers, other students, or irrelevant topics.

Don't overwhelm parents by presenting too many problems.

Don't make idle disciplinary threats.

Don't "gang up" on parents by bringing in teacher reinforcements whose purpose is to sit in the meeting for your moral support.

Don't run over the allotted time and make parents wait.

Don't end a conference about a problem without a plan to solve the problem.

Teacher-to-Teacher Tip

"Try to affirm that you are working with parents and not against them. Also, try to avoid conflict over minor issues (especially those in the past), in order to focus on the big picture and what can be done to improve things in the future."

– High-school teacher, Texas

Learn To Love Teaching Again

Parents as Volunteers

Parents in the classroom: this sounds scary to some teachers. But in actuality it is one of the best ways to forge teacher-parent partnerships that benefit all parties (parents, teachers, and students)! Here are some of those benefits:

- Teacher stress is reduced (because some of the more mundane tasks such as preparing and organizing materials are completed by someone else).

> **Chuckle!**
>
> *The good news is that Abigail's mother has volunteered to help in the classroom.*
>
> *The bad news is that Abigail's mother has volunteered to help in the classroom.*

- As students see their parents making time to help in the classroom, students get the message that their parents value education and want to be a part of theirs.

- Students see their teachers and parents working together for a good classroom experience. This increases students' good feelings about the teacher.

- Parents grow closer to their children and closer to the academic expectations for and performance of their children.

- It is harder to be confrontational when they are part of the school's story. Parents who visit schools to volunteer see more of the whole picture and understand more completely the daily challenges in the classrooms. These parents will be your biggest supporters when the parking lot chatter begins.

- Studies show a connection between parent involvement and both better attendance and higher academic success. Studies confirm that when the parents are more involved, students get better grades in English and math, and their reading and writing skills improve (Epstein, 2008). Also, when parents are involved, students and parents have more positive attitudes towards education (Mattingly, et.al. 2002).

Roadblocks to Successful Parent Volunteerism:

Roadblock #1: Time (parents finding the time to volunteer)

Between home and work responsibilities, coordinating the schedules of two households (in cases of divorce), extracurricular activities, and trying to find the time for quality family activities, many parents find it difficult to parse out the time and energy to volunteer at school. Yet the old adage about finding the time to do what is important to you rings true. Help parents see that interaction with their child's school life is important, and help make it possible for them to take part.

Getting Past the Roadblock

A consistent complaint from schools is that parents just do not sign up or show up, whether at school functions or for volunteer opportunities. Here are some ways to get volunteers—even in the face of all the other commitments:

- Provide all kinds of opportunities for volunteering. Create a list of possible involvement that fits many different schedules, skills, budgets, and personality styles. Include requests for before and after school help, weekend projects, and tasks that can be done from home. Include ideas from guest speaking to providing popcorn for a class celebration. Make sure there are opportunities for families who might feel uncomfortable participating, or who might have a language barrier. See "50 Ways to Use Parent Volunteers," found in the Tools section at the end of this chapter.

- Send out an "Interest Survey" to parents at the beginning of the year. Use it to find out about the skills, interests, and availability of parents. Make the forms short and to the point. Once you have this information along with a reliable phone number and email address, keep track of it and put the forms to use. See an example in the Tools section at the end of this chapter.

- Still can't get parents involved? Here's a secret about how I get parents to volunteer—a secret so simple, you'll probably be surprised. Ready? **Ask them.** I am not being facetious. I discovered this secret after trying the tricks we all attempt—posting requests on the school website, getting room parents to make calls, sending emails, and begging in school newsletters. Parents want to help, mean to help, but rarely respond to these "cattle call" invitations, figuring someone else will do it. However, we found that when parents are approached on a one-on-one basis, they won't (or can't) say no.

My colleague would go out on the afternoon home line, chat with parents as they waited in their cars, and come back to the office with her volunteer roster filled. A first-grade teacher would only have to stand outside her classroom in the morning for a few minutes with a handful of paper phonics books that needed to be cut apart and stapled before a willing volunteer was found. Parents rarely say no when they are reached by phone either, though the same is not true if a message is left.

> ### Teacher-to-Teacher Tip
>
> *"Keep a notebook for parent contacts. Enter dates and summaries of phone calls or face-to-face conversations. When you send a note or email, staple a copy in the notebook. It makes life much easier when you have a record of all contacts!"*
>
> *– Elementary teacher, 22 years experience*

Learn To Love Teaching Again

Hello, Mrs. Bumples! We're here to help monitor those tests!

Like many educators, my staff and I complained that it was always the same parents providing all of the assistance. Now we saw an added bonus: we had folks volunteer who had never graced our hallways before! Suddenly one parent found opportunities to take a few early lunches to help out with recess. Another parent could spare the use of a truck to help transport the new science lab tables. A non-English-speaking mother and father took care of the flower garden in front of the school. By asking folks directly and by providing volunteer opportunities to fit all kinds of schedules, we saw a 95 percent parent participation rate. Relationships between teachers and parents benefited. The parents felt they were connecting and making a difference in the school, the children saw that their families valued their education, and the stress level of my staff improved.

- And here's a final reminder—one that I cannot overstate: Be sure your parent volunteers are recognized and thanked for each project in which they participate.

Roadblock #2: Attitude (yours!)

"I can do things much more quickly by myself."

"I don't need another person to babysit in my room."

"My door is closed once the bell rings. What I do in there is my business. I don't want parents in my classroom snooping around."

Okay, so maybe you aren't a teacher with an attitude like this. But many teachers are. Take a casual survey of any school, and you will find that a huge percentage of teachers see relationships with parents as problematic. Many teacher education programs fall short in the area of preparing new teachers to deal well with parents. When the teacher's attitude is negative or wary, parents feel it—and volunteer efforts will probably not work very well.

Getting Past the Roadblock

- If you are an effective teacher, you have nothing to hide. Welcome parent volunteers and use them to do important tasks that further student achievement and excitement in the classroom.

- Understand that parent volunteers bring rich gifts and talents to your classroom. See their involvement as a way to enrich your students' lives at school.

- Realize that, with good organization, a parent volunteer system really can lighten your load and reduce your stress.

- Be well prepared. Greet the parent at the door with written directions and all materials ready. If the parent knows exactly what to do, things will go more smoothly. Think through the assignment of duties for the parent as well as the location (working in the teacher's lounge is always a bad idea, for instance), and be ready to make adjustments as needed.

- Greet the volunteer with a warm smile. This will make you feel more relaxed and will put the parent at ease. Focus on making this a pleasant experience for the parent.

- Have a pile of already created student thank-you notes, or thank volunteers in your classroom newsletter. When the volunteer feels appreciated, the experience of having him or her in your room will become more comfortable for you, too.

- Don't be intimidated. Remember that you are in charge. Give the parent clear parameters for relating to students (that is, disciplining and such). Don't be afraid to gently remind them of these protocols when necessary. Don't be afraid to change the volunteer's tasks if you observe that the current "assignment" is not working. At our school we asked Mrs. Greggs, an involved parent with extra time on her hands, to help monitor a restroom break for the kindergarteners. All went well until I heard her loud voice in the hallway yelling at students to behave and threatening them with consequences she was unauthorized to assign. We redirected Mrs. Greggs to shelving books in the library, and she excelled in the quieter and more organized environment.

New Teacher Tip

It is not appropriate to have volunteers grade papers, enter grades, work with attendance records, or do any other work with confidential student information. Check your school or district privacy guidelines on this, and be sure to protect the privacy of your students and their families.

Learn To Love Teaching Again

Partnerships without Parents

One glance at Savannah told you she was a child of neglect, and almost-certain abuse. She was an unhealthy pale, an obvious product of a constant diet of food high in sugar and fat. Savannah's appearance went beyond disheveled; the other students ostracized her because of her strong odor—the odor of an unwashed body and cigarette smoke. Savannah's parents were uneducated and barely employed. Though technically present, the parents had little to do with Savannah. After school, she cared for her toddler sister while her mother watched television and smoked. It seems her mother interacted with Savannah only by screaming at her.

Despite this grim home situation, Savannah attended school joyfully and smiled easily at teachers and other school staff. Savannah tried desperately to make friends among her peers, but the children could not get past the slovenly appearance and lingering smell. And, to be honest, much of the staff reacted to Savannah the same way.

What about the children in your classroom who have no available parents or guardians, or whose parents or guardians are just incapable of participating in the educational process? Parents may be incarcerated or in the throes of devastating illnesses. There may be domestic distress or substance abuse in the home. The financial situation may be so bad that the family is simply in survival mode. (But do not assume that negligent or absentee parents are unique to lower socioeconomic strata.)

For whatever reason, some parents just don't or can't care about what goes on in school. Yet a classroom teacher, no matter how well-intentioned, cannot fill all the gaps for every student. Most of us enter this profession with two traits in common: we are natural nurturers and we are high achievers, expecting much from ourselves. When we get no help or response from home, we become overwhelmed, angry, and frustrated. Or we just feel helpless. When that happens, it is time to look for a student mentor.

Pairing Students with Mentors

Savannah was so sweet and eager to please, but academically was far behind her fifth-grade peers. Homework was never complete; Savannah had no home supplies, no facilities, parental support, or encouragement to do the work. She was a full-time caregiver for her baby sister in the afternoons and evenings. The only opportunity Savannah had to be a kid was at school, and she soaked up the minimal crumbs of attention thrown to her by her teacher and fellow students.

Look around your school and find someone who is willing to take on a supportive role with a student who so desperately needs it. The school secretary is a natural choice, as is a specialty teacher, school counselor, paraprofessional, or cafeteria worker. Make a deal with another teacher at your grade level; you'll mentor one of his students if he mentors one of yours. And don't forget administrators! As principal I was brought in as a mentor a number of times by my teachers. I always welcomed the opportunity, delighted in knowing that at least a small portion of my day would be spent doing what I loved doing—interacting with students. When you approach a possible mentor, explain that you are looking for a small commitment of time, just minutes only a day. The only requirement is someone who is willing to show the child support.

In our district, the elementary school formed a partnership with the high school across the street. A group of students came over during lunch periods and were assigned one child. Each high schooler played checkers, read a book, played soccer, or enjoyed recess with that mentee. This turned out to be a win for both sets of students. We were very clear; these were not tutoring sessions, but supportive and encouraging relationships that really helped the students feel special. We did not do a formal study, but I can say that the classroom teachers were happy with the arrangement and their stress levels lessened for their kids involved in the program. The teachers were able to take a break from the nurturing of those students for 30 minutes twice a week, and in all cases the students came back into the classroom happier and more cooperative.

To create a bond between the mentor and the student, suggest some informal getting-to-know-you activities, such as:

- helping to staple papers with the school secretary,
- playing a few games of *Crazy Eights* with the principal during lunch,
- assisting with a classroom task like cleaning the whiteboards after school with a fellow classroom teacher, or
- setting out gym equipment with the physical education teacher before school.

The school nurse was chosen as Savannah's mentor because of some health issues on record, as well as suspected abuse. It took only a little time and attention from Nurse Cheryl before Savannah began stopping to chat with the health worker each morning before school. Almost immediately Savannah's daily attendance improved, and she was no longer tardy to school.

Once the relationship has been established between the student and the mentor, the mentor can easily ask the student how his day is going or how he did on his science test. The role of the mentor then becomes one of encouragement, gently reminding the student to stay for an after-school study group or congratulating her on a good grade. The students thrive on the positive attention, and often work to live up to the higher expectations their mentors have of them. The stress level of the teacher goes down as the burden of the child is shared, and the child's attitude and self-esteem improves.

A student mentor will never make up for the desperate home lives many of our children face each day. But a student mentor can make a difference. Listen to stories from adults who came from terrible childhood situations; they invariably pinpoint one person in school who believed in them, and cite that belief for being a factor that changed their lives. Think back on the person in your education who made the most difference to you, and consider how that person affected your life. When someone takes the time to care, big changes can happen for students.

Because of their daily interactions, Nurse Cheryl was able to approach Savannah about her personal hygiene from a health standpoint. Since it was clear that anything sent home would be destroyed or misused, personal hygiene items (lavender body soap, a toothbrush and toothpaste, deodorant, a face cloth, and so forth) were placed in a pretty gift bag on a bathroom shelf of the nurse's office. Additionally (and with the mother's permission) a few clean white blouses and socks were provided. Savannah would come into the nurse's office, clean up, and change her shirt and socks. (After school, Savannah came back to the nurse's office to don her original clothes. Nurse Cheryl washed Savannah's clothes so that there were always fresh items available.) After a few days of this routine, the staff noticed Savannah being asked to join the games with other girls on the playground.

Student mentoring helps everyone involved: the teacher's stress is reduced as the burden is shared; the student's grades and behavior often improve, the student feels noticed and successful (maybe for the first time!), and a wonderful relationship with a caring adult is developed.

The Effect on the Parent-Teacher Relationship

If you take the action to provide a mentor for a student, how will it affect your relationship with the parent(s)? It is possible that you will see no effect. In many cases, the issues are so complex that the only results you know about are those you observe with the student. However, student mentoring often does have benefits for parents and does help to begin a working teacher-parent relationship. Many parents begin to feel better about the school or more comfortable coming to school. Their trust in the teacher rises. They have more hope for their children and perhaps even more pride.

Before the school staff set up the mentoring relationship, contacts with Savannah's parents had been troublesome. Her mother or dad would arrive at the principal's office or the classroom yelling inappropriately. They seemed terribly uncomfortable in the school building, and had no idea how to begin to fit in.

A few months after the mentoring began, something changed. Savannah's mother would actually come into the school just to pick her up, or ask the teacher how Savannah was doing in class. She seemed to feel proud of the extra attention Savannah was getting. It appeared that since everyone at school thought Savannah was special, her mother could think she was special, too. She walked a little taller and smiled a little more. Then came a big surprise! Savannah's mother volunteered to help with some projects at the school.

In a non-fairy-tale ending educators know all too well, Savannah and her family disappeared shortly after the school reported some suspected abuse. The school staff could not change the realities of Savannah's family life. But in those two years with her, we were able to give her a supportive partnership that filled some of the roles of advocating parents. The experience of being valued and the increased belief in herself were gifts that we knew would continue to support her when the caring folks at this school no longer could.

Falling in Love Again

There is no way to overstate the benefits of having good partnerships with our students' parents. It is absolutely necessary if you are to offer the best educational experiences for your students.

Everything works better when home-family connections are strong and mutually supportive. Each improvement you make in this area will give measurable results in your comfort level and your stress level. And when you get to watch students doing better, safe in the knowledge that parents AND teacher are pulling together FOR them, you'll feel a surge of delight. And when you no longer have to hide from parents but feel they are your advocates, you'll be able to relax and enjoy your job a whole lot more!

Me Moment

During intense mental activity (such as problem solving) you may notice your forehead tends to feel much warmer. Conversely, as your mind and body relax, you may notice your forehead becomes cooler. You can induce tranquility by applying a cool (not cold) compress to your forehead. Try this when you have a minute at school and definitely when you arrive home after a stressful day. This might help you sleep better, too. About ten minutes before going to bed, apply a cool compress to your forehead (NO cold cans of soda or frozen peas, please).

Chapter 3 **Tools**

Two Stars and a Wish

We celebrate . . .

_____
_____
_____

We celebrate . . .

_____
_____
_____

We'll work to . . .

_____
_____
_____
_____

We plan to . . .

(what the teacher will do) _____

_____

_____

(what the parent/guardian will do) _____

_____

_____

parent signature _____ *teacher signature* _____ *date* _____

November

Mr. Tuliano's Class News

What a Great Class!

Thank you for giving me the opportunity to teach your children! We are having a great school year.

Help Wanted...
We will need 2 parent volunteers for our big Thanksgiving project.

Please contact Mrs. Garcia, our room mother, at 222-333-4444 or roommother1@yahoo.com, if you are able to help.

Our Class Wish List

We are going to be working on several projects this month. Mr. Pringle, Tamara's dad, donated 2 boxes of craft sticks. Thanks, Mr. Pringle!

We still need the following items for our log cabin project:

• 4 bags of extra-large pretzel sticks

• 3 cans of white frosting (for holding the logs together)

November is a busy month for us. As you can see on our calendar below, we have two field trips planned this month.

Monday	Tuesday	Wednesday	Thursday	Friday
		Field Trip to Jones Farm		
				Log Cabin Project
Field Trip to Museum		Thanksgiving Project		
	Timmy's Birthday		Happy Thanksgiving NO SCHOOL	NO SCHOOL
		Kenya's Birthday		

News You Can Use

May Issue

What We've Been Working On

By Sylvia Caper & Matt Stole

Science: *We are studying about reptiles. Mrs. Peppercorn brought in a frozen rattlesnake that her husband caught at their farm. She saved it in the freezer. We opened it up and found bones of rabbits and rats. It was really cool!*

Math: *We're working with exponential numbers and scientific notation.*

Social Studies: *Everyone has been working hard on projects for their assigned states. We take turns explaining our posters and brochures to the class. We've learned surprising things about every state!*

Language Arts: *We are about to finish reading the book, "**Anne Frank: The Diary of a Young Girl**" in class. The test covering the book will be on Friday the 14th.*

May Dates to Remember

By Colby Alba & Steve Hanna

May 12 – Field Day

May 17 – Field Trip to Museum

May 21 – Bring a large brown paper sack for cleaning out lockers

Shining Stars

By Myrna Garza & Sue Lang

● **Kendra Parker's soccer team** won first place in the district competition.

● **Congratulations, class!** We had perfect attendance during the month of April. Way to go!!!

● **Thank you, Mrs. Sanders,** for donating your digital camera to our class. We have been using it every day. Stop by and see our great pictures in the hallway outside of our classroom. We also plan to take the camera on our field trip to the museum.

The bus ride to City Hall

50 Ways to Use Parent Volunteers

 At School:

- help with outdoor maintenance or cleanup
- help in math lab or computer lab
- practice math problems with students
- help students select books in the library
- chat with a student at lunch or recess
- practice a skill with a group of students
- compile, organize, or clean classroom supplies
- give classroom talk about profession
- give a presentation about topic of interest
- set up supplies for science experiment
- set up supplies for art project
- reorganize or clean classroom supplies
- organize items in student take-home folders
- read to students or listen to students read
- cut, staple, glue, fold, laminate, assemble
- prepare for, help with, or clean up from:
    parties, celebrations, talent shows, picture days, rummage sales, bake sales, book fairs, field days
- help with music, movement, drama, art experiences
- restock art supplies
- work with students on computer
- make copies
- keep classroom scrapbook
- join class on nature walks
- maintain the school garden
- take a turn as room parent
- assist teacher at recess duty
- assist classroom daily work time
- tutor individual students
- chaperone events
- return books to library
- join in on field trips
- create or assemble bulletin boards

 Away from School:

- provide a student internship at place of business
- bargain hunt for classroom supplies
- gather resources for upcoming unit
- host a field trip at their place of business
- gather equipment and supplies for big projects
- call, send, or email reminders to other parents
- make simple games
- collate and print newsletter
- make party decorations, games, food, favors
- coordinate volunteers for field trips or class events
- assist with fundraising
- compile school directory
- make play dough
- work on classroom website
- find speakers for curriculum units
- gather resources for projects
- write grants to fund new programs
- collect and place book orders
- organize classroom pictures

TIPS

1. Make a list of volunteer opportunities.
2. Organize your list by time needed, frequency (once, monthly, weekly, etc.), or location (work at home, in-school help, etc.)
3. Send home the list with a form that parents can return.
4. Prepare packets, notebook, or tub of materials parents will need for a task. Include specific instructions.

What Are Your Talents and Interests?

Parent Volunteer Survey

We value your participation in our classroom and school. There are many ways to help. You can help before school, after school, in school, at special events, at home, or in your place of work. Your volunteer commitment can be shorter or longer, one time, once a week, or twice a year. There are all kinds of opportunities to match your interests and schedule.

How Can You Help?

Look at the attached list of our areas and jobs for which we need volunteers. Then complete this form.

Your name_____

Phone number _____   Email: _____

Would you like to volunteer

_____ in the classroom?   _____ at outside events?   _____ at home?

What is the best time for you to help?

_____ weekdays   _____ evenings   _____ weekends

Approximate times: _____ _____ _____

Name some of your particular interests, talents, areas of knowledge and expertise:

_____

_____

What things on the list seem like activities that might be right for you?

_____

Is there anything that you would like to do that is not listed?

_____

Teacher:_____Grade_____Room_____

Teacher's Checklist for Parent Communications

Any time I talk to or write to a parent, I will . . .

____ begin by making sure it is a convenient time for them to talk.

____ speak or write with a patient, caring (but never condescending) tone.

____ state my reason for the call right away.

____ speak or write respectfully.

____ speak in language they can understand (no educational jargon).

____ listen more than I talk.

____ ask for their opinion or view on the problem
(if the subject is a problem).

____ ask for their help (if it is a situation that needs help).

____ restate what I hear them say.

____ clearly say what it is I need from them.

____ make a point to communicate my advocacy for the child.

____ let them know how they can reach me for further comment
or discussion on the topic.

____ conclude by reviewing or summarizing the purpose
or the decisions made.

____ thank them for their time.

____ follow up with a written summary
of our conclusions as to what they
agreed to do and what I agreed
to do (if the communication
involved action to be taken).

Teacher Self-reflection
on Relationships with Parents

Questions	My Answers
What regular patterns are in place for making connections with parents?	
What have I done to show respect and an open door to parents?	
What processes do I have in place for parents to be involved in my classroom?	
How often do I communicate in some way with the parents as a group?	
On average, how often do I have contact with each student's parents?	
What portion of my parent contacts communicate good news about the child?	
How often do I ask a parent's opinion or ask for their help?	
After conferences or phone calls, do the parents and I each have a clear understanding of what we can do to help the student?	
How effectively do I engage parents in helping solve a problem regarding their child?	
How comfortable do I feel relating to my students' parents?	
How comfortable do the parents or guardians seem to be with me?	

● On reviewing my answers, I learned

_____

● Two goals for improving my relationships with parents:

1

2

102

Am I a Teacher or a Police Officer?

"One of my students was clearly out of control. I did not know how to handle her. But when I went to the administration for help, I was made to feel inadequate because I did not know how to deal with a classroom problem."
– Vincent T., Illinois

"I just could not believe the language used by a few of my sixth-graders! And when I brought it to the attention of their parents, I found that they weren't bothered by the language. If they didn't care, how was I supposed to discipline the students?"
– Dina K., Pennsylvania

"I have been in this school for almost a year now, and I cannot figure out the schoolwide discipline plan."
– Camille B., Colorado

"The assistant principal said to come and get him anytime I had a problem. But I only tried that once, because the reality was that it was a no-no to ask for help."
– Bev L., Maine

"No matter what I tried, the students were unmotivated. They appeared to be engaged only when they were acting out."
– Harvey A., Louisiana

New teachers enter the profession hopeful and full of high expectations. This is a good thing. In fact, new teachers often rejuvenate the more experienced and sometimes jaded teachers. But some of those expectations are unrealistic and quickly lead to new-teacher despair. The first year of "real" teaching may not look anything like student teaching—especially when it comes to managing all the details of a classroom while trying to get students to cooperate.

Some schools treat student teachers with kid gloves, isolating them from contentious family situations and extra duties. After all, it is the "real" teacher who handles all the problems. She (or he) is ultimately in control, her presence still recognized by the students even if she is physically out of the room. All the things that go into creating a well-run classroom (such as expectations for students, the creation of class rules, parental relationships, a process for home-school communication, and good classroom management procedures) are already well established before the student teacher sets foot in the classroom. Furthermore, student teachers are usually placed with master teachers, who may make the classroom management look easy.

One of the top reasons teachers give for choosing another profession is that the reality of the classroom experience did not match their expectations. They thought they were going to be stimulating young minds with exciting learning experiences. Instead, they began feeling like traffic directors and police officers.

First-year medical residents are not expected to perform neurosurgery. A beginning worker in a four-star restaurant does not plan the menu. A new pilot is not likely to fly a jumbo commercial aircraft as her first flight in command. Yet, a new teacher is expected to manage 150 I-know-everything high-school students, 125 hormone-crazed middle-school students, or 27 can't-keep-their-hands-to-themselves elementary students starting the first day on the job.

Over the years, as I interviewed scores of prospective teachers for my school, I was struck with their lack of training in all the processes and skills needed for managing a classroom. Combine poor preparation with the behavioral issues of today's students, and you have a combustible situation. And one component of this situation is always a stressed teacher!

Losing the Love

Do you battle students all day long, beg for attention, raise your voice or yell a lot, spend more time disciplining than teaching? If so, then it's no wonder that you are stressed! To walk into an out-of-control classroom every day is to hop a fast train to burnout. Because of struggles with handling students and the operation of the classroom, many teachers go home with headaches—discouraged and exhausted. They did not accomplish the learning goals for the day and they don't feel good about their students.

This is not just the case for new teachers. Plenty of experienced teachers are stuck in patterns of poor management. They may start every year with hopes for a better-behaved students, but instead find themselves caught in the same old cycle of struggling with students—year after year.

If you dread the moment when the bell rings and your students walk in, you are hardly in love with your profession. It truly is possible to leave every day (well, most days) feeling good about your students and knowing that some of those expectations you had are coming true. With some adjustment in attitude, preparation, and practices, you can run a classroom that doesn't drive you crazy, but is a productive, comfortable place for you and your students.

A Fresh Start

How much of your disillusionment with your job (and your stress) is connected to difficulties with students? Pay attention to this. At the end of each day, reflect upon your frustration level and assess the causes. Your encounters with students can be uplifting, rewarding, and joyful. You can drastically reduce the number of stressful incidents with better classroom organization and management. It's harder to change procedures midyear, especially if you're into a downward-spiraling pattern. **But even that is possible.**

Many years ago, a wise child psychologist, Haim Ginott, wrote a simple book with a powerful message for teachers (Teacher & Child, 1972). It rescued many a chaotic, contentious classroom. This is a basic premise of his work, in his own words:

> *"I've come to the frightening conclusion that I am the decisive element in the classroom. It's my personal approach that creates the climate. It's my daily mood that makes the weather. As a teacher, I possess tremendous power to make a student's life miserable or joyous. I can be a tool of torture or an instrument of inspiration. I can humiliate or humor, hurt or heal. In all situations it is my response that decides whether a crisis will be escalated or de-escalated and a student humanized or dehumanized."*

You might be asking, "What? Is this guy saying this is all about ME—that I'm the problem and not the kids?" If you read the entire book, you won't find Dr. Ginott blaming or accusing the adult as the problem in the classroom. You will find that he shows that the way the teacher IS and ACTS powerfully affects the way students behave and perform. In truth, many classroom-management issues are actually caused by the teacher. And so many can be prevented or alleviated by the teacher.

It would take another book to recommend all the classroom management techniques that I have seen work. Since this book is about keeping or rescuing your love of teaching, I'll suggest some basic management processes that I know can lead to greater classroom harmony, more productive students, and a more joyful teacher. In agreement with Dr. Ginott's discovery above—that the teacher is the decisive element—this chapter will focus on the following questions. Use them to evaluate your own procedures and how they alleviate or contribute to a well-functioning classroom:

How do you relate to students?

How do you communicate with students?

How do you get (and hold) their attention?

How do you monitor your students?

How is your classroom arranged?

How effective are your classroom rules?

How consistently do YOU follow the procedures?

How Do You Relate to Students?

Have you stopped to closely examine your attitude toward students—how you treat them, or how and where you learned to relate to students? If not, try this: Write a paragraph or a list that describes how you view students and describes how you relate to them. As you do this, ask yourself such questions as: "Do I see students as 'half-formed' beings to be managed and controlled by me, the all-knowing adult?" "Do I let stereotypes about social or ethnic or academic groups affect my view of a particular child or family?" "Do I listen to the labels put on students by other adults or students?" "Do I care—really care—about students as individuals?" "Do I respect each student?" "Is my care for students genuine?"

Your relationships with your students are the foundation of your classroom management. Healthy, respectful teacher-student relationships translate into minimal problems in the classroom.

Attitude—Students need to perceive themselves as significant, capable, and in control of their own lives. Do you see them this way? Do you truly accept every student? Keep your mind open to full appreciation of every student—without judgment.

Care and Interest—Do you really care about each student (even the prickly ones)? How do you show that care? One of the best ways to demonstrate care is to show a personal interest in the student. Really get to know the student's likes, dislikes, strengths, needs, preferences, hopes, dreams, fears. Get to know his learning style or her social challenges.

Teacher-to-Teacher Tip

"Do whatever it takes to track down a copy of **Teacher & Child***, by Haim Ginott. It revolutionized my relationships with students. His ideas revolutionized my communication with my own children, too!" (See* **Between Parent & Child***, by the same author.)*
– Longtime teacher and parent

Respect—Most lists of classroom rules contain one that says something like this: "Treat all other people with respect." Do you treat all students with the same level of respect that you expect from them? All your responses and communications convey the kind of respect (or nonrespect) and dignity that you afford a student. I can guarantee you won't have a student's respect if he or she senses anything less than clear respect from you.

Being Real—Students can spot a phony a mile away. No teacher can pretend care, interest, or respect without being detected—and pretty fast. Talk in your normal voice, not a "pretend" teacher voice. Don't insult your students with an artificial self; they need to be educated by a genuine human being.

How Do You Communicate with Students?

> *Talk to the situation, not to the personality or character.*
> Haim Ginott

How you talk to your students tells them how you feel about them. This applies to your entire approach—the tone and expression, the words and demeanor, and how you criticize or praise, reassure, demand, ask, explain, and evaluate. It applies to nonverbal signals as well as verbal talk.

Dr. Ginott based his advice to teachers and parents on the concept of congruent communication—a whole way of transferring messages, verbally and nonverbally, that is fitted to specific situations.

To explain the concept, Ginott describes teachers at their worst and best. At their worst, he says, teachers judge a student's character or personality. They label, belittle, and denigrate them. Though this is usually unintentional, it creates more problems than it solves. At their best, teachers address a particular situation. They affirm a student's dignity by treating her or him as a social equal capable of making good decisions. This approach leads to solutions instead of creating problems.

For example: A student does a poor job on a test or homework.

Instead of
> "You are capable of much better work than this. You're a smart kid. From now on I want you to work up to your potential."

The teacher says,
> "I'm concerned about your performance on the last few English assignments. Your work needs some improvement. Let's talk about how I can help."

Instead of
> "Why have you made such a mess? You've got a sloppy space here. Pick up all those papers right now."

The teacher says,
> "I see there are lots of papers on the floor. They belong on your desk."

Chuckle!

Teacher: Cassie, your essay has dozens of mistakes. Let's get together so I can help you correct them.

Cassie: You'll have to schedule that get-together with my dad. He's the one who wrote it.

If the basis of your work with students is a caring, respectful, and authentic relationship, it is natural to communicate respectfully. These principles will help you to be aware of and practice communication that shows your acceptance and increases students' self-worth:

- Describe a situation. If necessary, state an alternative.
- Avoid "you" messages, especially those that denigrate a student's person, character, opinions, feelings, or experience.
- Do not shame, blame, threaten, belittle, order, moralize, bribe, or preach.
- State your expectations clearly.
- Keep sarcasm out of your communications.
- Do not label students.
- Praise students for what they DO, not for what they are.
- In every communication, accept and acknowledge the student's feelings.
- Invite cooperation rather than demanding it.
- Attend to your body language. Make sure it shows acceptance and care.

How Do You Get (and Hold) Their Attention?

If you observed a dozen classrooms, you'd find that many of the teachers spend the better part of each day trying to grab or hold the students' attention. This is no small skill. And if a teacher can't do it well, a lot of time is lost. It is made more difficult, of course, by the reality that students learn very early to shut out the voices of adults. So you must have some workable ways to get students to attend to important information and directions. Beyond that, you need ways to keep students engaged in classroom learning. Here are some techniques to try if yours are not working:

- **Find attention-getting strategies that work for you.** The exact method (a bell, hand signal, special phrase, etc.) is not as important as its effectiveness and your consistency. State the expectation clearly and make certain students understand that you expect compliance every time. Role-play and practice your expectation. If the students' reactions begin to slip, then retrain and repractice, or switch to a different technique. For several examples of attention-getting techniques, look in the Tools section at the end of this chapter.

- **Don't shout.** Teachers often try to talk over student noise. The kids get louder, the teacher gets louder, and pretty soon colleagues from five doors down hear the screaming of the elements of the periodic table or some other lesson. Make a mental note to stop and check your volume and pitch. If you find yourself shouting to be heard, take a deep breath. Gain control by some effective attention-getting procedure that you established with your students.

- **Plan activities that truly engage students.** When lessons, assignments, and other adventures are relevant, timely, varied, and interesting to students, students will want to know what's going on! Active learning (meaning students' minds and bodies are actively involved in the learning) captivates students and keeps minds from wandering. If you find yourself constantly battling for student attention, stop and examine the kinds of experiences you are planning.

> **Chuckle!**
>
> *A veteran teacher gave this tip for getting the attention of her high-school students: Tell them that you are about to explain a new, guaranteed cure for zits.*

How Do You Monitor Students?

> **Teacher:** *Deidra, sit down now and get to work . . . Stop talking in the corner over there! . . . Who is tapping that pencil? . . . Rachel and Sije, please go back to your seats . . . Deidra, I asked you to begin your work a few minutes ago . . . No, there are no drinks of water right now . . . Jon, open your book to page 49, please—you cannot do this assignment without looking at that map . . . We just had a bathroom break . . . Deidra, how many times do I need to ask you to get to work?*

Don't assume that independent practice time for the students means a coffee break for the teacher. If a teacher sits at her desk (with or without the coffee) while students work alone on assignments or in small groups, that "break" is likely to look like the scenario above.

An effective teacher will walk the classroom, circulating among the students, dealing with any problems or misunderstandings. By moving throughout the classroom, the teacher can:

- clear up any student confusion.

- ensure that all students are on task.

- redirect behavior when necessary.

Learn To Love Teaching Again

- note any students with gaps in understanding.
- encourage even the most reluctant learner.

And all this can be done in a quiet way that respects individual student privacy and doesn't turn small problems into big ones.

Independent or small-group work puts responsibilities on students. At any age, they need some reassurance as they take on their work tasks. They need the safety and security of a present, watchful teacher. They can perform better when they know you are nearby to answer a question, help with a problem, keep other students from bothering them, keep group work from getting off track, and help them keep on task.

New Teacher Tip

Do not let any rules violations slip. Respond right away. State objectively what happened; review the consequences; then apply the consequences. Every time you let something slide, your classroom takes a slide, your management takes a slide (backwards), and you'll regret it. Be brave. It's not mean to enforce the rules. Students expect it from you, the adult.

Your roaming, involved presence also gives students the message that you are involved in their learning and that you want them to succeed. A great deal of private tutoring happens in these casual moments when a teacher circulates. Don't miss out on any of those opportunities.

How Is Your Classroom Arranged?

As principal, I have seen every classroom arrangement possible: desk circles, arcs, pods, learning groups, work centers, and the free-wheeling-sit-where ever-you-want display. A classroom arrangement is a matter of a teacher's personal taste, experience, and comfort level. Each teacher has to decide what works best for him or her and what best contributes to learning.

However, what many of us are not taught in our teacher training classes is the part that your classroom arrangement plays in classroom management. Many incidents, disruptions, annoyances, arguments, or crises that cause trouble are the direct result of the arrangement of furniture and students. Ask yourself these questions about your room arrangement to avoid some chronic management problems:

- **Do my students have adequate space around their desks?** If at all possible, seat students so that they cannot easily reach each other when seated. This will deter unwanted touching, poking, grabbing others' belongings, and such.

- **Is my classroom an obstacle course?** You and students need to be able to maneuver around the classroom readily. When pathways are narrow or cluttered, it is easier for students to bother each other; "inadvertently" touch, hit, or fall on each other; and trip over belongings. Students need to move and change locations at many times during a class. You need to move around the classroom easily to get to students, and you don't want to hurdle over backpacks or squeeze between desks. They have to do the same. The classroom that is an obstacle course breeds trouble.

- **Is the room unnecessarily cluttered?** Clutter causes visual confusion, tripping accidents, and a feeling of chaos. Remove everything from the room that is not absolutely necessary and keep items not in use in cabinets or closets. Students have enough distractions already. Don't let the room decor or contents add to the distraction.

- **Are there any hidden pockets wherein students go unobserved?** The teacher needs to be able to see all students at all times. (My husband, out of high school for 20 years, still boasts of the daily poker games in the back corner of French class.) Hidden pockets encourage hidden activities.

- **Can all students see me at all times?** Students need clear visibility of all instruction areas without the inconvenience of twisting or turning. Effective teachers are not limited to teaching from the board in the front of the room. Be sure that all students can see all lesson presentations. Many discipline problems result when the classroom arrangement keeps students from fully engaging in an activity.

- **Are materials readily accessible?** Students need to be able to access commonly used learning materials such as paper, pencils, calculators, math tools, computers, reference materials, and books. If these materials are difficult for students to get to, learning will be disrupted.

See pages 122–124 in the Chapter 4 Tools section for sample seating arrangements, room arrangements, and some tips on using principles of feng shui as you set up your classroom.

How Effective Are Your Classroom Rules?

What are the best classroom rules? How do we make them? Who should make them, and when? How many do we need? What is the best way to enforce them? There are hundreds of sources, loads of advice, and endless opinions on these questions. There is no one right answer to any of these questions. What's critical is that you develop them thoughtfully, end up with rules that make sense and work for your classroom, and consistently keep them. Here are ten of the most workable strategies I've found for creating and using rules that will be effective.

It's the class consensus!

Classroom Rules
Ms. Lewis's 8th Grade
1. Wear no shoes.
2. Eat often in the classroom.
3. Gum allowed at all times.
4. Turn in homework whenever.
5. Cell phones allowed.

1. Keep them simple. Too many rules overwhelm students; the list loses its effectiveness. Choose a list they can remember. In most cases, five or fewer rules are enough. (To start your thinking, ask this question—it covers most situations: "Will your behavior hurt other people, hurt others' feelings, or hurt others' belongings?")

2. Collaborate. Work with your students to determine classroom rules. When they take part in making the rules, students take ownership of the process and are much more likely to follow them. Students usually come up with the same rules the teacher would have crafted. Often, students' rules are much harsher, so you may have to temper them.

3. State rules clearly. The rules should be easy to understand and stated concisely. The actions described should be observable. If you have a rule such as "Treat others with respect," make sure students know what that means. If your rule is "Honor each others' personal space," demonstrate precisely what personal space is.

4. Keep them positive. Have a list of "Do's" as opposed to "Do nots." Display positive policy in an easy-to-understand format. For example: "Work quietly," instead of "No talking." OR "Use walking feet," instead of "No running." OR "Raise hand to speak," instead of "No interrupting."

5. Set realistic expectations. Set rules that students can actually follow. Make sure they are age appropriate. Rules and limits should leave room for children's creative ideas or different situations.

6 State consequences clearly. Students must know the exact consequences that will result from violating a rule. Use proactive measures as the first step in consequences (that is, non-verbal signal, verbal redirection, proximity control).

7. Post the rules. Put rules in writing and put them in a prominent place where they are visible all year long. Post the consequences along with the rules. Some teachers also use "rules contracts" which provide a written agreement signed by student and teacher. For samples of rules contracts, see the Tools section at the end of this chapter.

8. **Teach and practice the rules.** Once rules are set, teach them with your words and actions. Have students role-play the behavior stated in the rules. Review the rules (and consequences) periodically. (I recommend five minutes every day for the first two weeks and five minutes a week each month after that.) To help young children understand why there are some things they cannot do, read books that share examples of such actions. Also encourage puppet play and pretend scenarios to teach these ideas.

9. **Monitor and enforce rules.** Train all members of the class to note when someone is following a rule. Don't let the importance of the rules lapse as time goes on. When a rule is broken, respond quickly with the agreed-upon consequence.

10. **Incorporate school or district rules.** Many schools and districts have rules that apply to all students. Make sure students understand these rules, and that you will hold students responsible for them.

How Consistently Do YOU Follow the Rules?

Do you "walk the walk," or just "talk"? Monitor your own behavior regarding classroom rules. Make certain that you model the behaviors described in the rules (such as treating everyone with respect or using appropriate language). Avoid any phrases that label students, border on name-calling, or appear taunting or denigrating. Watch out for words and expressions that may be amusing in adult social situations but do not translate into the classroom. Be mindful also of how you say things. Avoid belittling sarcasm. Consider the feelings of a child who hears her teacher say:

Teacher-to-Teacher Tip

"Do not set a classroom rule unless you are willing to enforce it."
– *Experienced middle-grades teacher*

"You need to use the restroom **again**?"

"Molly, I already answered that question. **Everyone else** in the class heard it!"

"Looks like your father **helped** you with your homework last night."

You set the tone of your classroom; the students will follow your lead.

What Do You Expect?

It's a funny thing about expectations. The chapter has stressed the importance of realistic expectations. Teachers are overwhelmed when the job turns out to be more challenging or frustrating (or less prestigious or rewarding) than they expected. Students are frustrated by expectations that don't match their developmental level. But, expectations have power. IF an expectation is realistic, even though not seemingly likely or possible, it can inspire a teacher or a student to achieve something they did not envision.

Twentieth-century sociologist Robert K. Merton proposed the theory of the self-fulfilling prophecy. A self-fulfilling prophecy is a prediction or belief that, although not true, becomes true. Here's how it works.

1. A person has a false belief that something will happen in the future.

2. This belief evokes behavior that the person would not normally have taken.

3. The original false (or seemingly impossible) assumption becomes true.

Merton cited as one example the story of the Last Nation Bank, a solid financial institution in the 1930s. Someone circulated a false idea that the bank was on the verge of financial collapse. That belief caused customers to withdraw their money, which in turn caused the failure of the bank.

In 1968, Robert Rosenthal and Leonore Jacobson applied this theory to the classroom. In their published report, *Pygmalion in the classroom: Teacher expectation and pupils' intellectual development*, they described an experiment conducted in an elementary school. They hypothesized a direct correlation between the expectations of the teacher and the level of student achievement. An intelligence test was administered to all students. Twenty percent of those students were then chosen at random, with no relation to the test scores. Teachers were told that these students had the highest intellectual potential and were expected to blossom academically during the school year. Tests were re-administered eight months later. There was a significant increase in test scores for the students who were labeled with the greatest potential, though not among the other eighty percent of the students. Teachers expected the selected students to thrive. This led them to pay more attention to these students and their learning activities. And the students did grow and thrive.

In addition, the teachers in the Rosenthal and Jacobson study were asked to rank students on intellectual curiosity, personal adjustment, social adjustment, and the need for social approval. Teachers rated that same "top" twenty percent as happier, better adjusted, and more intellectually curious.

This theory has been retested and reaffirmed since Rosenthal and Jacobson. We can see examples of this all around us in education. Good teachers don't even need to read the research to know this is true. It is played out in individual families and classrooms, in schoolwide or districtwide programs.

Falling in Love Again

When teachers expect students to succeed, the most amazing thing happens: teachers subtly and overtly convey belief in the students. It's easier to believe in yourself when someone believes in you, and the increased sense of self-worth translates into great strides for students. So believe in your students. Give them the gift of a well-managed, emotionally and physically safe classroom where the conditions are great for learning. The combination of these two conditions is POWERFUL. And when you work in an orderly, comfortable setting with students who have hope, you will find yourself enjoying your days. You can take off the police hat and badge, and throw away the handcuffs. You'll have taken several more steps away from teacher burnout and toward renewing joy in your profession.

Me Moments

- Take a few minutes each day to journal your thoughts. Journaling is a great way to let go of your stress.

- Every time you want to buy fast food, put the money in a jar instead. The money that you will save will add up quickly! Use your money for a back massage, foot massage, or manicure. You (and your body) will appreciate the pampering.

- Buy a bracelet with large beads. (Or make your own bead bracelet.) Move one of the beads over on the string every time you use reinforcing language in speaking to someone. Try to make it around to the last bead each day. Saying positive words all day is a winning situation for you and the other person. Each time you say positive words, you are energized (and so is the other person). You will be surprised how much energy you will have at the end of the day!

Chapter 4 **Tools**

Get Their Attention!

Use these tips as you create your own repertoire to match your students' age level and your personal style.

Simple things that grab their eyes or ears:

Buzz an electric doorbell.

Use a fun word or phrase.

Clap a pattern.

Shake a maraca.

Flick the lights.

Play some music.

Talk to the wall.

Put on a mask.

Sing or hum a song.

Put on a hat.

Strum a drum.

Strike a tambourine.

Do a cartwheel.

Clash some cymbals.

Hold up a red light.

Set a timer.

Whisper.

Toot on an instrument.

Stand on a stool.

Do a dance.

Other tactics:

Give Me Five— When students see you hold up five fingers, one at a time, they do this: eyes on speaker, mouth closed, ears listening, hands and feet still, show high-five sign.

Card Shuffle— Get a deck of cards. Write each student's name on a card. When you need to call on someone, shuffle the deck and choose a card. Reshuffle before each use. Students will pay close attention, because their card can be pulled at any time and may be pulled more than once.

Calming Music Box— Wind up a music box. Let students know they are to be quiet and ready by the time the music ends.

Teacher Hands Up— YOU raise your hands. As students notice, they raise their hands too until all hands are raised. Hands up means, "Stop talking and listen."

Silent Countdown— Count backwards from five to zero with your fingers or any other items you hold up (such as rulers). By the time you reach zero, they are to be quiet. Mix this up and surprise students with the items you will use. Sometimes paint your hand or wear a funny glove or use straws or salamis.

Ball Toss— Ask a question or give a direction. Toss a beach ball as you say a name. That person must catch the ball and answer. Students will NOT know when to expect the ball, so they will ALL have to be on their toes.

Classroom Rules

Teacher's Self Checklist

	Definitely	Somewhat	Not much
There are a reasonable number of rules— easy to remember (4 to 5 at the most).			
The rules are based on realistic expectations.			
The rules are positive (not a list of "Don'ts").			
The rules are stated in clear, observable terms.			
My students were involved in developing rules.			
The rules were posted prominently in the classroom as soon as they were developed.			
The rules have been taught and practiced using words and role-playing.			
All students have signed a rules contract, with copies kept in the classroom and sent to parents.			
Students and I all watch for and compliment others who are following classroom rules.			
Consequences for not following the rules are posted with the rules.			
I help students remember rules and guide their behavior so that they can successfully follow them.			
When rules are not followed, I consistently apply the consequences.			

Note: Use this near the beginning of the year. Make necessary adaptations so that within a week or two you can honestly place all checkmarks in the "Definitely" column.

Classroom Rules Contract

 1. Keep the classroom clean.

2. Raise my hand when I want to speak.

 3. Look at and listen to someone else who is talking.

 4. Treat everyone else kindly.

5. Keep my hands to myself instead of touching others or the belongings of others.

I agree to follow these rules.

| yes | no |

Your signature:

_____

Teacher's signature :

_____

Classroom Rules Contract

I understand that I am expected to:

- treat students, teachers (including substitute teachers), school property, and everyone's belongings with respect.

- take responsibility for all of my actions.

- be inside the classroom door when the bell begins ringing.

- act in ways that are safe for others and me.

- do my own work, without cheating of any kind.

I understand that the consequences for not following a rule are:

warning

loss of recess or other privileges

time out from the group

after-school detention

in-school suspension

Detention Today: 3:15 - 4:45 pm

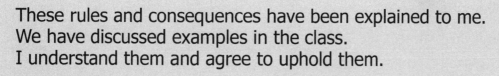

These rules and consequences have been explained to me.
We have discussed examples in the class.
I understand them and agree to uphold them.

Signatures:

Student _____

Teacher _____

Seating for Success

There is no one perfect seating arrangement for a classroom. The best arrangement is one that works for the kinds of learning activities you do. When planning seating, consider your students before yourself. Be flexible when it comes to seating for success and think outside the box. Consider these models or arrange your own variations of these ideas.

Note: If possible, face desks so that all students can view the board and any projection screen.

Desk Row Seating Arrangement

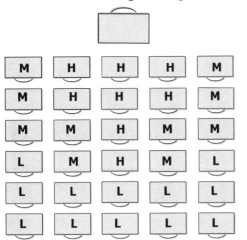

Desk Row Seating Arrangement
Ideal for monitoring student behavior
Not ideal for cooperative or collaborative learning

Cluster Seating Arrangement
Ideal for cooperative and collaborative learning
Not ideal for testing

Semicircle Seating Arrangement
Ideal for debates and discussions
Not ideal for meeting with students one-one

Note: This seating arrangement is not ideal for large classes.

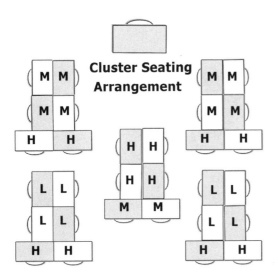

Cluster Seating Arrangement

H = High Interaction
M = Moderate Interaction
L = Low Interaction

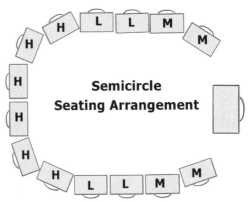

Semicircle Seating Arrangement

Seating for Success, continued

Note: If possible, face desks so that all students can view the board and any projection screen.

Table Row Seating Arrangement
Ideal for pair work
Not ideal for testing or monitoring students

Table Row Seating Arrangement

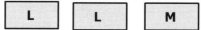

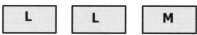

Pair Seating Arrangement
Ideal for monitoring students and one-to-one/two feedback
Not ideal for testing and may be problematic if students
do not get along with their partner

Pair Seating Arrangement

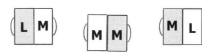

Learning Centers Seating Arrangement
Ideal for collaborative learning and differentiated instruction
Not ideal for testing and may be problematic if students
are not able to move with minimal disruption

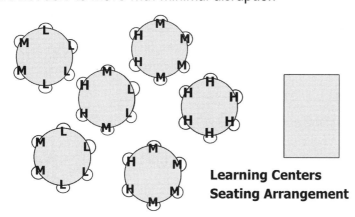

**Learning Centers
Seating Arrangement**

Note: Don't forget to talk with the custodian, so he or she is aware of the reasons behind your desk arrangements. There is nothing more frustrating than arranging your room for the next day, only to return the next morning to have all your desks facing forward in rows.

Interaction levels adapted from McCorskey and McVetta (1978)

Feng Shui Tips for the Classroom

Feng Shui (which literally means "wind and water") is the art of designing for a flow of life and energy. Some principles of feng shui can make the classroom a more comfortable place for students and teachers and can enhance student concentration, good behavior, and achievement.

Place the teacher's desk facing the door, with the back of the desk against a wall. (But don't think you should be sitting at your desk all the time!)

Provide soothing music or other soft sounds such as a metal chime.

Keep the entryway to the classroom unobstructed.
The path into the classroom should be open and welcoming.

Clear away clutter. Store supplies behind doors or curtains. Keep your desk and students' desks clear of excess "stuff." Avoid excess furnishings. Include only what you really need.

Use bright blues and greens to calm students. Add splashes of yellow or orange to areas where you want students energized.

Place seats in clusters or semicircles with plenty of space between them.

Bring in nature. Desks can face a window, or you can create a sense of nature by adding plants and pictures of nature on the walls of your classroom.

Soften sharp edges with a drape of fabric. Add curves to a row, position a shelf at an angle, or place a screen diagonally to create a quiet place.

Try to use natural light and avoid the use of florescent lights.

Add some water! The sound of water is soothing, as is the sight. Try a tabletop waterfall, small aquarium, or fishbowl.

Teacher's Pet

They're Begging Me to Say Yes

You know you are a teacher under stress when you agree to be the advisor to the How-To-Use-Your-Cell-Phone-To-Cheat-On-Tests Club.

Groan

Injured Athlete's Newsletter

Twitter Club Manual

Procrastinators' Club

Right now, I can't breathe! I have a research paper due in three days for a college course I am taking. I attend class two nights a week. (Imagine! I actually thought that would be doable!) Thursday afternoons I advise the chess club. And Mrs. Parker just asked me to help her meet some yearbook deadlines, as I was yearbook supervisor two years ago. I hate to say no because she has helped me out of some jams. Now I need to get to school early for yearbook meetings. And then—at a faculty meeting today, I mentioned that the front of the school looked shabby and might be a good place for a student garden. Guess what? I am now the head of the School Beautification Committee. I am completely stressed. I have no time to grade papers, let alone have a life at home. This job is burning me out. I am thinking of going back to my old job as a bank teller.

– Catherine Berg, middle-school teacher

If you want to send a bunch of teachers scurrying to the dark places beneath their desks, just utter a few of these things in their presence:

student newspaper advisor

chess club

Future Teachers of America

Future Professionals of America

art club

marathon-runners' team

French club

intramural soccer

4-H club

jazz band

IT club

holiday choir

student fund-raising committee

cheerleading squad

dress-code enforcement team

Oprah wannabes

students against tucked-in shirts

mall shopping marathon team

boycott-the-lunchroom committee

Burger Connoisseurs of America

cell phone photography club

Okay, so maybe I got a little carried away with the club titles. But for some teachers, the prospect of a student club sponsorship (or advisory job) causes more stress than lesson plans, teacher evaluations, or even high-stakes testing.

Learn To Love Teaching Again

Losing the Love

It's just a fact of life in a school: there are dozens of extracurricular events and organizations that need help or supervision. Somebody has to do this! And let's face it—the skills and the nurturing personality that brought you into the teaching profession are highly sought after by myriad causes outside school, too. All of these "opportunities" involve worthy goals, and have the potential to be satisfying for you under the right conditions. But the bane of a teacher's existence is being overcommitted. And when you get stretched beyond your limits or torn in different directions, burnout is a guaranteed result.

A teacher who can't balance and choose duties wisely is soon in trouble. Teaching alone is demanding. If you can't say no to extra jobs that are not right for you at the time, you will surely lose all delight in your main job.

Extra-Duty Blues

The first faculty meeting of the year is ending. The principal dismisses the teachers and turns to you. Casually, he says, "And you won't mind running the Four-Syllables-Only Spelling Bee this year, will you?" The inside of your head is screaming, "No! No! No!" But you turn to him, smile, and say, "Of course. I would be glad to help."

And your colleagues breathe a sigh of relief. This time it is you, not them.

The assigning and performing of extra duties has become a sore point between school administrators and teachers. Schools want to offer (and parents expect) a variety of extracurricular activities to round out student academics and to offer supervised opportunities where students can try new experiences or pursue their interests. These activities benefit students and families in many ways:

- increased social interactions
- opportunities for students to negotiate relationships with different people
- safe, positive after-school activities as an alternative to being home alone
- a chance to learn new skills and progress in previously learned skills
- a balance to the isolation of hours alone at computers or video games
- ways to increase physical or intellectual activities

There are benefits for teachers, too. Among these are:

- chances to build relationships with students
- stretching their abilities into new areas
- pursuing and developing personal interests
- the rewards of watching students grow in some new ways
- in some cases, additional financial compensation

In most schools, however, the demand for teacher supervisors is greater than the pool of teacher volunteers. And many teachers resent the pressure put on them to accept extra duties for which they may be neither qualified nor compensated. Often this issue can become quite political. Many contract negotiations and even teacher strikes include disputes over the hours or compensation related to extra duties. The "extras" that teachers protest even include such activities as open house, curriculum nights, and social functions—in addition to all the many duties of a coaching, supervisory, or advisory nature.

Such responses are not surprising. Teachers are overwhelmed by the "extra stuff." Listen in on an interview about this topic between an administrator and a first-year teacher.

> **Dr. Cole:** *What types of duties are assigned to you?*
>
> **Michael:** *Each morning, another new teacher and I must watch all the middle-school students in the gym. It is a wild scene. I'm so afraid that something bad is going to happen. I have already talked to the principal, but he just shrugs his shoulders and pretty much says to handle it. Since the last time I talked to you about this, I have segregated the boys from the girls. They hate it, but it seems like it's a little better. After this year, I'm hoping to be replaced by someone else. What makes me the most angry is that there is another new teacher who hasn't been assigned to any duties. I don't know how she got out of it. I think she flirted with the principal or something.*
>
> **Dr. Cole:** *Do you feel that you had no choice but to say yes to such duties?*

Teacher-to-Teacher Tip

"I used to hate playground duty. Now I put on my running shoes and walk around the playground. Sometimes kids walk with me. I am able to watch all the kids in my designated area and get exercise at the same time."

– Vicki T., Oklahoma

Learn To Love Teaching Again

Michael: I **know** I had no choice. The principal said, "Here's your duty," so I had no choice in the matter. I was pretty forceful with him one time when I had just about had enough. But he acted as if it was going to hurt my evaluation. I am a first-year teacher; I know he doesn't have to renew my contract next year. We also have to rotate lunch duty. I don't mind that, because all of the teachers in our team have to rotate. Thank goodness, none of us have after-school duty. The kids are expected to get on the buses and head out. Usually the assistant principals will stand watch outside.

> ### New Teacher Tip
>
> *Teachers are expected to take up the slack by taking on additional responsibilities. Even when you are new, don't be intimidated into saying yes to a duty that you don't think is right for you. Be assertive. Speak up. Offer to take something more suited to you. Discuss the situation. Learn to say no when it's appropriate.*

Dr. Cole: What about extracurricular duties?

Michael: Teachers are given an extra amount added to their salary for extracurricular duties. The football coach and his assistant are given around $5,000 extra to coach after school. I haven't been asked yet to do any extracurricular duties. A friend of mine, who has taught forever at another school, was told that he had to coach the girls' soccer team. He was paid extra money, too. I'm not sure how much, but he still didn't want to do it. His principal was pretty persistent, so he didn't feel like he had a choice, either.

Michael is in a bind. There are some duties that are clearly assigned, and it is not an option to say no if the administrator closes off the discussion. Or, perhaps the consequences of saying no are not an option to you. However, in many other cases, the job comes in the form of a request that, though it may be uncomfortable to do so, you could decline. It's worth some time to learn how to say no to the things that **are** within your control.

I can't figure out why the principal keeps asking me to take on all these new clubs and projects.

It's Hard to Say No

The assigned and volunteer supervisory tasks are not the only extra tasks that come along. Colleagues, relatives, and all kinds of other friends and acquaintances "invite" you to help them out for several hours, one day, a week, or longer. There are fund-raisers and PTO meetings, baby showers, community events, soccer coaching stints, and . . . . The list is very long. And no matter how pressed we are, some of us just resist saying no.

Why We Can't Say No

There are some good reasons why we say yes, even when we mean no. Here are a few:

Chuckle!

Accept that some days you're the pigeon, and some days you're the statue.
— Dilbert's Words of Wisdom

- We want to be liked. We fear that someone will think we're haughty or disagreeable if we refuse a request for help.

- We don't want to reject anyone or appear to be rude. Kind souls that we are, we don't want to hurt anyone's feelings.

- We want to help. Most of the time the help really IS needed—for something worthwhile. We don't like to turn someone away, especially when the task helps kids.

- We don't want to jeopardize our jobs. Pressures from colleagues, particularly administrators, raise fears. We want to be seen as professionals who pull their weight. And we don't want to lose the confidence or approval of superiors, that's for sure! (And for sure, we don't want to lose our jobs!)

- We don't like conflict or disagreement. Someone might interpret a "no" as dissent, and plenty of us people-pleasers stay as far away from confrontation as possible.

New teachers are particularly vulnerable to the burden of extra assignments, as these extra duties are sometimes included as conditions for renewal of their contracts. The more-experienced staff members are burned out, or have learned how to say no. So administrators are desperate to fill the supervisory slots. Sometimes candidates for jobs who show willingness to take on extra duties have a better chance than other prospective teachers of getting the job! Yet new teachers are even more susceptible to increased stress from extra assignments. Here are some of the reasons:

- The new teacher will say always yes. He is enthusiastic and energetic. Or she wants to make a good impression. But maintaining that high level of energy for a long list of duties is a recipe for early burnout.

- When starting out in the profession, a new teacher has not had the chance to build a strong support system among colleagues. So this teacher may feel "out on a limb" or isolated while supervising a club or activity. This loneliness can pave the way for stress.

- New teachers have not had the time to develop the good time-management skills they need to juggle the multiple responsibilities.

Paperwork, student challenges, parental communications, and school deadlines can be overwhelming and create stress on their own, without the addition of time-consuming extra duties.

Though new teachers are highly susceptible to the pressures to take on more and more duties, no teacher is immune. Well, if you have developed a steel shell over the years, or if you've perfected the mean snarl—you may be. But few are. So all teachers can stand a few lessons in saying no.

Teacher - to - Teacher Tip

"Over the years, I learned to say no to the principal's request for volunteers. I knew those extra duties would be stressful because I had young children of my own. Say yes to extracurricular tasks when the time is right in your life. Now that my children are grown, I say yes more often—and I am having fun with the students in these activities."

– Joyce P., Colorado

Check Your Assertiveness Style

Take this quick four-question survey to get some insight into your assertiveness (or lack of assertiveness) style. This is just for the purpose of self-reflection. There are no right or wrong answers.

1. You spent all weekend working on a new interactive bulletin board. You're excited; this will get the students jazzed about the upcoming measurement unit! The teacher next door knows how much effort and money you put into the project. Yet she makes an uncalled for, disparaging remark. How are you likely to react?

    a. Say nothing and turn away. Your feelings are seriously hurt.

    b. Calmly tell your colleague how you feel about her remark. Maybe she is having a bad day and does not realize how she is treating others.

    c. Make a snide comment that you overheard how poorly her students performed on the standardized tests, or that you noticed the dull appearance of her classroom.

2. On the day of your evaluation, everything that could go wrong does. Shortly after class begins, Scott gets sick. While the other students gag and squeal, you get another teacher to take him to the nurse's office. You call the custodian for a cleanup, and try to continue with your lesson. Just as students are reasonably back on task, a voice crackles across the intercom asking for Belinda Cabot (your student) to come to the office with homework assigned and ready to go home. Then the fire alarm goes off! Upon your return to the classroom, just when your students have the energy levels of motorized Ping-Pong balls—the teacher evaluator walks in! You just know you'll be getting a substandard evaluation. How are you likely to react?

   a. You explain that the day's circumstances were out of your control and see if the evaluator is willing to come back on another day.

   b. You wait until you see the report, then confront the evaluator. You point out all the other teachers who, unlike you, truly have poor classroom management skills.

   c. You try to play for sympathy and give a slightly whiny, tearful excuse to the evaluator.

3. The reading teacher borrowed a favorite teaching-strategies book last month, and has finally returned it. Many of the pages are ruined with a huge coffee stain. How are you likely to react?

   a. You say nothing and suck it up. You do not want to make your colleague angry.

   b. You loudly make a big deal out of the damage, embarrass her, and have her promise to replace the book.

   c. You make a sarcastic joke about the ruined pages, sending her a clear message that you will not be lending her anything again.

   d. You tell her kindly that you are disappointed that a favorite book is damaged, and let go of your anger about it.

4. Your colleagues admire (or at least notice and comment on) your

   a. laid-back attitude.

   b. sense of humor.

   c. tolerance level.

   d. sense of drama.

Review your answers. What do they tell you about yourself? Are you willing to stand up for yourself? Do you let others walk all over you? Is your approach more a cowering Edith Bunker or a roaring Godzilla on a bad day? In situations like these, do you tend to be defensive? passive-aggressive? calm? spiteful?

Learn To Love Teaching Again

The following examples demonstrate a few different ways a teacher might respond in a situation where she doesn't want to say yes.

The principal asks Ms. Nguyen to oversee a new Reading for Success Program. But Ms. Nguygen already advises the Photography Club and is a teacher representative for the PTO.

Nonassertive response: *Ms. Nguyen answers meekly, "I suppose I can take on one more task." As soon as the principal leaves her classroom, Ms. Nguyen runs next door and complains to a peer. When a birthday card is passed around for the principal, Ms. Nguyen "accidentally" drops it outside in a pile of dust and then "forgets" to sign it.*

A nonassertive reaction is rarely an honest reaction. True opinions are pushed aside, and the respondent seems to acquiesce passively. Nonassertiveness often increases the stress of the teacher and leaves her with feelings that can include loneliness, helplessness, poor self-concept, and depression. While the nonassertive teacher seems to be saying yes, her repressed anger can leak out in sarcasm, backbiting, and seemingly unrelated arguments.

Aggressive response: *Ms. Nguyen stands up. Her body stiffens. She gets red in the face. She wants to bang the desk, but restrains herself and clenches her fists. Raising her voice, she shouts that she will not do one more thing for the school, that while her pay is not even close to her husband's she is still continually asked to perform extra duties, and that there are other teachers who just do not pull their weight. Other staff and students passing in the hallway stop and shake their heads as they listen to her rampage.*

Though an aggressive reaction (even if it is passive-aggressive) certainly lets others know how someone feels, it often leaves guilt and frustration. Those on the receiving end of the aggressive response may react with anger, hurt feelings, or humiliation. An aggressive response may fool the teacher into thinking she is controlling the situation, but the truth is her perspective is not clearly articulated in her outburst. In fact, the result will probably be negative for her. In many cases, respect is lost when aggression is demonstrated.

Positive Attitude Tip

Be who you are and say what you feel, because those who mind don't matter and those who matter don't mind.
– Dr. Seuss

Appropriately assertive response. *Ms. Nguyen listens quietly to the principal. When he is finished speaking, she reminds him of the other duties that she has already taken on and the time commitments those duties entail. She explains that her work has already been increased with the addition of the new Tier Two Vocabulary class this* *year. She suggests that a new commitment would diminish her performance on those other tasks. Ms. Nguyen ends by saying she would be happy to consider the position for the following year.*

An assertive response is an honest expression of feelings. Assertiveness is not hostile, threatening, or demanding. It is a way of expressing needs and wants without causing disrespect to the opposing party. It usually results in feelings of positive self-esteem and confidence. This strategy leaves the way open to continued good communication.

Your assertiveness style will play a part in the responses to "requests" to take on duties beyond your classroom. As you prepare to practice appropriate "no-saying," it will be helpful to you to have identified the way you usually react. Decide if your style is helpful and productive. If not, think about how you might change it. To further examine your current ability to say no, use the self-reflection tools and tips in the Tools section at the end of this chapter.

Learn to Say No and Mean It

You really can learn this. And as you do, you will select tasks that are suited to your time, interests, and talents. And then your life will be less stressful. Don't assume that the advice here is intended to keep you from ever saying yes. You will have to, if you intend to keep your job. Remember there are plenty of good reasons to help out for worthwhile and necessary activities. When the time, workload, and reasons are right, you will be saying yes!

No, I have to finish my dryer-lint sculpture that day.

Drop the Guilt and Fear

Earlier in the chapter, I referred to some of the reasons you might fail to say no when you should. Guilt and fear are two of the most powerful. Get rid of these. Yes, I know, it's not that easy. But keep these things in mind as you try:

- If you say yes when you mean no, you take on a task that you don't really want. Then you'll probably resent this the whole time you do the job. You'll rob yourself of time to do other commitments well, to take care of yourself, to do your main job well, or to be with your family. This does no one any favors.

- You have the right to protect yourself and your time. You do not have to justify your choices. You have the right to take care of yourself and your family. There's no need to feel guilty about that!

Learn To Love Teaching Again

- If you say no, it does not mean you are disagreeable, rude, or cranky. It just means you can't do this right now. Speaking up for yourself does not mean that you have bad manners.

- Saying no once doesn't mean you will always say no. You will say yes to some things. You may even say yes to this in the future. There will be plenty of opportunities to help out.

- You may fear looking selfish or disinterested, or hurting someone's feelings. Some people may choose to view it that way. Take other opportunities to show that these people are wrong about you.

- Do you fear not being liked? Ask yourself this question: "If I take on yet another job and do it poorly, how will that affect my likeability?"

- If you have good reason to fear for your job or professional advancement, then you may have to say yes. Even in these cases, you can try to discuss the options or negotiate the matter.

Plan Ahead for the Request

You know you are going to be asked to sponsor the Future Debit Card Users of America this year. In fact, you hear the principal determinedly heading down the hallway right now. Looking around the classroom, you realize there is no place to hide. You desperately scour your brain, searching for a way to say no.

You mentally run through your excuses, but the counterarguments fly back at you:

This position would be too hard. (Sure, find one person who ever told you teaching would be easy.)

To be a club sponsor is not in my job description. (Face it; everything is in your job description.)

But I don't know anything about this organization! (Join the club.)

I am planning my wedding, working on my master's, taking a cake-decorating course, training a new puppy; and I just cannot focus on anything else. (Hire a wedding planner and buy a goldfish. This argument won't get you very far.)

Chuckle!

Third-grade teacher Anna Cooke was asked to run the Spelling Bee. She agreed—reluctantly. Mrs. Cooke gathered the students who wanted to participate. Opening the official Spelling Bee list, she asked for a volunteer to spell the first word. There was a moment of silence. Then one student hesitantly stood up and asked to buy a vowel.

> *I'm busy that weekend. I'll be getting my karma adjusted.*

"Why?" you whisper through clenched teeth, "Why didn't I get ready for this? I knew it was coming!"

You definitely can get a handle on this "saying no" issue if you think about it before the requests come. Don't get caught off guard. Have a plan. Here are some ideas that will help:

1. Before you get asked to do something, think about the big picture. Think about what you are already doing and what you would like to do. Perhaps even volunteer (before you are asked) for the things you would most like to do.

2. If you know a request is coming, think through the following questions ahead of time.

   - **How much time will this activity entail?** When you consider what time you have, be sure to include all commitments, including those outside school.

   - **What personal benefits are likely?** What can you gain from doing this? Will you learn something new? Will this further an existing interest? Will it fulfill a passion? Will it add value to your résumé?

   - **What personal risks are involved?** Will you be alone with students before or after school in an empty part of the building? Are there good procedures for emergencies that could arise? Does the district's insurance policy cover the activity? Are you equipped to handle the risks?

   - **Is there a stipend offered with the activity?** What are your financial needs in relation to this offer? Is the amount of money enough to compensate for the additional time and effort?

3. If the request catches you by surprise, ask for some time to consider this. Then ask yourself the same kinds of questions before giving your reply.

4. Do you want to say no as sponsor to the Future Debit Card Users of America? Organize your thoughts ahead of time. Know exactly what you are going to say.

5. Make a list of all the school projects you have taken on. Have this ready to share with the principal (or other person asking). This person may not realize she is asking you to do double, triple, or quadruple duty.

135

6. Do you feel that an additional duty will decrease your effectiveness with your existing duties? If so, be ready with examples. Be ready to show the extent of your dedication and determination to do a good job with your current commitments.

7. Practice saying no. Have a good list of ways to say no, and practice the actual words you will say. They'll be automatic when you get the surprise request. For a list of ways to say no, see the Tools section at the end of this chapter.

8. When asked to do something, listen to the entire proposal first before responding. Sometimes knowing you are going to be approached sets off an internal panic and a screaming inside your head: "NO WAY! I AM NOT GOING TO DO IT!" That internal conversation can disrupt the external conversation. Maybe you are only being asked your opinion. Or maybe the job is not as encompassing as you assumed. Understand exactly what is being asked of you before you offer your response. And if you are not ready to respond right away, ask for some time.

Say It Well

What makes the difference is **how** you say no. In most cases, the person making the request will understand overcommitment, burnout, family responsibilities, or your other reasons. They have the same concerns for themselves.

- Show care for the person who is asking. Express appreciation that this person considers you capable of the task. Thank them for their own involvement in the project. Let them know you understand that their task of finding helpers is a job that has its difficulties. For some help with this, see ideas in the Tools section at the end of this chapter.

- When you say no, do so clearly, firmly, and kindly. Give a brief explanation or no explanation. Don't belabor the issue with long excuses.

- Don't second-guess yourself after you have said no. If you have planned and practiced and considered the topic of extra duties ahead of time, you should not need to rethink a decision.

- Don't be a person who always says no. Say yes to things you can do and have time to do. This will make it easier to say no later when you have to.

Say It Definitively

Avoid wishy-washy or middle-of-the-road answers, such as: "I'd love to do this, but . . . ."

> "I guess I *could* think about it."
>
> "Let me see what I can do."

If you mean no, say no. Many people fall into the trap of the "sort of, but not definitely" no.

I couldn't possibly head up that committee. I have no matching socks.

Example:

> **Mrs. Borgman:** *I have a new project I would like you to take the lead on. The school council has voted to create a wildlife sanctuary in the courtyard. There will be a small budget, and you can solicit some parent volunteers to help out.*
>
> **Mr. Alonzo:** *But I don't have much time after school. I'm assistant basketball coach, which, with equipment preparation and off-season drills, has turned into an all-year job.*
>
> **Mrs. Borgman:** *That's all right. This project can be worked on in the mornings before school begins.*
>
> **Mr. Alonzo:** *But a wildlife sanctuary . . . I have done only a little home gardening, and worked at Barry's Landscaping just part-time for a couple of years.*
>
> **Mrs. Borgman:** *Yes, with your experience you'll be perfect!*
>
> **Mr. Alonzo:** *I don't know much about wildlife . . .*
>
> **Mrs. Borgman:** *Put up a hummingbird feeder and some plants that attract butterflies. You'll be fine!*
>
> **Mr. Alonzo:** *I did have that back surgery last year . . .*
>
> **Mrs. Borgman:** *This apparently is no longer an issue, since you coach basketball. What a perfect match!*
>
> **Mr. Alonzo** *(with a sigh):* *I'll get my shovel . . .*

Do you see Mr. Alonzo's problem? Every time Mr. Alonzo answers Mrs. Borgman, he gives an excuse. (Your students would say "TMI"—Too Much Information!) His comments give Mrs. Borgman fuel for counterarguments, and she finally wears him down.

Keep it simple. If you want to say no, say no. Make a firm stance and repeat it more than once if necessary. Offering explanations and detailed stories only weakens your position. Let's revisit Mr. Alonzo, as he now heeds this advice.

Mrs. Borgman: I have a new project. I'd like you to take the lead on this. The school council has voted to create a wildlife sanctuary in the courtyard. There will be a small budget, and you can try to solicit some parent volunteers to help out.

Mr. Alonzo: I am already overcommitted. I will not be able to help with this project this year.

Mrs. Borgman: But the sanctuary can be worked on in the mornings before school starts.

Mr. Alonzo: I am sorry I can't help you out. It sounds like a wonderful project. I just do not have the time this year.

Spanish Club every Thursday at 3:00? Sorry, that's the exact time that I floss my hamster's teeth.

Mrs. Borgman: But with your experience you'd be perfect!

Mr. Alonzo: I appreciate your confidence, but I cannot commit to this project this year.

Mrs. Borgman: Just put up a hummingbird feeder and some plants that attract butterflies. You'll be fine!

Mr. Alonzo: I already have a heavy load of commitments this year. Ask me again next year, and I will be sure to leave time on my schedule.

Mrs. Borgman (with a sigh)**:** I'll get my shovel . . .

Say YES to This!

Jana's Italian mother-in-law (a great cook) is coming for the weekend. She'll expect some good food. The problem is, Jana is not that great a cook. Well, actually, Jana eats a lot of ramen noodles and salad out of a bag. But she's determined to impress "Mom." So she tracks down manicotti recipes on the Internet. She's never made this dish, so hasn't a clue as to which version to choose. Furthermore, she doesn't have the right pots and pans. She's never heard of some of the spices. She runs around buying ingredients and gathering supplies, spending a lot of money in the process—and brings them all to her kitchen.

And then she stands there wondering—"Now, what?" She can bumble along, over-boiling noodles, undercooking the sausage, making a sloppy sauce, and hoping to end up with something edible. If only she had someone to actually teach her how to do this! (She should have waited for her mother-in-law to show her how to do this.)

This scenario parallels the experience of many teachers beginning a new teaching assignment. They spend a lot of money, not knowing what "recipes" really are best. They start and stop, look for more information, eat up time, and end up wondering, "Now, what?" Frustration rises, enthusiasm sinks, and stress sets in. They need a helping hand—early in the new venture. This is where a good mentoring program can make all the difference.

Now You're Telling Me to Say Yes?

It may seem strange, yes! Here you are in the middle of a chapter about learning how to say no. And the author is telling you to say yes. Well, first of all, the chapter is not only about saying no. It is also about when to say yes. If you are a new teacher, or if you are an experienced teacher, a mentoring relationship is definitely an opportunity to consider accepting. New teachers, or anyone changing positions or taking on new responsibilities, should get help to learn the ropes and avoid mistakes. The mentor benefits as much as the mentee—to the surprise of many a mentor. Guiding another teacher gives you an incentive to examine what works, try new things, feel good about what you have to offer, and enjoy the partnership with another professional. Teachers who mentor generally become better teachers.

Mentoring Makes a Difference

Teacher mentoring programs have been around for many years, and today more than half of the states require mentors for new teachers. Many mentoring programs, wisely, expand to provide mentors for any teacher new to a position or new to a set of responsibilities. Local school campuses, school districts, and state governments all recognize the value of mentoring programs.

In a September 2008 press release from the state of Alabama, Governor Bob Riley said of the state's new mentoring program: "It's probably one of the more successful programs we've had in education." In 2007,

Teacher-to-Teacher Tip

"Here are some things to do as a mentor:

- *Go shopping with my mentee to help find things for the classroom.*
- *Suggest some good organization or filing strategies.*
- *Make a list of all the forms and information to be completed during the opening weeks of school.*
- *Create a mentor book with information needed (so he or she won't have to keep asking).*
- *Answer any questions to help understand the program and procedures."*

– Maria Hannah, experienced mentor

all of the state's 2,900 beginning teachers were assigned veteran-teacher mentors. Here are some of the results:

- Over 84 percent of the mentees rated their mentors as important or extremely important in a positive first-year experience.

- Almost 83 percent of the mentees stated that their mentors assisted with procedures for classroom organization and student management.

- 88 percent reported that the mentorship program provided emotional support and a boost in teacher confidence.

- Additionally, retention rates were improved. Typically Alabama lost 30 to 50 percent of its teachers in the first five years of employment. Nationwide 10 percent of teachers quit the profession after the first year. After one year of mentoring, only 2 percent of Alabama's first-year teachers said they had no plans to return.

Researcher Jonah Rockoff studied the $40 million mentoring program designed by New York City and the New Teacher Center at the University of California at Santa Cruz. The program was developed to satisfy a state law requiring that all teachers with less than a year of teaching experience receive a "mentored experience." A goal of many mentoring programs is, obviously, to develop better teachers for the students. And usually another goal is to reduce new teacher turnover. Here are some results of the New York City mentoring program:

New Teacher Tip

You can be trained to teach, but still not be prepared to teach. If you work in a school with a mentoring program for new teachers—rejoice!

- Among the teachers (mentees) participating in the New York City program, 97 percent continued teaching until the end of the school year, 90 percent returned the following year to teach somewhere in New York City schools, and 80 percent returned to teach at the same school.

- Mentors who had taught (and worked as a mentor) in a teacher's school raised that teacher's propensity to return to the same school the following year. Also, having a mentor who had previously taught in the same school reduced teacher absences by 0.6 days.

- When standardized test scores in grades 4 through 8 were used as a measure of student achievement, and after controlling for student demographics, the hours of mentoring provided had positive effects on reading and math achievement.

Effective Mentorship

An effective mentor . . .

- shows the mentee "the ropes" of the school—policies, procedures, expectations, guidelines, rules, locations, supplies.
- visits the mentee's classroom regularly, offering encouragement and praise, as well as insightful commentary on areas in which improvement is needed.
- promotes the mentee's participation in school events and professional-development opportunities.
- assists the mentor in both short- and long-term instructional planning.
- shares teaching methodologies, curriculum resources, and classroom strategies.
- provides a listening ear and a positive and supportive attitude.

In addition . . .

The mentor teacher is committed to the process of mentoring. Optimally, the mentor believes in the process and is devoted to filling in the gaps for new teachers. The mentors understand the role that this relationship plays in new-teacher retention. They make themselves available and work to build a trusting partnership.

The mentor accepts the new teacher. The mentee will make mistakes, will ask the same question more than once, and will need guidance at the end of a trying day. The mentor works to make the mentee feel comfortable and safe, and does not make judgments on personal issues or teaching styles. The new teacher is treated as the professional she or he is. Finally, the mentor does not try to make his protégé into a replica of himself.

The mentor demonstrates effective instructional and management skills. One of the goals of a mentorship program is for the mentee to see how a good classroom is run. While the methodology and techniques the mentor demonstrates may not be the only way, they should reflect best practices.

The mentor reflects a positive attitude. If you do not have hope as an educator you cannot provide the education your students deserve. The new teacher should learn from the mentor that despite its many challenges, teaching is truly a wonderful and rewarding profession. The only way students will think positively about their education is if their teacher believes in them. The only way a mentee will think positively about herself and education is if the mentor believes in her.

Time is reserved for weekly communication. Mentors and mentees need to touch base often. Quick hallway questions and teacher-lounge words of wisdom are not enough. Planned time needs to be set aside for prolonged conversation and reflection.

Learn To Love Teaching Again

When a Good Idea Goes Bad

A mentorship program at Happytown School seems set up for success. All parties (administrators, veteran teachers, new teachers) understand the need for mentoring and are on board. Mentorship teams are created, partners join hands, cheers are heard throughout the nation. And then things go downhill. Two months in, the new teacher mentee is frustrated and still unable to get her questions answered, and the veteran teacher mentor is annoyed by how much of her time this program is taking.

Set up a mentorship program with care. The program needs ground rules and clear expectations. (For example: Can the mentee e-mail her mentor on the weekend and look for an answer before Monday morning? Just how many three a.m. phone calls is the mentor expected to take?)

Ideally, each mentoring relationship should be guided and nurtured by an administrator. As a principal, I liked to have three to four meetings a year with my mentor-mentee partners. The first was a social get-together at a local restaurant, a get-to-know-you gathering. For the other meetings, I selected a topic or shared a short professional article and had the partners work through classroom solutions.

Time must be allotted for preparation. I met a mentee who told me he felt as though he was constantly bothering his mentor teacher. It seemed that William's mentor gave him brief or incomplete answers and always acted too busy to devote any real time, so William gained little knowledge. Simple procedures had not been explained, so he was always "messing up," he said, and having to ask questions again and again.

How can such a good idea like mentoring go so horribly wrong? Here are some things that can go wrong, and some advice to keep them from going wrong.

1. **The incorrect teacher is selected to mentor.** Mentors should be chosen for their positive attitudes and effective instructional practices. Length of tenure in a school should not be a deciding factor. A mentor who is burned-out on teaching will poison the mind of any mentee. She will model poor techniques, will promote shortcuts whenever possible, and can, in fact, suck the positive energy right out of her protégé.

I went to lunch not long ago with two teachers from a small town in East Texas. One teacher was brand-new, while the other, Ms. Keyes, had several years' experience. The entire hour-and-a-half lunch conversation was dominated by Ms. Keyes showering the new teacher with war stories. She told about parents who were not to be trusted, the students' poor attitudes, the inept administration, the lack of supplies and support, and so on. I wanted to whip out my checkbook and personally send Ms. Keyes on a much-needed sabbatical!

2. **The mentor teacher is already overloaded with extra duties.** The mentor has to be available to the mentee. That is the way the program works. If the mentor is overburdened, he will not be able to give his protégé the time needed, leaving a frustrating situation for both teachers.

3. **The mentor suddenly becomes an evaluator.** A good mentor-mentee relationship is built on trust. The mentee must be free from the fear of making mistakes in front of the mentor; she knows this is a safe place to fail. No question is too small to ask. While the mentor can certainly assess the mentee's skills or procedures in an effort to offer constructive advice, teacher evaluation is truly off the table. If the mentor is in a position of judgment, the trusting relationship goes right out the window.

4. **The mentor takes the money and runs.** In some school districts the job of mentoring comes with a financial stipend. If a teacher is taking on the role of mentor just to make a little extra money, the results can be disheartening for the mentee who just does not get the attention he deserves. In a successful mentoring program, the teacher understands the higher purpose and takes on the role to support a new educator.

5. **The mentor knows it all—and isn't afraid to tell the mentee.** A mentor is chosen, at least in part, for her expertise and skill level. But that experience must be tempered with respect for the knowledge and enthusiasm that the new teacher brings in. The goal is not to create a clone of the mentor, but to guide and inform the mentee so that he can find his own way.

Don't let your good idea for a mentorship program fall into these pitfalls. Head these troubles off with good planning. For more help with mentoring ideas, see the Tools section at the end of this chapter.

Positive Attitude Tip

Whether or not she intends to, a leader leads by example. Mentors, repeat this many times until it is deeply embedded in your mind!

Pass It On

Pass-It-On Notebooks are empty loose-leaf binders that contain pages of information learned and tried by one teacher, administrator, or volunteer collected for the purpose of sharing with the people doing the same job next year. Create these in your school to keep next year's staff, mentor, or mentees from having to rediscover processes that have already been established!

Whether or not a mentor is provided, whether or not you know anything at all about the Croquet Club you have been asked to sponsor, wouldn't it be great to have guidance from those who have gone before?

The table of contents for the notebook will be different for each category (volunteer programs, clubs, classrooms, and so on). The actual items (schedules, forms, policies, permission slips, and such) may even be on a computer file instead of in hard copy paper. Provide contents on a disk or flash drive. Here are some ideas for contents:

- **A yearly calendar, marked with dates important to that activity:** Some committees actually begin their planning meetings before school begins, or even during the final days of the previous year's last semester.

- **Copies of notices that have been sent out:** So much time is spent creating something new. Use last year's copy. It is easier to tweak something already made than starting with a blank sheet of paper. If the drill team invites new membership to try out the Monday after spring break, simply change the dates and use the previous announcement.

- **Membership information:** It is helpful to have a record of who has participated in the organization, the tenure of its members, and the turnover rate.

- **Rules, regulations, bylaws, constitution:** Some school organizations are regulated by governing agencies, while others are more informal. Either way, records that guide membership, prerequisites for membership, or behavior of members are vital and not something that needs to be reinvented annually.

- **An anecdotal accounting of what worked and what did not work:** Let's go back to our friend Michael, who shared his story about morning cafeteria duty at the beginning of this chapter. Wouldn't it be helpful if Michael left some notes for his successor, describing how separating the boys and the girls improved the discipline problems?

Start a Pass-It-On Notebook habit in your school. Create a notebook for each extracurricular activity, committee, and program. It can help you get organized right now, and can smooth the path for anyone who does your job in the future.

Falling in Love Again

Relax! Your new skills can help you say no when they're pushing you to say yes, and to say yes to things that are fulfilling and comfortable for you! Just having a little freedom (even if you can't control all the assignments) knocks back the stress meter. This allows you to succeed at and enjoy the commitments you have. When you start asserting yourself with an attitude of caring for the people who are "after" you, you won't have to dread the requests for your time. And you'll be able to get back some of that romance you felt when you dove into teaching back at the beginning!

Me Moments

Feeling overwhelmed? Wondering if you are making a difference? Need a diversion? Pop some corn, kick off your shoes, and watch one of these movies:

Dead Poets Society – Troubled students find their lives changed after an English professor encourages them to go against the status quo. (1989)

Dangerous Minds – An ex-Marine discovers unusual ways to reach the disenfranchised students in an inner-city school. (1995)

Mr. Holland's Opus – The title character takes a teaching job to pay his rent. He dreams of composing one memorable piece of music. (1995)

School of Rock – A down-and-out rock star takes a job as a substitute teacher for a 4th grade class in an uptight private school. (2003)

Mona Lisa Smile – During the 1950s a young professor takes a position at a women's college that students attend as they wait to find husbands. (2003)

Sister Act 2: Back in the Habit – Nuns work together to save a doomed Catholic school from closing. (1993)

Freedom Writers – A young teacher takes inner-city teens raised in violence and gives them a voice of their own. (2007)

Take the Lead – Through dance, a young man vows to teach inner-city youth respect, dignity, confidence, and teamwork. (2006)

The Man Without a Face – Story about the relationship between a troubled young boy and his disfigured teacher. (1993)

(continued next page)

Lean on Me – A new principal uses unorthodox methods to reach the students of a school drowning in drug abuse, gang violence, and despair. (1989)

Renaissance Man – A failed advertising executive takes a job teaching thinking skills to Army recruits but finds no structure in place for instruction. (1994)

Akeelah and the Bee – A young girl from south Los Angeles tries to make it to the National Spelling Bee. (2006)

Music of the Heart – A young teacher fights the school because she wants to teach the violin to inner-city children. (1999)

The Emperor's Club – A passionate and principled high-school teacher tries to make a difference in the life of a difficult student. (2002)

Blackboard Jungle – A good-hearted teacher joins the faculty of a school filled with thugs. (1955)

Stand and Deliver – A math teacher adopts an unconventional methodology as he attempts to turn gang members into top math students. (1988)

Only the Strong – An ex-Special Forces soldier returns home to find his high school steeped in drug abuse and violence. (1993)

Half Nelson – An eighth-grade teacher in Brooklyn befriends a student as she understands the struggles the teacher faces. (2006)

Madam Sousatzka – A Russian immigrant takes over the life of her gifted young piano student. (1988)

To Sir with Love – An engineer accepts what he believes will be a temporary job at an East End London high school. (1967)

The Miracle Worker – Through perseverance and love, teacher Annie Sullivan finds a way to reach Helen Keller, who is deaf and blind. (1962)

Up the Down Staircase – Amid overcrowded classes, broken windows, no chalk, teenage dropouts, and a suicidal student, a new teacher finds herself in an inner-city school and tries to make a difference. (1967)

The Prime of Miss Jean Brodie – A young slightly eccentric school teacher with liberal views instructs girls during the period between the two world wars. (1969)

Chapter 5 **Tools**

Welcome to the faculty!

No, I can't.   I really don't have time.   I'm swamped this week.

Oh, all right.

Can You Really Say No?

You may think you are in control of your time. You think you are managing the projects you take on. Yet you feel stressed and fatigued. Are you really taking on more than you know? Do you just think you are saying no?

Use this tool to tally how many times you say yes and no at school and in your personal life. Try keeping track for a week to test if what you think you do matches what you actually do. Make a checkmark each time you say yes or no during a given day; then tally your marks and write the total number at the end of the day. Answer the self-reflection questions on the next page and plan what, if anything, you want to change.

✔At School

Days of the Week	Times Said Yes	Times Said No
Monday		
Tuesday		
Wednesday		
Thursday		
Friday		
TOTALS		

✔Outside of School

Days of the Week	Times Said Yes	Times Said No
Monday		
Tuesday		
Wednesday		
Thursday		
Friday		
TOTALS		

Can I Say No?

No.

What am I?
A teacher
or a mouse?

Teacher Self-Reflection

1. In which column do I have more tally marks?

yes_____   no_____

2. Are the totals similar in both my professional and personal lives? _____
If not, how can I explain the different results?

3. What pattern, if any, emerges? (For example, do I say yes more
often at the end of the week when I feel worn down and tired?
Or do I feel more confident about saying no on Tuesdays and
Thursdays, when I walk the treadmill before school?)

4. Am I surprised by these results? _____ Why or why not?

5. To what kinds of things do I most often say yes?

6. What have I learned from charting my responses and from my
answers to questions 1 through 5?

7. Is there anything I plan to do differently in my responses to
requests for my time and talents?

8. When will I repeat this exercise for another checkup on myself?

25 Ways to Say No

Begin by saying something courteous
such as . . . Thank you for asking, but...
I appreciate that you thought of me for this job, but...
It's nice to know you have confidence in me to do this, but...
This is a good thing you are doing, but ...
Thank you for your efforts on this wonderful event, but...
I admire you for doing this, but....
I know how important this is, but...

1. I need to remain focused on the responsibilities I already have.

2. I fear that if I take on anything else, I won't do a good job at ____.

3. Now is a terrible time. Maybe you could check back with me in ____ weeks.

4. I don't have any experience with that kind of thing, and I know I'd be uncomfortable.

5. I'd rather say no at the beginning than take this on and do a poor job.

6. I know someone who would be much better at this than I am. I suggest you ask ____.

7. If I take on one more thing, I'll be robbing time and energy from my students.

8. This is not my strength. Maybe there's another job that would work better for me.

9. I need to hang on to some time to take better care of myself.

10. I might be able to do this next year (or week, month, semester), but not now.

11. I am right in the middle of ____. Could you check with me in a few weeks?

12. If I take on one more commitment, I'll have to be committed!

13. This would just be too much for me.

14. I am not very good at that kind of thing.

15. I just can't take on anything else right now.

16. I can't give this my full energies at this time.

17. I wouldn't be able to do a good job at that.

18. I need to keep some time for my family.

19. I'm overcommitted already.

20. It's not a good time.

21. I am stretched really thin as it is.

Sorry,
I need some
time to unwind!

22. I just can't do that.

23. My calendar is full.

24. Not now.

25. No.

✔ Mentor's Checklist ✔

As a mentor to _____,

I have done the following with and for my mentee:

_____ held a "getting-to-know-you" meeting.

_____ given a "welcome-new-teacher" gift.

_____ set goals together for the school year.

_____ set dates for monthly meetings.

_____ discussed expectations for the mentor and the mentee.

_____ given a recommended shopping list.

_____ recommended a "to-do" list for the first month of school.

_____ reviewed school procedures (such as for lunch, attendance, media center use).

_____ explained before-school and after-school activities.

_____ reviewed the personnel manual together.

_____ oriented him or her to school facilities, equipment, and supplies (such as the copy machine and code, faculty lounge, location of supplies, and so on).

_____ reviewed all campus and playground rules.

_____ given a copy of the Internet and e-mail rules and procedures.

_____ helped my mentee to access e-mail, the electronic gradebook system, and so forth.

_____ reviewed the after-hours security procedures for entering and exiting the building.

(continued on next page)

Mentor's Checklist ✔ (continued from previous page)

_____ reviewed the student code of conduct with my mentee.

_____ explained the fire and safety drill procedures.

_____ explained procedures for filling out report cards.

_____ reviewed procedures for reporting suspected child abuse.

_____ reviewed procedures for reporting suspected drug abuse, alcohol abuse, bullying.

_____ made recommendations for communicating with parents.

_____ explained the schedule and expectations for parent-teacher conferences.

_____ discussed the procedures for referring a child who may have a disability.

_____ reviewed the procedures for individualized education program or student-learning-plan meetings.

_____ reviewed curriculum standards and expectations.

_____ shared information about clubs and extracurricular activities offered to students.

_____ explained procedures for scheduling and taking field trips.

_____ reviewed and prepared him or her for giving state-mandated tests.

_____ given a copy of the form for reporting damaged furniture and equipment.

_____ discussed special initiatives and programs (such as Response to Intervention).

Mentor's Signature_____

Mentee's Signature_____

Date Completed _____

Surprises that Encourage

To give a boost to a new teacher or mentee,
leave a note and goodie.

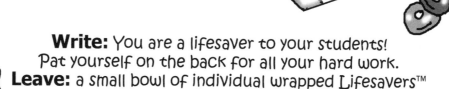

Write: You are a lifesaver to your students!
Pat yourself on the back for all your hard work.
Leave: a small bowl of individual wrapped Lifesavers™

Write: You plant the seeds
of knowledge in your children.
Leave: a bag of sunflower seeds

Write: Because of you,
our kids are not dum dums!
Leave: a bowl with Dum Dum™ suckers

Write: Hugs and kisses
for everything you do.
Leave: a bowl of Hershey Hugs and Kisses™

Write: You deserve a carefree weekend.
We are lucky to have you at our school.
Leave: a package of Carefree™ gum

Write: You've been presenting
refreshing ideas to your students.
Now take time to refresh yourself!
Leave: a 6-pack of sparkling water

Quotes to Inspire

Encourage a mentee or any colleague with a quote. Who knows, it might even inspire a great discussion or writing activity for their students, too! Leave one on their desk or hang it in an unexpected place.

They may forget what you said, but they will never forget how you made them feel."

– Carol Buchner

One must never, for whatever reason, turn his back on life.

– Eleanor Roosevelt

If you want to live more, you must master the art of appreciating the little everyday blessings of life. This is not altogether a golden world, but there are countless gleams of gold to be discovered in it.

– Henry Alfred Porter

It isn't the load that weighs us down; it's the way we carry it.

– Anonymous

Spoonfeeding in the long run teaches us nothing but the shape of the spoon.
– E.M. Forster

For a long time it had seemed to me that life was about to begin—real life. But there was always some obstacle in the way, something to be gotten through first, some unfinished business, time still to be served, and a debt to be paid. Then life would begin. At last it dawned on me that these obstacles were my life.
–Alfred D. Souza

Everyone has inside of him a piece of good news. The good news is that you don't know how great you can be! How much you can love! What you can accomplish! And what your potential is!
- Anne Frank

Don't wait for your ship to come in; swim to it.
– Unknown author

When you come to the end of your rope, tie a knot and hang on! – Franklin D. Roosevelt

But I Was Hired to Teach Pre-Algebra

You know you're a teacher under stress if you wander around all day mumbling acronyms.

ADA CFR FBA MDR
OCD ? OSERS
SLD FERPA
USC
NCLB NAEP

IEP

Winston, who failed sixth grade, has a debilitating stuttering problem. As his science teacher, what is your responsibility to meet Winston's needs?

Harriet suffered a traumatic brain injury when she was young, causing recurring epileptic seizures. As a reading specialist, what is your responsibility to meet Harriet's needs?

At twelve years old, George still cannot read. In school, he is able to memorize what the teacher says during lessons. So he squeaks by. As his math teacher, what is your responsibility to meet George's needs?

Thomas finds school challenging, as he has attention problems and particular difficulty with math. As his history teacher, what is your responsibility to meet Thomas' needs?

Caryn has ADHD and dyslexia. As her music teacher, what is your responsibility to meet Caryn's needs?

And you thought you were hired to teach students how to solve for *n*!

If you have been in a classroom very long (maybe longer than five minutes), you know (well) that teaching does not follow any ideal model. The norm for most classes is that students are often on different pages (literally and figuratively), and they can't all "get" a concept with your one wonderful method of sharing it—or can't even all sit in their seats.

Do you think your job is to teach pre-algebra or fourth-grade subjects or high-school history or middle-school physical education? If so, drop that delusion. Your job is something far more wonderful. It is not to teach a subject—but to grow human beings. So, to the label "pre-algebra teacher," add these roles: counselor, nurse, psychologist, mentor, cheerleader, disciplinarian, model of proper manners and good decisions, peacemaker, crisis manager, arbitrator, positive role model, and diagnostician. And if I have not lost you yet, you can add "legal expert" and "learning-style specialist" to the list.

Learn To Love Teaching Again

Losing the Love

If you are like most teachers, you have a heart for all your students. You want to help every one of them succeed. But here you are, mired in the reality of trying to be all things to all students. You are overwhelmed by the many different needs—many of which you were not prepared to address. Teachers work and sometimes struggle just to prepare the lessons needed to adequately teach their subject areas. And they have to be ready to adapt each lesson to a variety of learners, including those with special needs. Add to this job the laws, expectations, regulations, meetings, and paperwork accompanying some specific identified needs. This combination adds up to feelings of inadequacy, frustration, or ill preparation. And with that equation—you, the teacher, may end up feeling despair for the students (and for yourself) and anger at everybody from administrators to your teacher-training instructors years ago. The final result is overload and stress.

Every child has needs, and all the needs are special. With or without official "labels," each student deserves to have his or her learning style, gifts, and challenges understood, embraced, and adequately addressed. When the teacher gains the right tools for addressing these needs, there is hope for relief from the stress of this classroom reality.

The Alphabet Soup of Education

There is just one answer to all the questions that opened this chapter: Your responsibility as a teacher is to understand and take part in addressing all of those needs. Notice the "take part" phrase in that sentence. You cannot and should not be expected to fix or alleviate every need of every child. You must have support. But neither can you ignore a child's learning style, abilities, or disabilities just because you are the physical education teacher or the math teacher. All that every child is, does, and feels are parts of the fabric of the classroom.

> Why is the alphabet in that order? Is it because of that song?
>
> Steven Wright, actor and writer

Beyond the professional, moral, and personal obligations to students, today's classroom includes legal considerations. As a result of education and civil rights law, general education teachers are almost sure to encounter students with legally identifiable disabilities in their classrooms. Teachers need a working knowledge of these. In addition, they must be prepared to set up inclusive classrooms, incorporate necessary modifications, and adjust to needed accommodations. Yes, this can feel burdensome. You may feel as if you've been dropped into an alphabet soup of labels and acronyms. When you are well informed and well prepared, the care of human beings and the process of meeting their needs will be far more joyful. Here are some tips to help you handle the many needs with less stress and more success.

1. Check your attitude.

You will never have a class that doesn't present a wide variety of needs (academic, personal, social, emotional, physical) as well as a variety of learning styles. Don't think of these as "weirdnesses" or "problems." Think of students as individuals, each with talents and each in need of a teacher who learns what they need and helps them get it. Don't whine about the "difficult" learners you are assigned. Dive in and do your best to figure out how to teach every one of them. I guarantee that a hopeful, positive attitude about even your most challenging students will cut way down on the heartburn, sleeplessness, and frustration.

2. Get to know each of your students.

Build personal relationships with the students. Really get to know each student. Watch. Listen. Ask questions. Learn first-hand everything you can about who the student is, how she or he learns, what her gifts are, and what the roadblocks are to learning. You'll have much less stress and do a better job if you start from a place of knowing and valuing the whole of each child.

3. Take off the "labels" glasses.

Children are not "things" with labels. Avoid seeing them with acronyms stamped on their foreheads. Yes, you will need to know the legally defined "diagnoses" in order to fully participate in intervention and learning plans for the child. But the label tells you about one part of who that child is. A disability label can lead you to think of the whole child as "disabled," and you could miss all kinds of other important attributes and information. You cannot provide the best educational experiences for a student if you are blinded by the label.

4. Be informed.

Learn everything you can about different kinds of learners, as well as their learning styles and challenges. If you haven't had training in such areas as special education designations, learning styles, multiple intelligences, and differentiated instruction—get

Learn To Love Teaching Again

busy. There is plenty of information available through educational sources, workshops and seminars, colleagues, journals, the law, and the Internet.

5. Learn the language.

Mrs. Hanson loved history. She was thrilled with her new teaching assignment in middle grades U.S. history. She had all kinds of exciting learning experiences ready to engage her students in this upcoming election year. But at the opening professional development meeting, the principal started talking about learning styles, meeting students' needs, and something called *differentiated learning*. He brought up IDEA, NCLB, AYP, FAPE, RTI, SLDs, IEEs, and IEPs. Mrs. Hanson was puzzled. She thought she was just going to teach history. Her stress level begin to rise. She wondered what she had gotten herself into.

You may have had a similar experience—of hearing a conversation where everyone was gleefully slinging around abbreviations and acronyms like mashed potatoes on a food-fight day in the middle-school cafeteria. You can ease this stressor right now, with some help from your very own cheat sheet of some education abbreviations and terms. Look for "Learn the Language" in the Tools section at the end of this chapter. Take some time to review it. You might even want to memorize the terms. When you hear someone use an educational acronym that you don't know, don't be shy. Ask the person to tell you what the term means. You don't want to be the only teacher who thinks that FAPE stands for "fantastically astounding principal's explanation."

6. Know the IDEA law.

Laws about the education of children with special needs are today's reality. Instead of fearing them, grumbling about them, or criticizing them—get to know them. While the onus of legal responsibilities falls on the shoulders of administrators, teachers must, now more than ever, understand the intent of the laws that protect students with disabilities. And they must know what the role of a regular education teacher is with regard to teaching students with disabilities.

So become as familiar as you can with the IDEA law (the Individuals with Disabilities Education Act). Read the law or summaries of it. Keep a copy of the basic law definitions and requirements in a place where you can easily access it. See definitions of IDEA disabilities in the Tools section at the end of this chapter. Review the information provided on the upcoming pages of this chapter. Ask questions of your special education teachers and administrators. This will keep you from feeling clueless among your colleagues. But that's not the important point, really. If you know the law, you will have a much better chance of effectively helping your students. You will come to meetings with useful suggestions for classroom modifications. You will understand what is being asked of you as a teacher. And you will be able to effectively communicate with the student's parents and with colleagues who are working with you to help the child succeed.

7. Learn your school's policies and procedures.

Hmmm. My book on teacher stress recommends a good support system.

Mattress SALE Today!

Best support in town!

Get familiar (REALLY familiar—not just a scan) with the policies, procedures, definitions, and processes in your school and district. Know it cold! Know how the process works to identify and help a student with special needs. Ask to see, in writing, your district policies and procedures. Talk to your learning specialist or special education teachers. If you feel poorly informed, suggest to your principal that a workshop on this topic would be helpful for teachers. Do this before the school year begins. Review any changes each year.

8. Build a support system.

Don't even begin to take this on alone! Helping a child with special needs is a team endeavor. Ask for help. Learn from all the administrators and specialists. Find experienced teachers who can share experiences with you. You do a greater service to your students when you have a solid system of help for yourself.

9. Build a good relationship with parents.

This book has already advocated (and given ideas for) the good work of establishing trusting relationships with parents. This is even more critical with parents of special-needs students. Parents know their children better than school personnel. So they can be of great help in identifying needs. You'll have the best chance of learning what parents know and observe if you already have an established relationship of mutual respect. When a student is being or has been identified with a disability, the teacher is so important to the parent. The process of meetings, IEPs, specialists, and decision making is often intimidating to the parent. You, the teacher, are the one they trust. So you can help them navigate this scary, sometimes complicated process. Do the best that you can to inform, help, and assure parents through this process.

10. Take your record keeping seriously.

A student will have the best chance of success if you keenly observe behaviors, progress, or difficulties and document them well. Don't get behind on record keeping. Do it thoughtfully. Don't skimp on important information.

11. Fiercely guard students' privacy.

The law requires confidentiality. But many educators either do not know or do not scrupulously follow the guidelines for keeping information, notes, and records private. (By the way, "not knowing the rules" is not a legally defensible argument. It is your responsibility to know.) Ask for your district's policies on record confidentiality. Keep all your notes locked up. Take great care with any records you view or create. And keep control of your mouth. Do not talk about students' designations or behavior incidents or information from their records—with anyone except the legally prescribed parties.

Guide to the IDEA Law

What follows is a summary of the laws related to students with disabilities and the laws' impact on the classroom teacher. The intent is not to exhaustively explain every aspect of special education law. Nor is it to offer legal advice. The purpose here is to help you build or reinforce a knowledge base. This is a good review for veteran teachers as well as newcomers to the field. Keep in mind that state law may create variations on federal law. A state can also give its public school districts some flexibility in interpreting and implementing sections of the law.

> It is a lonely existence to be a child with a disability that no one can see or understand. You exasperate your teachers, you disappoint your parents, and worst of all—you know that you are not just stupid.
>
> Susan Hampshire

The information will be divided into categories, and will answer the kinds of questions in each category that teachers often ask.

Special Education as Defined by IDEA

Special education is specially designed instruction that is intended to meet the individual needs of the student with a disability and that must be provided at no cost to student families. Additionally, *specially designed instruction* means that instruction will be adapted:

. . . to address any needs of the student that may occur because of his disability.

. . . to ensure access to the general curriculum, so that a student with a disability can meet the educational standards set out by the local educational agency.

Eligibility for Special Education and Related Services

- **Qualifications**—In order to qualify for special education and special services under IDEA, a child must meet the following criteria: The student must be between the ages of 3 and 21 and have been evaluated in accordance with IDEA, and as a result be determined to have one or more disabilities as defined by IDEA. Or, if a state allows, a student can qualify for eligibility by meeting the criteria for developmental delays. It must also be shown that the student needs special education and related services as a result of his disability. (Identifying and evaluating a child is a process that is referred to as *Child Find*.)

- **IDEA-specified disabilities**—The law includes these:

autism	other health impairments
deaf-blindness	emotional disturbance
deafness	specific learning disability
hearing impairments	speech or language impairments
mental retardation	traumatic brain injury
multiple disabilities	visual impairments, including blindness
orthopedic impairments	

  For definitions of these disabilities, see the Tools section at the end of this chapter. Also, consult the text of the IDEA Act itself.

- **Response to intervention**—Prior to the reauthorization of IDEA in 2004, the preferred method of identifying a child with a specific learning disability was to show a severe discrepancy between aptitude and achievement. In 2004, IDEA subtly created a push for a model that uses a child's responsiveness to scientifically based intervention as a dominant identification criterion. States and districts have scrambled to adopt and implement a "Response to Intervention" model that is also used for behavioral interventions. The teacher who works with the child is in a key position to use the agreed-upon interventions and note the child's response to the interventions.

- **Right to appropriate education**—IDEA is an education law and a civil rights law. All children with disabilities are entitled to a free appropriate public education (FAPE), regardless of the severity of the disability or cost of providing special education and related services. The key word in FAPE is **public**. If the Child Find process determines that a child is eligible for special education and related services, the public school district in which the child resides must provide FAPE.

- **Enrollment in a private school**—If the child's parents decide to enroll the child in a private school, they give up their right to receive special education and related services. In this case, the district is no longer obligated to provide FAPE, but the parents can decide at any time to enroll their child in a public school and once again be entitled to FAPE. A private school does have the right to deny a child with a disability enrollment and/or special education and related services. Most private schools make every effort to meet the needs of their students, but cost may be a barrier to needed services. A portion of the IDEA funds that a public district collects is held by the district to offer services for eligible children who have been enrolled in private schools by their parents' decisions. Private schools can access services, if they choose, through a consultation process with the public district.

- **Another route to services**—A student who does not meet the requirements of IDEA for special education and related services could qualify for services (not special education) under Section 504 of the Rehabilitation Act of 1973 (a civil rights law, not an education law). The intent of this law is to prevent discrimination against persons with disabilities. Section 504 considers a student to be a person with a disability if he or she: has a physical or mental impairment that substantially limits one or more of the person's major life activities (that is, walking, seeing, hearing, speaking, breathing, learning, working, performing manual functions and caring for one's self), has a record of such an impairment, or is regarded as having such an impairment. Section 504 eligibility excludes age restrictions and is based, not on specified categories, but on the functional impact of a person's physical or mental impairment.

> A student in my class does not qualify under IDEA, yet her impairment affects her ability to learn. Is there any assistance for her?

- **Initiating an evaluation**—If a student is enrolled in a public school, the following persons or entities may initiate a referral for an initial evaluation: the child's parent(s), the school district, the state educational agency, or another concerned state agency. For a student with a disability enrolled in a private school, it is the child's parents who must request and give consent for an evaluation for special education and other related services.

> Christopher, one of my kindergarteners, has been diagnosed with autism. The parents have asked me how to ensure that Christopher receives the support he needs at school. How does the family begin this process?

- **Parent consent for services**—Although a parent can refuse an initial evaluation, a district can still evaluate the child. However, the district cannot provide special education and related services without parental consent.

- **Timeline for evaluations**—With the reauthorization of IDEA in 2004, the timeline for completing an initial evaluation is now 60 calendar days. Check with your state educational agency however, because IDEA does allow for a state to establish a different timeline. There is no specific requirement under Section 504, but the expectation is that the initial evaluation should be completed within a reasonable amount of time.

- **Refusal to evaluate a child**—Suppose your principal refuses to evaluate a student that you believe has a disability. If you are a private school teacher, remember that your principal is not required by law to accept special education and related services from the local public school district.

New Teacher Tip

The district is responsible for completing initial evaluations. However, you are the one that can provide data on the student's responsiveness to intervention and other classroom performance. If you are asked for evaluative information, write it clearly and contribute it promptly.

If you are a public school teacher, you might remind your principal that the school is required by IDEA to identify all children with disabilities and provide FAPE to such children. Under Section 504, the school cannot discriminate against a student when the student is regarded as having the particular impairment that you observe. Be prepared to give your principal (and parents) facts and data that support your professional opinion for the need to have your student evaluated for special education and related services. Don't be afraid to reference the law (IDEA and Section 504). You don't have to cite regulations. Simply let your principal know that you know the law.

Or, you could talk with the child's parents first. If they are willing to consent, ask them to request an evaluation in writing. This removes you from being the one who is pushing for an evaluation. If the parents refuse to consent to an evaluation and the principal doesn't want to evaluate the child, you have done what you can do and your hands are pretty much tied.

What can I do when I know a student needs to be referred for an evaluation, but my principal says, "no"?

Learn To Love Teaching Again

Individualized Education Programs (IEPs)

- **The IEP**—An IEP is a document that includes essential components of an appropriate educational program for a student with a disability, as agreed to by school representatives and the parents. There are no specifications as to the length of an IEP document, but it must contain the following components:
  - a statement of the child's present level of academic achievement and functional performance
  - a statement of measurable academic and functional annual goals
  - a description of how the student's progress will be measured and when periodic reports will be issued
  - a statement of the special education and related services to be provided
  - if appropriate, an explanation of the extent to which the student will not participate in regular classroom activities with students who are not disabled
  - a statement of any needed accommodations
  - the projected start date of the services and accommodations
  - beginning no later than the first IEP when the child is 16 years old, appropriate postsecondary goals (Some states may require a younger age for this component.)

Teacher-to-Teacher Tip

"You reap what you sow. So don't throw lots of things into an IEP just because you want to help the student. Avoid using standard checklists. Just focus on what this student actually needs and what you can do for the student. Remember, you will be responsible for implementing the IEP!"

— Experienced special education teacher

- **Developing the IEP**—To develop an IEP, the IEP team should consider:
  - the current records of the student
  - the student's current IEP, if applicable
  - recent evaluations
  - the student's strengths
  - parental concerns
  - the academic, developmental, and functional needs of the student
  - the use of positive behavioral interventions, if the student's behavior impedes his progress
  - any language needs, if the student is limited in English proficiency
  - Braille support materials, if the student is blind or visually impaired

- communication support materials, if the student is deaf or hearing impaired
- assistive technology support, if applicable

- **IEP timeline and team**—A meeting to develop an IEP must take place within 30 days of determining that a student is eligible for special education and related services. IEP Team members must include:
  - parents of the student
  - at least one general education teacher
  - at least one special education teacher
  - a school district representative
  - a person who is qualified to interpret the instructional implications of the results of the evaluation (However, another member of the team can serve in this capacity as well, with the exception of the parents or child.)
  - other caregivers or individuals who have knowledge of the student, or special expertise in a relevant topic concerning the child
  - the student, whenever appropriate

Decisions are made by consensus at IEP meetings. An IEP should never be written prior to the IEP meeting.

- **No guarantees**—A student's IEP is not an educational contract and there are no guarantees that annual goals will be attained. The school is, however, obligated to make a good faith effort to help the student reach IEP goals.

- **Plans in private schools**—Students with disabilities who are enrolled in private schools by their parents have a services plan (SP), which is also referred to as a personal learning plan (PLP). A services plan only relates to the services that are agreed upon during consultation between the public district and the private school.

Placement and Related Services

- **The placement decision**—A placement decision is an agreement by the IEP team about where the student's IEP will be implemented. The decision does not need to cite a specific teacher or classroom, as that is recognized to be an administrative choice. During a placement discussion and decision, the IEP team should consider several questions to affirm that placement was properly decided, made in the least restrictive environment, as close as possible to the student's home, and based on the student's IEP. The placement is reconsidered annually, but the student's needs may lead to placement being changed even within a school year.

> Lief's parents want him to stay in my classroom for most of the day, but the administration thinks he would be better served in Ms. Rubin's special education class for his core subjects. How is something like this decided?

- **Parent wishes**—Although services cannot be denied because of factors such as cost, these kinds of issues can affect placement decisions. Because several factors need to be considered during a placement decision, the preference of the parents cannot be an overriding factor. Parental preference should be considered, but not given predominance.

- **Placement in a neighborhood school**—The placement should be at a school as close as possible to the student's home. Weight is given to the educational program that provides an appropriate education in the least restrictive environment. If this means that the most appropriate placement is a school that is farther away, the district must provide transportation.

- **Placement in a private school**—The district may determine that a private school or facility is the least restrictive environment to meet the student's identified needs. In this case, the public district would be responsible for the cost of the placement, special education, and related services. The student would be served under the same requirements as if she were placed in a public school. For example, the student would have an IEP and not a services plan (SP).

- **Mainstreaming, inclusion,** and **least restrictive environment**—These terms relate to student placement. Many educators use them interchangeably, but they do not have the same meaning.

Mainstreaming is the participation of students with disabilities in general education classes, to the extent appropriate, without the use of modifications that change the learning expectations. (For example, a student who is mainstreamed may attend a special education classroom for part or most of the day and attend a general education classroom, with nondisabled peers, for science, physical education, or library.) With the reauthorization of IDEA, there is a stronger push for students with disabilities to participate in a general education classroom for the majority of or the entire school day. *Mainstreaming* is a statutory term and does appear in IDEA.

Inclusion is the participation of students with disabilities in general education classes, to the extent appropriate, with the use of modifications and accommodations. A student with a disability may attend an inclusive classroom for one or more periods during the day. Some students with disabilities participate in full inclusion, which means that they attend all classes with their nondisabled peers. Full inclusion is not a right. In fact, *inclusion* is not a statutory term and does not appear in IDEA.

I prefer to be in the mainstream.

Least restrictive environment is a term found in IDEA that means a student with a disability must receive his education, to the extent appropriate, with his peers that are nondisabled. Special classes, separate schooling, or any other removal of a child with a disability from regular education classes should only occur if the nature and severity of the child's disability are such that education in regular classes, with the use of supplementary aids and services, cannot be satisfactorily achieved.

Least restrictive environment is a continuum of services, with the general education classroom being the least restrictive, to a residential facility or hospital being the most restrictive. According to the needs of the student, he may move up or down on this continuum, within a school year if necessary. Decisions made during the development of an IEP will include the least restrictive environment for the student's education. The general education classroom should always be the most desirable and preferred placement. In order to be appropriate, it must be a setting wherein the student with the disability can be satisfactorily educated, and where the IEP can be implemented. That classroom placement must not bring harm to the student or the quality of services provided to her, and must not impair the learning of classmates.

- **Related services**—These are support services provided for a student with a disability to enable him to benefit from special education. The most common related services include: speech and language therapy, physical therapy, occupational therapy, counseling, and behavioral therapy. Assistive technology can also be a related service, if it is "an item, piece of equipment, or product system which can be used to increase, maintain, or improve the functional capabilities" of a student. Not every child with a disability needs related services. The decision to provide related services is made on an individual basis, and should be included in a child's IEP. If a child only needs related services and not special education, the child will not qualify as a child with a disability under IDEA. The child may, however, qualify for accommodations under Section 504.

Tobia's parents do not speak much English. I worry that they may not take advantage of all the assistance that is available for him. Is there anything that protects the parents through this process?

Procedural Safeguards

- **IDEA-prescribed safeguards**—The law provides a set of guarantees that certain processes and procedures will be followed when it comes to decisions and services regarding children with disabilities and their families. The safeguards are meant to ensure that parents of children with disabilities maintain meaningful involvement in decisions about their child's educational placement. These safeguards include rights of parents to examine records, participate in meetings, and be notified of changes; rights of students who do not have parent representation; rights to have written communication provided in the native language of the parents; provisions for student medication; and a system for filing and processing complaints.

- **Educational records**—Both IDEA and Section 504 federal regulations guarantee parents of children with disabilities (and older children, themselves) the right to inspect and review records. The Family Educational Rights and Privacy Act (FERPA) provides parents and older students the right to inspect and review educational records. FERPA applies to public and private educational agencies. According to IDEA and FERPA, the term "records" refers to records (print, handwritten, taped, and filmed) that are directly related to a student.

  Natural or adoptive parents who live with a child are considered "parents" under IDEA. But others may also be considered as parents and as such, are provided the same procedural safeguards. This would include: natural or adoptive parents, legal guardians, a person acting in the place of a parent, a surrogate parent, or a foster parent. If a parent has been awarded physical and legal custody of a child under state law, he or she is then recognized by IDEA as the sole person to act as parent.

- **Rights of students in private schools**—If a public school district places a student in a private school setting through an IEP, then the rights provided by IDEA are retained. If parents place a child with a disability in a private school setting, the rights to special education and related services are forfeited. However, the public school district must still identify and evaluate all children residing within district boundaries through the Child Find process.

Positive Attitude Tip

Don't let the IDEA law overwhelm you! Keep the above handbook nearby for details. And remember these six principles that the law guarantees to students with disabilities:

1. Free appropriate public education (FAPE)

2. Child Find, including appropriate evaluation

3. Individualized education programs (IEPs)

4. Least restrictive environment (LRE)

5. Parent and student participation in educational decisions

6. Procedural safeguards

– ASK Family Resource Center (2008)

Disciplining a Student with a Disability

- **Different rules**—In general, a student with a disability cannot be suspended for more than 10 school days if the misconduct was a result of the student's disability. IDEA does recognize special circumstances. A principal may remove a student with a disability to an interim educational setting for not more than 45 school days, without regard to whether the behavior is determined to be a manifestation of the child's disability—if the student carries a weapon to or possesses a weapon at school, on school premises, or to or at a school function under the jurisdiction of the SEA or district; knowingly possesses or uses illegal drugs, or sells or solicits the sale of a controlled substance, while at school, on school premises, or at a school function under the jurisdiction of the SEA or district; or has inflicted serious bodily injury upon another person while at school, on school premises, or at a school function under the jurisdiction of the SEA or district.

Next week I am getting a student in my class who, by former teacher accounts, consistently acts out and disturbs the other students. This student happens to have a learning disability. How does having a disability affect how he is disciplined?

- **Functional behavioral assessment**—A functional behavioral assessment (FBA) is a problem-solving process that seeks to find the purpose for a student's behavior. An FBA should help the IEP team to look beyond the student's behavior and focus on the function of the behavior, such as social-affective, cognitive, and/or environmental factors that are associated with the occurrence of the behavior.

- **Manifest determination**—When a student with a disability is to be disciplined, both IDEA and Section 504 require a review of the child's behavior to determine the relationship between the misconduct and the student's disability. This process is called *manifest determination* or MD. The team making this determination is made up of members of the student's IEP team and other personnel with knowledge about the student. If there is any decision made to change a placement of a child with a disability due to a violation of a code of student conduct, the district, parents, and relevant members of the IEP team must meet to review all relevant information within 10 days. If it is determined that the student's behavior is a manifestation of his disability, the law outlines specific steps that must be followed, including steps to remedy problems that resulted in the behavior.

- **Expulsion**—A school can expel a student with an identified disability. However, the school must continue to provide FAPE in another setting.

Learn To Love Teaching Again

*Don't be too hard on yourself or your
students. When a student with a
disability acts in inappropriate ways,
the behavior is more often than not
a function of some other issue. Look
for the function, and you will be more
effective in addressing the behavior.*

The Inclusion of Students with Special Needs

*"If a doctor, lawyer, or dentist had 40 people in his office at one time,
all of whom had different needs, and some of whom didn't want to
be there and were causing trouble, and the doctor, lawyer, or dentist,
without assistance, had to treat them all with professional excellence
for nine months—then he might have some conception of the classroom
teacher's job."*

– Donald D. Quinn, teacher, author

Mrs. LaRoche was halfway through her first year of teaching fourth grade at my elementary school when she came to see me. In her hand was a faded piece of tubular material that looked as though it had been through the laundry a few too many times. Mrs. LaRoche was an excellent teacher who, despite her inexperience, was one of my best. She had an instinctive wisdom with the students that impressed even her most jaded peers.

"What is that thing?" I asked, as Mrs. LaRoche placed the raggedy cotton material on my desk.

Suddenly Mrs. LaRoche, the cool, calm and always-in-control teacher, burst into tears. "That," she said, pointing, "that is Jerome!"

It turns out that the cloth on my desk was actually the remnant of the sleeve of new student Joseph's old pajama top. Joseph had Asperger Syndrome. To provide himself comfort, Joseph obsessively carried that sleeve with him everywhere, gave it a name, and used it as a way to help cope with the social pressures of fourth grade. Mrs. LaRoche had been patient. She had been tolerant, but the stress of trying to work with Joseph and the ever-present pajama sleeve finally pushed her to a breaking point.

> He told me that his teachers reported that . . . he was mentally slow, unsociable, and adrift forever in his foolish dreams.
>
> Hans Albert Einstein, on his father, Albert Einstein

I bought Mrs. LaRoche a diet root beer (her favorite), gave her a box of tissues, and then rolled up my sleeves. We had to find out everything we could about Joseph—his joys, his fears, his strengths, his challenges, his triggers. We had long discussions with Joseph's parents, spoke to his therapist, and read everything we could find about Asperger. Integrating Joseph into the classroom was not easy, and often she was frustrated, but Mrs. LaRoche stuck it out. She learned how to accommodate the classroom so that Joseph felt comfortable. She learned when to push Joseph and when to back off, and spent many hours working through peer issues. By increasing her knowledge base of Joseph's condition, Mrs. LaRoche was able to lessen her own stress. And along the way his teacher discovered that she shared a wicked, off-the-main-road sense of humor with Joseph.

One and a half years later Joseph threw out that old pajama sleeve. Four years later, he graduated successfully from our school. And four years after that, he graduated from the local high school. He had several friends and was accepted, quirks and all, by his classmates. While Mrs. LaRoche cannot claim complete responsibility for Joseph's success, without a doubt she could have been part of his failure. Had Mrs. LaRoche continued to deal with Joseph at a heightened stress level, Joseph would not have been successful academically. He would not have made what turned out to be long-lasting friendships, and both he and his teacher would have been miserable the entire school year. And by the way, though they were no longer in daily contact, Joseph personally invited Mrs. LaRoche to his high school graduation.

The LRE (Least Restrictive Environment) component of the IDEA Act results in more inclusion for children with disabilities. Though the school's special education department may have official responsibility for these students, many of them spend some or most of the day in a regular education classroom. This creates a definite difference from the classrooms of the past, and presents a challenge that our predecessors did not have to deal with in the same way.

Benefits of the more inclusive classroom for these students are widely recognized. However, trying to meet the wide disparity of student needs can daunt even the most

Learn To Love Teaching Again

experienced teacher. Teaching students with disabilities is not easy and does not always end in success. But inclusion is part of the reality of today's classroom, and even if that inclusion is just for part of the school day, a teacher can feel overwhelmed.

For any teacher in this situation, knowledge is power. If you understand the strengths and limitations of each disability, you will be better prepared to provide the support that all classroom students need. A win-win situation is created: the student achieves a level of success, and you can feel that you have made a difference. For further details on teaching students with disabilities, visit the websites listed in the resource section for Chapter 6, found at the end of the book. You will also find additional resources in the Tools section at the end of this chapter.

Teacher - to - Teacher Tip

"It's a no-brainer! The more prepared you are; the more information you have about a child's specific disability, needs, and behaviors; the better your connection with the child and his or her parents—the greater will be the progress and happiness of the student. And, by the way, you'll be far more comfortable, too. Check your anxieties at the door. Overcome them with knowledge and care for that child."

– Experienced classroom teacher

Responding to Student Needs

One day at school I asked my colleague Brenda if she remembered a certain phone number. Suddenly her fingers started flying.

"What are you doing?" I asked, puzzled.

"Trying to remember the number," she mumbled.

I realized then that she was pretending to hold her cell phone in her left hand while punching in the numbers with fingers of her right hand. In no time, she reeled off the correct phone number.

"Aha!" I thought. "Brenda is a kinesthetic or tactile learner."

If you ask me a phone number, I am likely to roll my eyes to the ceiling or quickly snap my eyelids closed in what appears to be an abrupt catnap.
I am a visual learner, and I am seeing those numbers in my mind's eye.

I didn't always make such connections about learning styles. When I began teaching, I insisted every fourth grader write down every word I put on the board. It made sense to me; that's how I learned. When I needed to study, I wrote and rewrote copious notes. In my naïveté I assumed everyone learned that way as well. There certainly is nothing wrong with teaching fourth graders to take notes, and for some, it is the introduction to a lifelong tool. But I had no clue about different learning styles.

By the time I taught eighth-grade English many (many!) years later, I finally got it. I had a complete dog-and-pony show ready before each class. I prepared rhythmic chants to practice parts of speech. I played soft music during writing times. I let students choose their spaces to work on assignments and tests. We played games to review vocabulary, and drew pictures when writing definitions. I used color markers on the whiteboard. I underlined, I circled, I drew arrows, and I drew diagrams. Some of the students, like Antwone, ate this up, copying my notes with colored pens and markers of his own.

I also learned to leave a student like Jennings alone. Jennings never took a note. In fact, if I insisted he write in his notebook, Jennings would be distracted and miss vital information. He was a bright auditory learner. He listened to every word I said, and was able to assimilate and apply information in original ways. I

Teacher-to-Teacher Tip

"Ever since my first year of teaching I have given my students a Multiple Intelligence Quiz twice a year. It empowers students to know their learning strengths. It reduces my stress because all my students are actively engaged in learning. I heartily recommend this!"
— Tanisha, Pennsylvania

had to work to stay one step ahead of Jennings, while making sure the rest of the class received the instruction they needed. This kept me on my teaching toes. Jennings aced every exam, without ever cracking a book. His projects were sloppy, but he could stand before the class and speak intelligently and with great depth about many subjects.

Learning differences and needs are not exclusive to those students who are identified as qualifying for special education or related services. Every classroom will be comprised of a mélange of learning styles. Think about yourself. How do you learn? It's a good idea to figure this out, because you can be sure that your own personal learning style will affect your style of instruction. It is likely that you choose and excel at the teaching strategies that suit your own learning tendencies.

Learn To Love Teaching Again

Know Your Own Learning Style:

Try out these simple tests to gain some insight into your own learning style:

Test 1

When you . . .	Do you . . .	Or do you . . .	Or do you . . .
try to concentrate	become distracted by movement?	become distracted by noise?	become distracted by surrounding activities?
spell an unknown word	close your eyes and try to "see" the word?	sound out words phonetically?	write the word, with your finger or a pencil?
meet someone you have met before	remember a face, but not the name?	remember a name and your last conversation, but not the face?	remember what you did the last time you were together?
read	prefer passages that use descriptive language?	prefer dialog?	prefer action scenes? or not really enjoy reading much at all?
tackle a new task at work	prefer diagrams, demonstrations, models, and slides?	prefer discussing the parameters of the job aloud with someone?	prefer to just leap in and learn by doing?
put something together	read the directions and look over the diagrams?	ask someone else to do the job?	bypass the directions and figure it out as you go along?
talk with someone	dislike listening for too long?	enjoy listening, but find yourself eager to speak your point of view?	use your hands and gesture as you explain something?
discuss business	prefer a face-to-face conversation?	prefer a telephone or email conversation?	prefer to talk while doing something active, like walking?
You might be:	a visual learner	an auditory learner	a kinesthetic learner

Adapted from Colin Rose (1987). *Accelerated Learning.*

Test 2

Do you enjoy . . .	Do you . . .	You might be . . .
books? crossword puzzles? word games? tongue twisters?	hear words in your head before you say or write them? find English and history concepts easier to understand than science and math?	a linguistic learner
courses like math and science? looking for structure or patterns?	compute numbers in your head easily? think abstractly?	a logical learner
mazes and jigsaw puzzles? drawing or doodling? reading materials that contain illustrations?	have vivid dreams? navigate well, even in unfamiliar surroundings?	a spatial learner
regular physical activity? spending a lot of time outside? riskier activities, like racing or skydiving?	find it difficult to stay still for a long period of time? use hand gestures or other body language when you speak?	a bodily-kinesthetic learner
listening to music? humming while performing a task?	remember a tune after hearing it once? often have a tune playing in your head for a long stretch of time? find it easy to keep time with a piece of music?	a musical learner
teaching others? team and group sports? group activities? social activities and games?	prefer going out on a weekend to staying home? consider yourself a leader?	an interpersonal learner
reflecting and meditating? hobbies or activities that you do alone? attending events that improve personal growth?	have specific life goals? consider yourself independent-minded and strong-willed?	an intrapersonal learner
being outdoors? examining the wonders and patterns of nature?	notice the connections within the environment? like to discover, identify, or categorize natural features?	a naturalist learner
pondering big questions? figuring out why things are the way they are?	think a lot about issues of life, death, and ultimate realities? like to read and examine philosophical theories?	an existentialist learner

Adapted from Colin Rose (1987). *Accelerated Learning.*

Learn To Love Teaching Again

When you design learning experiences for your students, avoid sticking too close to your own personal comfort zone. If you do, you'll find it is not really all that comfortable. You'll be stressed, because some of your students won't be learning well. Yes, it may seem counterintuitive that students benefit when you stretch beyond what is familiar for you. But when you do, you can diversify teaching strategies to address individual student needs. Students will be more successful, and you'll have less frustration.

Not long ago, a veteran-teacher friend sighed and spoke of the stress she was feeling now that she was required to use differentiated instruction.

CST?
Chronically-stressed teacher?
Caught seven truants?
Curious science teacher?
Capable scuba trainer?

"Beth," I pointed out, "you've been differentiating instruction for years! What about the needs-based reading groups you created a few years back? And remember the small-group instruction you have always had for math? What about the team teaching with your grade-level colleagues, where you taught the same objectives in several different ways?"

Suddenly Beth smiled. "You're right! " she said. "I guess this isn't so hard after all!"

Tips for Teaching to Student Needs

Good teachers naturally teach and meet the needs of various types of learners in their classes. Keep these practices in mind; they will help you remember to focus your instruction on the needs of your individual students:

1. **Get to know each learner.** Gather as much information as you can about how the student learns. Listen to parents, previous teachers, and the students themselves. Observe closely. Keep a chart or list of key attributes of each learner.

2. **Set up your classroom to support learners.** Make sure it supports the needs of learners. This includes your room arrangement, the kinds of materials you use, the lighting and acoustics, the traffic-flow patterns, the schedule—and even your classroom policies and procedures. Some of the greatest distractions to learning come from classroom processes that clash with student learning styles.

3. Supply your toolbox. Gather a wide variety of ideas for meeting various learning needs. Review these helpful tools, found in the Tools section at the end of this chapter:

- How Does the Student Learn?
- Tips for Working with IDEA Students
- ADD and ADHD Instructional Accommodations: A Quick Guide
- Multiple Intelligences Hunt
- Tips for Teaching Students with Multiple Intelligences

4. Learn to differentiate. Differentiation of instruction is a lifeline for students (and the teacher) in any classroom. This means presenting the same concepts or related skills in different ways, adjusting expectations for individuals, or asking for different kinds of products and processes. Take a course, attend a seminar, get help from other teachers, and read everything you can find. For some good books on the topic, consult the reference list for Chapter 6 found in the Reference section at the end of the book.

5. Build a repertoire of varying instructional approaches. Make a checklist of learning activities. You can use the list found in the Tools section at the end of this chapter, or create your own in collaboration with your colleagues. Review the list at least once a month to remind yourself of the variety of strategies available to adapt to each student's particular needs and styles. When planning for the whole class, be sure to include many different kinds of activities so that you touch the learning modes of all learners.

6. Be aware of your own learning preferences. Several times a year, stop and reflect on your instructional style. Make sure you are not stuck in a rut—imposing **your** learning style on your students.

> ## Teacher-to-Teacher Tip
>
> *"For years I came home from school mentally exhausted. When I asked a colleague why she always seemed energized, she gave me this great advice that I want to pass along. She said she actively participates in every experience she assigns to students. It helps me remember to consider all learning styles. I am no longer depleted. I am fired up! Try it!"*
> – Kathleen, Texas

7. **Believe that you can do this!** Be encouraged by the knowledge that thousands of students, with legally identified learning needs or without official "labels," are helped by teachers who focus on the students' individual needs. The students described at the beginning of this chapter—Winston, Harriet, George, Thomas, Caryn—all flourished under the care of teachers who took the time to know and plan for them to learn in the ways that worked best for them.

Falling in Love Again

Every child is unique. The colorful mixture of gifts, struggles, abilities, challenges, and modes of learning can bring you delight. It all depends on how you view the "garden" of differences, and on how well prepared you are to tend the treasures that "grow" there. When you take full advantage of the available support, learn the characteristics and needs of different learners, understand the laws and appropriate procedures for working with various children, and equip yourself with techniques for loving and teaching the variety of students placed in your hands—you can manage it all without chronic distress. Armed with the right attitude, good preparation, and solid support, you will lose your fear of all those "special" needs. And when you lose the fear, you can enjoy the students and find fulfillment in meeting their needs.

Me Moment

Does your mind toss and turn with issues from your work week or workday? Are you having trouble turning off that DVD player (with surround sound) that perpetually rocks and rolls in your brain? Is your mind exhausted—and your body in constant stress mode? Relax your mind and distract it from the worries, dilemmas, or decisions with music.

Think of a song that peps you up, or makes you feel happy, or is just fun to sing. Hum, whistle, or tap out the rhythm to the song as you walk down the hallway.

Chapter 6 **Tools**

I'm so confused!

Know the Language

Classroom Teacher's Guide to Special Needs Acronyms

Sure,
I'll have this
list memorized
by tonight.

ADA – Americans with Disabilities Act

ADD – attention deficit disorder

ADHD – attention deficit hyperactivity disorder

AYP – adequate yearly progress

BIP – behavioral intervention plan

BMP – behavioral management plan

CFR – Code of Federal Regulations (rules created by regulatory agencies, such as the U.S. Department of Education, that regulate and carry the full force of statutes; often helps to clarify the intent of a statute)

DI – differentiated instruction

ED – U.S. Department of Education or emotionally disturbed

ELL – English language learner

ESL – English as a second language

FAPE – free appropriate public education

FBA – functional behavior assessment

FERPA – Family Educational Rights and Privacy Act

IAES or **IAEP** – interim alternative educational setting

IDEA – Individuals with Disabilities Education Act

IEE – independent educational evaluation

IEP – individualized education program

IFSP – individualized family services plan

ISAP – individual student assistance plan

ISS – in-school suspension

LD – learning disability or learning disabled

LEA – local educational agency (school district)

LEP – limited English proficiency

LRE – least restrictive environment

MD or MDR – manifestation determination or manifestation determination review

NAEP – National Assessment of Educational Progress

NCLB – No Child Left Behind (Act)

OCD – obsessive compulsive disorder

OCR – Office for Civil Rights

ODD – oppositional defiant disorder

OHI – other health impairment

OSEP – Office of Special Education Programs

OSERS – Office of Special Education and Rehabilitation Services

OT – occupational therapy

PT – physical therapy

RTI or RtI – response to intervention

SEA – state educational agency (state department of education)

Section 504 – Section 504 of the Rehabilitation Act of 1973

SED – serious emotional disturbance

SLD – specific learning disability

SP – services plan (replaces the IEP when a student with a disability is parentally placed in a private school)

Title 1 – Title 1 of the Elementary and Secondary Education Act of 1965 (reauthorized as the No Child Left Behind Act)

USC – United States Code (federal statute/law)

How Does the Student Learn?

Tips for Instructional Strategies for Different Kinds of Learners

When teaching auditory learners, try to . . .

- read directions out loud.
- ask students to repeat the direction.
- include oral drills.
- allow projects that include student presentations using songs or poetry.
- allow the use of a tape recorder for note taking.

When teaching visual learners, try to . . .

- use handouts, charts, diagrams, and tables to deliver important information.
- encourage students to take written notes.
- allow the use of highlighters, colored pens, and markers to emphasize critical points.
- use flash cards and graphic organizers.
- give written instructions.

When teaching kinesthetic learners, try to . . .

- allow frequent movement breaks.
- teach key ideas with a physical body rhythm (such as the memorization of the periodic table while tossing a ball from hand to hand).
- permit a small activity while the student is practicing to a rhythm, such as squeezing clay, tapping a pen quietly on a leg, or chewing gum. Yes, chewing gum. I promise the world as we know it won't come to an end.
- use manipulatives whenever possible.
- have students physically point to key concepts housed in text.

When teaching verbal-linguistic learners, include . . .

- choral speaking.
- debate.
- reading out loud.
- dramatizing.
- journaling.

When teaching logical-mathematical learners, include . . .

- predicting.
- coding.
- using manipulatives.
- solving puzzles.
- sequencing.

When teaching visual-spatial learners, include . . .

- graphing.
- painting.
- using charts, diagrams, tables, graphic organizers.
- photographing.
- creating 3-D projects and computer design projects.

When teaching body-kinesthetic learners, include . . .

- hands-on activities.
- dramatization.
- crafts.
- small-group work.
- movement.

When teaching musical learners, include . . .

- rap and poetry.
- background music.
- rhythm.
- singing.
- patterns.
- use of percussion instruments.

When teaching interpersonal learners, include . . .

- cooperative learning.
- peer instruction.
- group work.
- sharing.
- brainstorming.

When teaching intrapersonal learners, include . . .

- individualized, independent studies.
- independent reading.
- assignments with lots of personal choice.
- journaling.

When teaching naturalistic learners, include . . .

- outdoor learning.
- use of insects or animals as lesson basis.
- use of a microscope or telescope.
- plant and animal identification.
- gathering collections from nature.

 Learn To Love Teaching Again

Tips for Working with IDEA Students

Autism

Characteristics include diminished verbal and nonverbal communication skills, resistance to change in daily activities, repetitive activities and unusual responses to sensory stimuli

Teacher Tips: Be willing to make adaptations to your classroom routines. Teach socially appropriate greetings, but do not insist on eye contact. Use concise and concrete language. Be sensitive to the level of sensory input with which the student is comfortable.

Deafness

A loss of hearing severe enough that the child can not hear even when using a hearing device

Teacher Tips: Since many students retain some residual hearing, carefully consider placement. This not only means where the desk is situated, but also where to seat the student during cooperative group work, class discussions, and school assemblies. If the student wears a cochlear implant, be sure to keep background noise to a minimum during instruction.

Deaf-Blindness

A hearing and visual loss so severe that the child cannot be accommodated by an adapted visual or hearing program

Teacher Tips: Keep in mind that this student usually is not completely without vision or hearing; this disability category encompasses a range of loss. Become familiar with the strengths and abilities the student possesses. Work in tandem with the student's special education teacher, therapists and other support staff.

Hearing Impairment

An impairment in hearing, permanent or fluctuating, that affects the child's education

Teacher Tips: If the student lip-reads, stand where your mouth is easily visible. Speak clearly but normally. Avoid the use of idioms and colloquialisms. If an interpreter is used, speak to the child and not to the interpreter. Provide instructional information in written form to ensure understanding.

Mental retardation

Significant subaverage general intellect

Teacher Tips: Give instructions individually or in small groups. Keep directions simple and clear. Assign a peer for support. Use repetition. Celebrate accomplishments.

Multiple disabilities

A combination of impairments that interferes with the child's education so severely that the child can not be accommodated in one of the other disability categories. Deaf-blindness is excluded from this disability.

Teacher Tips: Since this is such a broad disability category, take the time to educate yourself on the particular strengths and challenges that your student may face. Plan for shorter blocks of instructional time and build in break times. Allow for extra time to move from activity to activity.

Orthopedic impairment

An orthopedic impairment severe enough to impede the child's education. Examples include the absence of a limb, cerebral palsy, and bone tuberculosis.

Teacher Tips: Allow extra time for movement between activities. Don't assume that this student cannot participate in an activity because of the impairment; be flexible and inclusive. Be sensitive to alternate bathroom needs, students who may become easily fatigued, or students who need to move or be moved periodically.

Other health impairment

Limited strength or vitality due to conditions such as leukemia, severe weakness, asthma, rheumatic fever, sickle-cell anemia, and heart ailments. ADHD is included in this categorization.

Teacher Tips: Students with OHI may miss school for elongated periods of time due to the nature of their illnesses. Be sure to not only provide instructional materials but also help students to continue to feel a part of the class, through notes, e-mails and phone calls. Your goal is to have them return to the classroom feeling welcomed and aware of any changes.

If the student has been diagnosed with attention deficit disorder, try to keep classroom distractions as minimal as possible. Consider seating, and place this student away from the classroom door or windows. Use visuals, and state instructions one at a time. Be prepared to repeat directions. Establish eye contact before giving instructions.

Severe emotional disturbance

Emotional conditions that can include inappropriate behaviors, a pervasive unhappiness or depression, and an inability to maintain appropriate social relationships. This category does not include students who are socially maladjusted.

Teacher Tips: Structure classroom rules with positive verbiage. Create a routine and try to stick to it. Reward appropriate behavior, and assign fair and consistent consequences for inappropriate behavior. Understand that your instruction with this student may need to include suitable social and self-help skills.

Specific learning disability

A disorder in a basic psychological process that can include understanding or using spoken or written language. Conditions can include dyslexia, dysgraphia, perceptual disabilities, developmental aphasia, and minimal brain dysfunction.

Teacher Tips: Talk with parents, the special education teacher, and any other caregivers to find out the particulars of the student's specific learning disability. Focus your instruction on the student's strengths. Be flexible and open to accommodations such as reduced assignments, oral tests, and extra assistance.

Speech or language impairment

Conditions include stuttering, language impairment, or voice impairment

Teacher Tips: Do not be afraid to ask this student to repeat a word or phrase. Do not finish sentences for this student. Encourage and model other forms of communication, such as facial expressions and body language. Keep a relaxed attitude when communicating and focus on what is being said, rather than how it is being said.

Traumatic brain injury

An acquired injury to the brain that adversely affects a child's educational performance

Teacher Tips: Practice patience. Realize that you may have to lower your expectations. Become informed; speak with the student's parents and other caregivers to learn as much as possible about any challenges or restrictions. Consider reducing the workload and give one instruction at a time. Be prepared to repeat directions.

Visual impairment, including blindness

A visual impairment that, even with correction, affects a child's educational performance

Teacher Tips: Always identify yourself and always use the student's name when directing the conversation toward him or her. Be aware of any physical changes to your classroom; close closet doors, pick up objects that fall on the floor, and don't rearrange furniture. Verbally explain what you are physically doing. Use an appropriate voice volume, as these students have normal hearing.

Quick Guide to Stress-Free IEP Meetings

1. Dress in a professional manner.

2. Arrive on time.

3. Bring any documentation or information that you have been asked to bring or that you are certain will support anything you plan to say about the student.

4. Present a professional appearance. Bring a clean notepad and new pen. (Don't come in with a pile of papers to correct or loaded with files other than the information needed. Be sure to leave the spiral notebook with paper tears hanging out and the pen with chew marks back in your classroom.)

5. Speak up if you have any concerns about the committee's decisions during the meeting, so that they will be recorded in the meeting minutes.

6. Leave at the end of the meeting with an IEP packet, or be sure you understand when you will receive one.

7. Request that a copy of the meeting minutes be sent to you.

8. Don't be afraid to ask (before you leave the meeting) for clarifications regarding your responsibilities in relation to the student.

9. You know your child's parent(s)—probably better than anyone else in that room. If you see that parents are confused or uncertain, don't hesitate to ask if they understand or if they need clarification. This will allow the diagnostician, special education teacher, or counselor to address their concerns or questions during the meeting and not weeks later.

10. After the meeting, let your child's parents know that you will work with them as a team and that you will keep them informed. Reassure them that everything possible will be done to help their child be successful.

Adapted from Texas A & M CTE Teacher's Tips

ADD and ADHD
Instructional Accommodations:
A Quick Guide

What should I do first? Math or Spelling?

Should I sharpen my pencil? Or get a drink of water?

Hi, Simon!

Hey, George!

Whatcha doin', Lulu?

If the student is easily distracted:

- Break assignments into shorter segments.
- Give preferential seating away from distractions.
- Provide opportunities for movement.
- Plan highly structured routines and teaching methods.
- Walk or stand near the student frequently.
- Frequently check on student work and redirect if necessary.

If the student displays organizational challenges:

- Provide an established daily routine.
- Contract with the student and use rewards for completing the contract.
- Frequently check student notebooks for organization.
- Provide due dates on written assignments.
- Break large projects into smaller parts with due dates for each part.
- Provide sticky notes for reminders.
- Provide sticky-tape flags to draw attention to certain pages.
- Provide colored paper clips to section materials.
- Keep highlighters available for the student to mark important information. This helps the student note key ideas and also provides a motor activity during reading.

If the student fails to get started quickly when assignments are given:

- Introduce the assignment in sequential steps.
- Check for understanding of instructions.
- Check on progress often in the first few minutes of work.

Adapted from Idaho Training Clearinghouse

Multiple Intelligences Hunt

Energize your students at the beginning of a class period or lesson. Since all the multiple intelligences are addressed here, each student will have a chance to "shine" with this warm-up activity. Give students a copy of the sheet below.

. . . .

Your mission: Find a different person in the room who can "do" one of the talents listed. Your classmate must demonstrate his or her talent and initial your sheet. Do not include yourself.

Find someone who can ...

Initials ————————— Classmate's Talent ——————————

	say the alphabet backwards.
	stand on one foot and rub their belly.
	sing or hum the first few lines of "The Star-Spangled Banner."
	tell the difference between warm-blooded and cold-blooded animals.
	find the next set of numbers: 6, 9, 12, 15, ___, ___, ___.
	explain why they think humans are on the Earth.
	draw a map that shows the way from school to the closest grocery store.
	describe a recent dream in detail.
	describe what the perfect party would be like.
	tell a funny story that happened recently.
	touch their tongue to their nose.
	do somewhat of a perfect cartwheel.
	sing or hum the first few lines of a current popular song.

Multiple Intelligences Hunt

Sometimes we're unaware of other people's gifts, but we can go on a "treasure hunt" (in this case, an "intelligences hunt") to discover one another's special talents.

. . . .

Initials ———————————— **Classmate's Talent** ————————

☐	whistle a few notes from Beethoven's Fifth Symphony.
☐	stand on one foot with his or her eyes closed for at least five seconds.
☐	recite at least four consecutive lines from any poem.
☐	draw a quick diagram explaining how an electric motor works.
☐	figure out how many shoes can fit in a student desk.
☐	complete this numerical sequence, and explain the logic: 36, 30, 24, 18, ___ .
☐	tell a funny (appropriate) joke.
☐	describe what the "perfect" zoo would look like.
☐	explain how life is a "journey."
☐	perform the nursery rhyme "Humpty Dumpty" as a rap.
☐	draw a picture of a cat and a dog in a hot air balloon.
☐	describe the differences between an amphibian and a reptile.
☐	draw a map that shows how to walk from school to the nearest post office.

Tips for Teaching Students with Multiple Intelligences

Children who are strongly...	Think . . .	Love . . .	Need . . .
Linguistic	in words	reading, writing, telling stories, playing word games	books, tapes, writing tools, paper diaries, dialogues, discussion, debate stories
Logical-Mathematical	by reasoning	experimenting, questioning, figuring out puzzles, calculating	things to explore and think about, science materials, manipulatives, trips to the planetarium and science museum
Spatial	in images and pictures	designing, drawing, visualizing, doodling	art, Legos, videos, movies, slides, imagination games, mazes, puzzles, illustrated books, trips to the museum
Body-Kinesthetic	through somatic sensations	dancing, running, jumping, building, touching, gesturing	role play, drama, movement, things to build, sports and physical games, tactile experiences, hand's on learning
Musical	via rhythms and melodies	singing, whistling, humming, tapping feet and hands, listening	sing-along time, trips to concerts, music playing at home and school, musical instruments
Interpersonal	by bouncing ideas off other people	leading, organizing, relating, manipulating, mediating, playing	friends, group games, social gatherings, community events, clubs, mentors, apprenticeships
Intrapersonal	via deep inside themselves	setting goals, meditating, dreaming, being quiet	secret places, time alone, self-paced projects, choices
Existentialist	by the big picture	analyzing "why" the world operates the way it does	to express feelings about the world, universe
Naturalist	through animals and nature	being in nature, categorizing domains, sciences	to be outdoors, exploring nature

Adapted from David Lazear's – *The Rubrics Way: Using Multiple Intelligences to Assess Understanding*

Learning Activities Checklist

Remember that students learn more and remember better when they

. . . are actively engaged with material—participating in some way

. . . are DOING rather than just hearing (speaking, writing, thinking, drawing, creating, moving, dramatizing, giving feedback)

. . . identify and articulate applications of a concept

. . . discuss an idea with someone else

. . . see implications for real life, relevancies to their own lives, and benefits to others

Include in learning experiences:

____ group decision making
____ problem solving
____ reading together
____ writing and sharing
____ role-playing
____ drawing to show understanding
____ flexible scheduling
____ flexible outcomes
____ questioning
____ making models
____ experimenting
____ journaling
____ creating displays
____ representing ideas visually
____ teaching an idea to someone else
____ setting an idea to music or rhythm
____ mapping or sketching concepts
____ ideas broken into chunks
____ analyzing
____ predicting
____ evaluating
____ use of technology:
       computers, visual projectors,
       interactive whiteboards, blogs,
       podcasts, websites, social networks

____ independent learning contracts
____ rubrics
____ cartoons, photos, tables, graphs
____ small-group discussion
____ small-group projects
____ choices
____ study guides of different kinds
____ graphic organizers
____ simulation games
____ learning stations
____ interactive teacher presentations
____ dramatizations and puppet shows
____ choral reading
____ "How-To" speeches
____ movement
____ music
____ debates
____ oral explanations
____ guided imagery
____ diaries
____ interviews
____ summaries, oral or written
____ visual classifications
____ self-reflections on work
____ portfolios

Racing to the Finish Line

You know you're a teacher under stress if you wear your running gear to school every day—and the stopwatch is always running.

Mr. Welter is preparing his students for a benchmark test tomorrow. In preparation, he's just taught a lesson on how to recognize the main idea in a passage and cite evidence to support it. He used a text about Shirley Chisholm, the Congresswoman from New York who served for seven terms, and who also was the first African-American major-party candidate for president.

One student raised his hand and asked why it took so long to elect an African-American president after Shirley Chisholm's nomination more than thirty years before. Another student wondered if gender had played a role. A lively classroom discussion spontaneously erupted. It was exciting—an example of authentic, dynamic learning. Students used concepts they had learned in class; they applied previously learned facts to the day's reading; questions popped up everywhere; different viewpoints were shared; and every last one of them was engaged with the learning.

But—*only minutes after it had begun, the teacher interrupted and put a stop to the discussion. "I would love to continue this conversation," he said wistfully, "but we can't. Perhaps some other time?" Mr. Welter passed out mock test questions about main idea and supporting evidence, so that the students could continue their test preparation.*

What's really discouraging about this common classroom scenario is that there never seems to be "some other time." There are curriculum goals to reach, textbooks to finish, benchmarks to meet, and (worst of all) the dreaded standardized test date looming ahead—and your students have got to be ready.

Learn To Love Teaching Again

Losing the Love

I would wager a year's salary that one of these tasks is near the top of every teacher's list of stressors: getting students to meet the standards, preparing students to do well on standardized tests, or getting students to make the expected yearly progress.

In this era of accountability, teachers are under enormous pressure to cover material (particularly material that will be on the state assessment) and to assure that their students make adequate progress. Those textbooks that should be finished, and those tests that are looming—they turn into demons nipping at the teachers' heels. And all the while, the teachers would just like to be left alone to TEACH! The demands of the current test-centered educational world discourage, depress, and defeat many teachers. They drive thousands away from the profession. Like so many other teachers, you may be exhausted and distressed from battling deadlines and grappling with accountability. You may feel as if your classroom has turned into a test-prep boot camp.

On Your Mark, Get Set, Go!

Starting the first week of school (or maybe before that), teachers seem to be dashing for a finish line. Anyone lingering near a school the week before students arrive can probably hear the starting gun. You actually **might** wear your running shoes at all times. (Maybe you should consider roller skates!) Time is a precious commodity in a classroom. There never seems to be enough of it—because there is so much to get done. Teachers know they must cover curriculum, get through the textbook, be ready for the standardized tests, and see that students make progress. At the same time, good teachers know that learning can't be rushed. They know that development never happens in a straight line. And they do not want to miss those wonderful moments of discovery when the race **should** stop so that something unexpected can be explored.

This chapter is about doing both—giving the students the experiences they need to grow as learners while meeting the deadlines and expectations. Covering curriculum and assessing progress are **not** at odds with quality teaching. The upcoming pages give several ideas for making it to the "finish line" without racing all the time—and without you and your students living full time in stress-response mode.

Let's start with a few cautions and considerations. Keep them in mind as you read through the other sections of the chapter. If you have these seven principles as **foundational rules**, you will have a much better chance for success at all of the rest—covering curriculum, getting the most out of textbooks, and preparing students to do their best on those state assessments.

1. Adjust your attitude.
Many teachers spend a lot of time and energy dreading and complaining about the curriculum, the standardized tests, the standards, and the accountability expectations. It's as if by whining about them, these burdens will disappear. There are plenty of valid arguments against using or finishing the textbook, working through a tightly set curriculum, and placing so much emphasis on standardized test scores and preparation. But in reality, these things probably **are** requirements in your school. So don't waste time griping. Save your energy. Work where you can in your school to set reasonable schoolwide policies related to these things. Beyond that, adopt the attitude that you can work within the framework to give students valuable educational experiences. Make those tests, textbooks, and expectations work for you—instead of their controlling and annoying you.

2. Clarify your goals.
The goals should **not** be to finish the textbook, or get through the next unit, or prepare for the test. The goals must be about nurturing individual human beings—giving them the setting, the tools, and the support to learn what they can and need to learn at their own paces and in their own ways. If you focus on the meaningful goals that are really what your job is about, you will figure out how to use curriculum, textbooks, and tests to move towards those goals.

Chuckle!

Two teachers on recess duty hurried the students inside, then headed back to the playground to put away the equipment. They were just taking down the volleyball net when they heard a low growl coming from the woods beyond the school. A large cougar stood at the edge of the schoolyard, poised to leap toward the teachers. Julianna McGraw tore off her backpack, dug out her running shoes, put them on, and took off.

"What are you doing?" yelled her colleague. "You can't outrun a cougar!"

Julianna shouted back as she ran, "I don't have to outrun the cougar—I just have to outrun you!"

Learn To Love Teaching Again

3. Don't dawdle. Value each instructional minute you have. Don't assume that the first week of school is lost time. Start right in with serious instruction. Give up the idea the students won't learn anything the week before holiday break, the week after holiday break, the week before the field trip, the week after the field trip, the week of Homecoming, the week with three assemblies, or the week before school is out. You may just find that you **do** have that "some other time" to continue an important discussion or explore that quirky idea. Pay close attention to principles 5, 6, and 7 below. They will help you make far better use of precious classroom time.

4. Do dawdle. Be flexible. There are times when the very best thing to do is to deviate from your plans—to grab a moment and teach something that is begging to be taught. When light bulbs appear over students' heads and all brain burners are lit—well, goodness, a teacher should to be able to take the chance, without getting stressed over what page the rest of the fifth-grade teachers are covering today.

Classrooms are not sports fields or boardrooms, where goals are recognizable and static. Classrooms are places in which

- kids impulsively run to the window when a helicopter is heard overhead.
- thinking is not done in a straight-line, orderly continuum but in waves, loops, and somersaults.
- the success of a seventh-grade math lesson for a student can depend on whether HE called last night.
- a visiting bunny rabbit can bring an entire school to its knees.

Of course, these things do not actually qualify as dawdling. They may take you on detours—but attending to them is just good teaching.

5. Be a good manager. Cut out some of the biggest timewasters of all with good classroom management. Hundreds of research studies and teachers' experiences testify that as much as half of the time in a classroom is wasted in nonteaching activities. These are things such as settling down, getting started, getting organized, resolving disputes, making transitions, or taking care of minor details. Consistent (and consistently enforced), reasonable classroom rules and procedures can cut that wasted time to a minimum. Scrutinize the patterns and practices that eat up time in your classes. Think about how you can change procedures in a way that trades wasted time for teaching time. If you have a smoothly operating classroom, there will be much more time to teach students what they need to learn.

6. Stay connected. The time you spend building (and nurturing) respectful, caring relationships with your students will pay you back with hours of time for good teaching. In most cases, when students are sure that you see them and know them as individuals, they will be more readily present to the learning experiences. Cut down on the time you spend battling students, miscommunicating, or struggling with respect issues—and watch how much faster you accomplish learning goals!

7. Keep students motivated. When your classroom is alive with dynamic learning activities, a lot less time is wasted. If students are motivated to learn and are actively engaged in their lessons, you won't have that feeling that you're racing through mud. Plan learning events that are relevant, inviting, and differentiated to students' many learning levels and styles. You will cover more of those important concepts in less time, because the students will remember what you teach.

The Stress of the Textbook

Lloyd Scott set a new world record at the Edinburgh Marathon in 2003. He had the slowest time—finishing the marathon in six days, four hours, thirty minutes, and fifty-six seconds. What was Scott's winning strategy? He walked the marathon in a 130-pound deep-sea diving suit. To train, he walked nine hours a day at a rousing clip of a half mile per hour. He took five days to complete the London and New York marathons. Scott lists among his other accomplishments running in the Edinburgh marathon while wearing a medieval suit of armor.

Textbooks— Do I love 'em or leave 'em?

(Signs of the Times, 2003).

Do you try to teach all of the content in a textbook before the year's end? If so, you will feel as if you are running a marathon wearing metal clothing from the Dark Ages. Even if you keep your class from afternoon assemblies, cut out all lunch periods, and allow no bathroom breaks (no matter what), you still may not make it though the textbook.

Some teachers (or even entire schools or districts) live and die by the textbooks. New teachers tend to rely on them heavily, and there is some wisdom to that. Following a textbook closely can provide a safety net (or security blanket) for a new teacher—until

Learn To Love Teaching Again

experience and confidence are gained. In this case, a textbook can indeed be a best friend. But, whatever your level of experience, ask yourself these questions:

- *Am I relying too much on my textbooks?*
- *Are page numbers reached in my textbooks tied to my worth as a teacher?*
- *Am I giving up my instructional confidence or authority to a team of textbook authors who may have experience in a different type of school community?*

This textbook race increases stress for teachers. Whether that pressure comes from the district or from the teacher herself, the strain to complete a textbook can cause a teacher to rush the teaching. The goal becomes the final textbook page, not effective instruction. Just look at the following topics covered in one world history textbook (and these take students only up to the 1400s)! Imagine trying to teach all of these to any depth:

Mesopotamia	The ancient Indus Valley
Ancient Egypt	The expansion of the Islamic faith
Hinduism	The ruins of Mohenjo-Daro
Pre-Columbian America	A day in the life of ancient Rome
Feudal lords	History of the Niger River Valley
China's Silk Road	Africa's Mali and Songhai
Greek theater	The fall of the Aztecs
Saharan trade routes	The fall of the Mayans
The Persian Empire	Feudalism of Japan
The Dark Ages	Humanism
The Renaissance	The Byzantine Empire

Note: If you walk by a history teacher's classroom door and see him or her sobbing uncontrollably because the stapler ran out of staples, you now understand. Don't say you know exactly what that teacher is going through. Just put a fresh box of tissues on the desk and back away slowly.

There are many definitions of effective instruction. Most contain components such as hands-on experiences, real-world connections, student engagement, brain-based strategies, building on prior knowledge, systematic presentation, differentiated activities, or ongoing formative assessment. However, I have never seen a definition of effective instruction that includes the strategy of finishing the textbook.

New Teacher Tip

Review the format and content of your textbooks. Then make a plan for using the portions that support your curriculum and state standards. Don't assume that you have to cover every page, or even every chapter. Also, ask a few veteran teachers how they use their textbooks.

Benefits of a Good Textbook

It would be wrong to completely vilify textbooks. This is some of the good news about textbooks:

- Textbooks let teachers know what grade-appropriate material to teach and when to teach it.
- Textbooks save teachers time, as activities and assignments are already created and ready for student use.
- Textbooks serve as a foundation for new teachers, as well as an assurance for principals that the correct curriculum is being taught by new teachers.
- Textbooks provide curriculum concepts that are aligned with state and national standards.
- Textbooks present information systematically, using instructional scaffolding.
- Your textbook is authored by experts in the specific content field.
- Textbooks can provide goals, objectives, assessments, assignments, accommodations, accelerated assignments, required prerequisite skills, homework suggestions, higher-level thinking challenges, rubrics, and the latest teaching strategies.

On the Other Hand

Some of those very same advantages can be disadvantages, too. Here are some reflections offered by real teachers:

PRO: *I don't have to reinvent the wheel.*

CON: *My fourth graders know nothing about geometry, because I never get to the last three chapters of our math book.*

PRO: *Textbooks save me my most precious commodity: time.*

CON: *The lessons often feel so "one-size-fits-all."*

PRO: *Someone who knows more than I created the plan for instruction.*

CON: *Is the "expert" really the expert for my students?*

PRO: *The learning activities are already prepared for me.*

CON: *The suggested assignments get stale. It seems there is not much variety.*

PRO: *If I use the textbook regularly, the sequence of information is all set for me.*

CON: *My students are bored if we use the textbook all the time.*

Wise Use of Textbooks

So, how heavily should you rely on textbooks? And should you race to cover everything? This book can't answer those questions definitively for every teacher. You'll need to weigh your needs, your students' needs, your school regulations, your curricular area, and your teaching style. But do consider the extent of your tie to the textbook(s) and whether or not it is right for your students. Here are some ideas and tips that can help you move toward your own answers, and at the same time, lower your heart rate by slowing down the textbook race.

- Your textbook is not the only tool in your instructional toolbox. It's a mistake to think that it is. It is not necessary to use every word, every activity, or every element of the textbook. Most textbooks were designed to give an array of choices to teachers and students. Use your textbook as a blueprint. It is a guide to curriculum, but not the whole story.

- Often a text is a great source of specific features, such as key ideas on a concept, pertinent vocabulary, relevant visuals, thoughtful questions, instructional sequence, statement of objectives, periodic review, test sections, a strong reference list, concise summaries of information, graphs, charts, diagrams, and tools for practice. Use the features that work well for your students.

Teacher-to-Teacher Tip

"I use my textbooks as major teaching tools. But I plan additions for each chapter: hands-on activities, creative experiences, and use of technology. These keep the interest of my students."
– Kurt R., Texas

- Your learners differ from one another. Some have trouble reading. Some learn best visually or auditorially. One problem with heavy reliance on the textbook is that it may inhibit differentiated instruction. Students who struggle with the written word or who read at a lower level can get lost with textbook assignments. View your classroom textbook with a critical eye and do not be afraid to modify or adjust instruction to meet the needs of your students.

- In many cases, the available textbooks are out of date. Examine yours carefully for obsolete or erroneous information. In many subjects (particularly math and science), the textbook may not be the best source of real-life experiences. Be free to compute, experiment, or explore with problems, test items, or examples from beyond the textbook.

- Supplement the textbook with many other resources—computer software, whiteboard programs, websites, podcasts, current news articles, video clips, visiting speakers, magazines, books (including recreational reading books that encompass your curriculum content), and student-based projects.

Here are some problems teachers have with their textbooks, along with some solutions that might help.

> Understand that most problems are a good sign.
>
> Problems indicate that progress is being made, wheels are turning, you are moving toward your goals.
>
> Beware when you have no problems.
>
> Then you've really got a problem....
>
> Scott Alexander, author

Problem

Mr. Hoffman: My school district requires that we use our social studies textbooks for 90 percent of our instruction. They have made a huge financial commitment to this particular company and do not want to see the money wasted. I understand that, and the textbooks are pretty good. But that means the students are exposed to only one view of the subject. I am afraid that their perspectives are skewed.

Solution

Continue to teach with your textbook as your school district requires. But use your other 10 percent of instruction well. Provide students a variety of other sources of information, with a variety of approaches. Also, be sure to include plenty of experiences that push students to analyze, evaluate, and question the material and make applications to the real world.

Problem

Ms. Vogt: Our textbooks are out of date. With the district budget crunch, it doesn't look as though they will be updated any time soon. On top of that, the questioning in the books is very low level and fact focused. I know my students need more.

Solution

Try to use your particular textbooks only as a reference. Supplement your instruction heavily with other resources. Perhaps you can work with your grade level teams to gather more current materials. Don't forget to share what you find. Create your own sets of questions that require students to use higher-level thinking skills. Assign student writing or projects that require them to research current facts and events. Get them involved in doing the "updating"!

Problem

Ms. Elam: Personally, I really like our science books. The information is topical and the presentation is clear and logical. However, the language of the text is just too high a level for my students. They do not understand even half of what they read!

Solution

Read textbook selections to your students. After each section, stop and summarize—in plain language—what the textbook has just said. Break down the text into small,

Learn To Love Teaching Again

digestible chunks. Pair a student who understands the textbook language with another who struggles. Talk about the material together as a whole class—a lot! In addition, track down supplemental materials on the students' reading levels. Add many other kinds of materials that present concepts in other modes—auditory, visual, and experiential. Gather more materials each year to round out the ways for exposing students to the concepts.

Problem

Mrs. Coons: The textbook is okay, but it doesn't take into account that my students have some background knowledge in the content. It seems we are starting at square one with every new topic. I swear the textbook companies must think that students have never been in school before!

Solution

As you preread your textbook in preparation for instruction, modify and adapt content. Do a quick review of the background knowledge your students already know, and move on to the new areas of study. But be careful here. Do not just assume your students know "old" information. Consider giving a quick pretest, either orally or on paper, just to be sure.

Problem

Mrs. Weiss: I have a problem with the format of our literature textbook. There are questions after each reading selection, but the answers are very obvious and can be found right in the text. My students can actually hold conversations with one another while completing an assignment, and still get all the answers right!

Heating bills at Jefferson School are way down this year. Nobody was using these history textbooks anyway.

Furnace Room ←

Solution

You will have to step beyond the textbook and create problem-solving and other extended activities for your students. Do not cheat them out of higher-level thinking opportunities just because those are not available in your textbook. Once you create these opportunities, be sure you save them for the following year's lessons.

The Stress of the Test

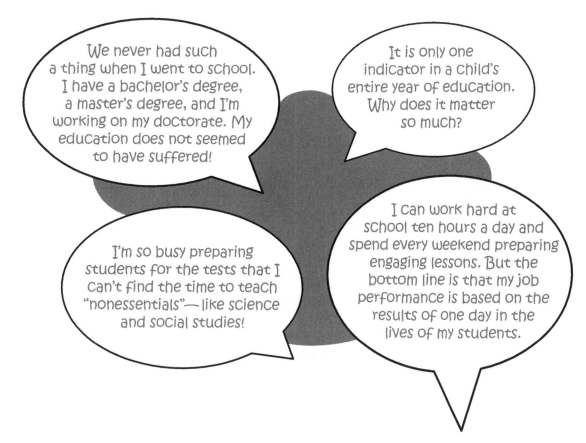

> We never had such a thing when I went to school. I have a bachelor's degree, a master's degree, and I'm working on my doctorate. My education does not seemed to have suffered!

> It is only one indicator in a child's entire year of education. Why does it matter so much?

> I'm so busy preparing students for the tests that I can't find the time to teach "nonessentials"—like science and social studies!

> I can work hard at school ten hours a day and spend every weekend preparing engaging lessons. But the bottom line is that my job performance is based on the results of one day in the lives of my students.

What are these teachers talking about? Let's all say it together now:
"High-stakes testing!"

And what does this mean for teachers? Shout it with me:
"High-stakes testing means teacher stress!"

Testing—it's a hot topic, a hot-button topic, and a topic that leads to hot-tempered discussions. The two authors of this book, alone, could fill a book with opinions we've heard and arguments we've overheard about standardized tests. You've probably participated in such arguments and voiced such opinions.

Yes, most educators agree that it is important to assess student knowledge. We know that we must devise ways to find out what students know, understand, and have learned. Good instruction is integrally tied to good, ongoing assessment. It is not so much the concept of testing that is the heated issue. It is the current trend of the all-consuming, all-or-nothing emphasis on standardized tests in the public school arena that causes so much stress to teachers (and, in most cases, to the students and their families also).

Learn To Love Teaching Again

Pressure Rising

Accountability and assessment have always had a place in education, but with the No Child Left Behind Act of 2001, things were booted up several notches. Not only was student achievement to be monitored on a yearly and measurable basis, but schools and teachers were held accountable as well. Goals of NCLB include:

- By the year 2014, every child will be able to demonstrate grade-level achievement in core subject areas.
- States are required to create academic standards that will achieve the above goal.
- State-created reading and math standards are to be assessed in grades 3 through 8, and at least once during high school.
- Beginning in the 2007–2008 school year, science standards were also to be tested.
- Gaps in education, especially among minority, special needs, and low income students needed to be addressed.

(U.S. Government, 2001)

The movement schools make toward achieving these goals is called AYP, or adequate yearly progress. The school's AYP is determined to a large part by its students' performance on state assessments.

For a public school teacher (or administrator), the stakes are high and the pressure is overwhelming. Test results can be tied to student placement, school ratings, funding allotments, and even teacher or administrator merit, pay, or job security. Under such pressures, stories abound of teachers giving students test answers, teachers giving students vitamins on test days, or school officials tampering with test answer sheets. Most teachers and administrators are not tampering with tests, but, at the least, they feel driven to teach with the test constantly in mind.

In the fall of 2008, the New York City Department of Education began to connect the performance evaluations of elementary and middle-school teachers to their students' scores on state math and reading tests. Teachers could earn an "average," "below average," or "above average" rating. Originally intended to be a consideration for tenure, the New York State Department of Education promised that the rating results would not be published for public consumption, nor would they be attached to pay raises or job advancement. (Fetig, 2010)

In the summer of 2010, things went further in California. The *Los Angeles Times* published ratings of teachers based on their students' performance on standardized testing—complete with teachers' names (Felch, Song, & Smith, 2010). Just a month before that, the Washington D.C. Schools Chancellor fired 165 teachers under a new evaluation system that held teachers accountable for student test scores. She also put another 17 percent of the district's teachers on notice that they could lose their jobs in the next year if they didn't improve on their records (Lawin, 2010).

Not every teacher operates under such extreme threats. But though teacher names are not generally part of the story, it has become routine (or even required) that the media publishes public school test results. All public schools in the United States operate under the current umbrella of the No Child Left Behind Act, and this includes the expectation for schools to demonstrate that students are making adequate yearly progress (AYP) as measured by the state tests. Funding, and—indeed—even the survival of the school itself, is tied to this progress. So is it any wonder that teachers and administrators are stressed? Is it any wonder that teachers "teach the test"?

I have the same dream every night—and the standardized tests are still six months away.

To encourage high scores, many states tie test results to school recognition, funding, merit pay raises for teachers and administrators, financial rewards for improved scores, money rewards for students who improve, and opportunities for career advancement. In some schools, the whole community gets involved in a campaign—complete with T-shirts and celebrations. Principals and district representatives have been known to promise to shave their heads, spend a day on the school roof, or wear a Barney (the dinosaur) costume for a week if test scores improve.

With the emphasis on test scores—resulting from one day or a few days once a year, curriculum plans and instructional goals are increasingly focused on the benchmarks, facts, or standards that teachers know will be on the test. Teachers might be comfortable with this if they believed that the tests were true representations of what students should be learning, and if they believed the test-preparation emphasis worked. But the stress is elevated by a general awareness that . . .

> . . . despite all the attention and energy focused,

> . . . despite all the dedicated classroom time,

Learn To Love Teaching Again

. . . despite the training given to students and parents on the importance of the tests,

. . . despite the monies spent on software programs that guarantee greater student achievement, and

. . . despite the additional compensation that may be the teacher's carrot to incite better student scores,

in many cases, neither the quality of education nor the test scores are improving.

Chuckle!

A team of sixth-grade teachers enjoyed some giggles over a few responses from their midterm tests:

- When you breathe, you inspire. When you don't breathe, you expire.
- Before getting a transfusion, you should find out if the blood is affirmative or negative.
- Algebraical symbols are used when you don't know what you are talking about.
- A magnet is something you find crawling all over a dead cat.
- Cells reproduce by a process called halitosis.
- To collect sulfur fumes in the lab, hold a deacon over a flame in a test tube.
- The pistol of a flower is its only protection against insects.
- John F. Kennedy rode a PT boat up the Delaware River to start the American Revolution.
- It is a well-known fact that a deceased body harms the mind.
- To remove dust from the eye, pull the eye down over the nose.

Accepting Reality while Teaching Well

Whatever you feel or believe about standardized tests, you have to deal with them. They are a factor in your job and the lives of your students—a factor that is not likely to disappear any time soon. Your stress about them will diminish when you accept the reality and make a plan for how you are going to handle it.

The best advice we can offer for life with "the tests" is this:
Get the emphasis off the test and onto the curriculum and instruction. Teach your students the things they need to know in ways that they can learn and remember, and they're likely to do just fine on the tests.

Here are some tips to help you do this:

1. **Know what your students need to learn.** Become friends with the scope and sequence chart of the curriculum for your grade level and subject area. Learn where individual students are on the continuum of learning in relation to grade-level guidelines.

2. **Know the district and state expectations.** Make sure you are well schooled on your state standards for your students' level and subject area. Get to know the district's requirements. Learn everything you can about the kinds of concepts and benchmarks upon which students will be judged. Become familiar with the format of tests your students will take.

3. **Establish a reasonable, appropriate curriculum.** Work with colleagues in your school to set or understand curriculum guidelines. Be purposeful about planning and teaching the big understandings and skills that students need. Resist the impulse to jump around and spend chunks of time on things that just seem interesting to you. This does not mean that you won't teach fascinating topics or build units that you know will appeal to your students. What it means is that you must connect those inviting topics to the things your students need to learn. Use strategies such as curriculum mapping, curriculum alignment, or backwards curriculum design to assure that your students will have carefully planned instruction.

- *Curriculum mapping* is a way to review, organize, and present the curricular-instructional plan for a whole school or district. The map will show the skills and objectives in each classroom, the instructional activities planned for each classroom, and a timeline for instructional goals, set in conjunction with the school calendar.

  When you work together to map your curriculum, you go beyond the recommendations made by "experts" from other places, companies, or states. Teachers at your school decide and show what is actually being taught in real-time in their classrooms. Mapping usually begins with a curriculum team that sets the vision for the school or district. They work to see if their vision is feasible, given the resources available. In the next step, all teachers provide information about the content, skills, and assessments—what they are and how they will be used in the classroom.

- *Curriculum alignment* is a way to compare what is being taught within grade levels and across all grade levels. The beauty of an all-school or all-district curriculum mapping project is that it allows for an easy look at alignment. *Horizontal alignment* assures that teachers of the same grade level follow the same sequence on the same timeline. This is especially

Learn To Love Teaching Again

useful when curriculum is tied to state standards and state assessments. *Vertical alignment* shows what content, skills, processes, and assessments are used across the grade levels. Examining this assures that there are no holes in instruction and that time is not wasted unnecessarily repeating content that students have mastered at a previous grade level. This also allows teachers to build upon previously learned concepts.

- **Backward design** (or backward mapping) is a process in which the end objectives are the starting point for planning. Once the teacher knows where the lesson is headed, he or she can identify how to tell when the students get to the goal and what learning experiences will help them get there. These steps summarize the process. (Also, see the sample "Backward Design Lesson Template" in the Tools section at the end of this chapter.)

> **Step 1:** Identify the knowledge, skill, or understanding that is critical for students to gain and use beyond the lesson. (What should students know, understand, and be able to do?)
>
> **Step 2:** Identify how you will measure whether or not the student has met this final objective. (What will be the evidence that the student has learned? How will you identify proficiency?)
>
> **Step 3:** Identify the specific, engaging activities that bring students to the place of meeting the goal, and the material that will support the process. (What will you do to make sure they know, understand, and can do the things you have identified?)

4. **Plan brain-rich instruction.**
   Brush up on principles of brain-compatible learning so that you can teach concepts in ways students will actually understand and remember. Reach for curriculum goals and cover the standards with experiences that engage the brain. Then you won't have so much worry about students' ability to retain and apply what they've learned to new situations—including test situations. (See "Lessons with the Brain in Mind" and "Invitation to Learning," a brain-based learning lesson plan template. These are found in the Tools section at the end of this chapter.)

My teacher says I need to make AYP. I'm not sure what that is, but maybe it's something I can make in shop class.

5. Share expectations with the students. Students have the right to know what they will be learning and where they are headed. Explain the benchmarks. They should know up front what criteria will be used in their evaluation. Tell them what constitutes a good performance. They will learn better when they know the expectations. Give them a list of curriculum goals or standards. Let them check these off as they master them or as they show they can apply them. Too often, these things are kept secret from the very people who need most to see and understand them—the learners.

6. Don't wait for the big test to assess students. Include regular formative assessment throughout the year. Use a variety of strategies to check up on what students know and can do. You will gain a wealth of information about where the students are. You'll see what they are getting and what they are missing. This will allow you to adjust your instruction frequently to assure that they are gaining the understandings they need.

7. Talk with students about the tests. Students have all kinds of anxieties about standardized tests. They overhear the comments and pick up the worries of parents and teachers. Often they are confused about what the tests are for, or what they contain. Explain why they must take the tests. Assure them that the test will ask about the kinds of things they have been learning. Practice asking questions in the ways the test will present them. Let students practice answering similar questions, making answer choices, coloring in the little bubbles, and discussing how they chose answers. Build their confidence in the process before they encounter it.

> ## Teacher-to-Teacher Tip
>
> *"I'll pass on a great idea I learned in college. It helps relieve my stess about preparing students for standardized tests. Take your students into four imaginary rooms of a 'learning house' with each lesson you teach. In these rooms, they are hooked on the lesson, learn information, bring the concept to life, and demonstrate what they learn. This 'house tour' helps students learn and process the concepts that will show up on their tests—in a very concrete and exciting way."*
>
> *– Jacqueline D., New York*
>
> See page 214 of this book for a sample lesson plan.

Falling in Love Again

Relax! Know your curriculum goals, standards, and expectations well. Know your students and their learning styles. Plan instruction that creatively and purposely covers the standards and concepts they need. Focus on active learning experiences that motivate and captivate students—so that they will remember what you teach. Work toward the growth of your students, and not for the test scores. This is the best way to assure that your students do well on their tests. When you feel that you know what your students need to learn and have control over how they learn it, your stress will recede. Positive, planned, forward-moving, dynamic curriculum is the best defense against the specter of the scary test. You can regain confidence that the textbooks and tests are your friends, and not your enemies. When you do, you will recover some of your affection for your content, your teaching process, and your job.

Me Moments

At a recent workshop, the leader began by asking the teacher participants to describe how they were feeling at this point in the school year. They answered: "stressed," "depleted," exhausted," "overwhelmed," and "discouraged." Then the leader gently nudged participants into playing a physical (and somewhat silly) game. After some initial reluctance, the teachers were drawn into the fun. When the game ended, the leader asked, "How are you feeling now?" Participants reported feeling "relaxed," "energized," "hopeful," and "happy."

This reminded me of the physiological toll that stress takes on our bodies. And it reminded me that movement loosens up all those clenched muscles and stimulates the brain chemicals that lead to positive feelings. So, for your own well-being, add movement to your school days!

- Park in the parking space that is farthest from the school, and walk briskly to your destination.

- Take the stairs instead of the elevator.

- Go outside at recess and shoot a couple of hoops or play a game with your students.

- Take the long way around to your classroom after lunch. Use the school halls for invigorating walks.

Chapter 7 **Tools**

Lessons with the Brain in Mind

Teacher Self-reflection on Lesson Plans

✔	*Given what we know about brain-based learning, I will ask these questions about each lesson or unit I plan:*
	Am I prepared to present the material in a safe, stress-free climate?
	Do the learning activities stimulate many senses?
	Is humor included?
	Are there chances for students to collaborate and discuss?
	Do the learning experiences arouse emotion of some kind?
	Has each student had a chance to translate the concept into another form or teach the concept to someone else?
	Are the concepts connected to visual images?
	Do my strategies relate the concepts to other familiar concepts or previously learned material?
	Are the concepts relevant and interesting to students' real lives?
	Do some of the learning experiences include movement, rhythm, or music?
	Have I given thought to the use of color to help fix ideas in students' long-term memories?
	Do the presentations include something new or unexpected to stimulate the students' brains?
	Is there challenge within the learning activities for each student?
	Is adequate help provided so that no student feels lost or stressed?
	Have I planned a time and way for students to reflect on what they have learned and make their own connections to their lives and knowledge?
	Will students know ahead of time what the goals and expectations are for the upcoming study?

Backward Design

Final Goal

Students will understand or develop:

Lesson-Plan Template

Backward design begins with the end in mind. Clearly identify the big understanding that students must gain. Then work backward to identify how you will know when they reach that goal, and what you will do to see that they do.

Assessment

When the lesson (unit) is completed, students will show their understanding by:

Lesson Activities

These activities will develop the skills and build the understanding, bringing students to the place where they can successfully show (through the assessment) that they have met the goal:

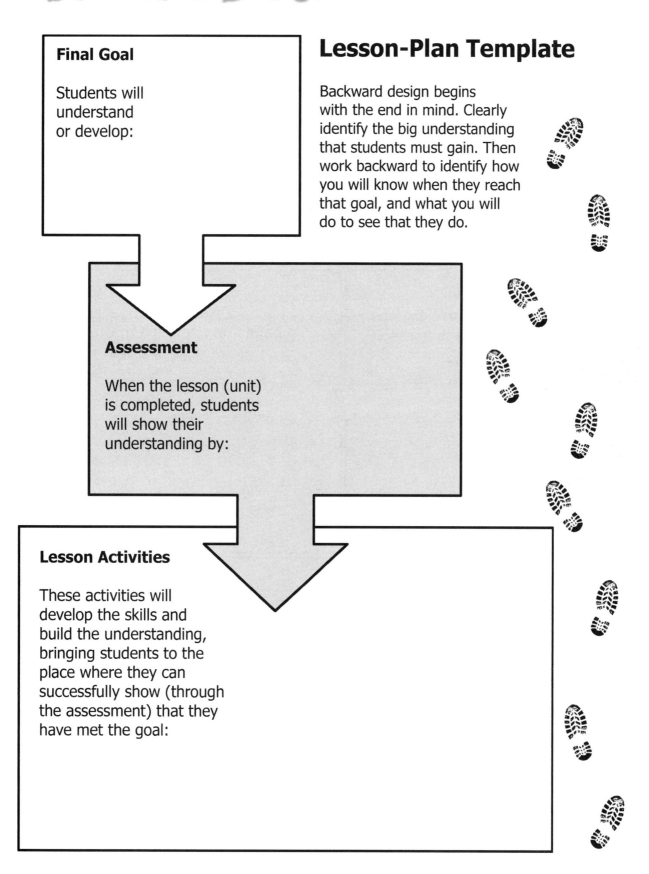

Invitation to Learning
Brain-based Learning Lesson-Plan Template

Lesson Title or Topic:_____

Each lesson will invite students into these rooms.

Entryway
a place to catch students' attention
I will capture students' attention by:

Office or Library
A place for students to hear, see, experience, or research a lesson

Ideas and information will be presented or found in these ways:

Kitchen
a place for students to do a hands-on approach to the lesson
Students will be actively engaged in the following ways:

Family Room
a place for students to reflect on and celebrate what they have learned

These are metacognitive strategies that will be used to get students thinking about their learning:

These are ways students will show what they have learned:

My Assignment Recipe

Describe your assignment in the form of a recipe to show what you did.

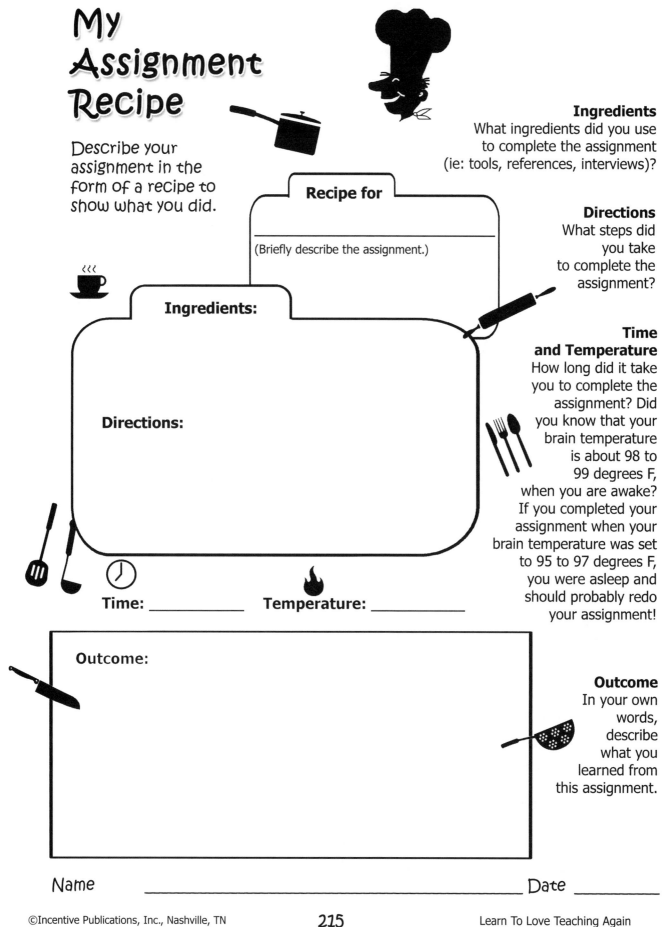

Recipe for

_____

(Briefly describe the assignment.)

Ingredients:

Directions:

Time: _____ Temperature: _____

Outcome:

Ingredients
What ingredients did you use to complete the assignment (ie: tools, references, interviews)?

Directions
What steps did you take to complete the assignment?

Time and Temperature
How long did it take you to complete the assignment? Did you know that your brain temperature is about 98 to 99 degrees F, when you are awake? If you completed your assignment when your brain temperature was set to 95 to 97 degrees F, you were asleep and should probably redo your assignment!

Outcome
In your own words, describe what you learned from this assignment.

Name _____ Date _____

Recommended Diet for Testing

Dear Parent,

Tomorrow the students will be taking a test on
_____.

To give your child the best chance to be at top
thinking performance, please see that he or she . . .

- has a dinner that consists of "brain-boosting
  foods." (See below.)
- gets plenty of sleep. (Consider making bedtime
  a little earlier.)
- has time to eat a healthy breakfast
  (of "brain-boosting foods").
- avoids the kinds of foods listed on the
  "stay away from" list.

Thank you for helping me to
prepare your child for
a successful test!
_____

Brain-boosting Foods

avocados	flaxseed oil
bananas	legumes
lean beef	Brewer's yeast
broccoli	oatmeal
brown rice	oranges
cantaloupe	peanut butter
cheese	peas
chicken	whole grains
nuts	Romaine lettuce
kale	salmon
eggs	soybeans
milk	spinach
tuna	Brussels sprouts
wheat germ	turkey
yogurt	wheat germ

Stay Away From

artificial food colorings
artificial sweeteners
sodas
corn syrup
sugary foods
high-sugar drinks
hydrogenated fats
white bread
sweet pastries
sugared cereals
fatty or greasy foods

The Principal Is Never Stressed—Right?

You know you are a principal under stress if you have an open-door policy, but your office is always closed.

On my first day as principal, the outgoing administrator reviewed all the critical policies and procedures. Then she closed her office door and lowered her voice to a whisper. "The most important thing you need to know is this," she said slowly and seriously. "Have a back door to your office. Always have a planned escape route."

I smiled and gave some vague response. But in my head, I scoffed, "My door will remain open. Any teacher, parent, staff member, or student will be welcome in my office at any time. It will be a place of friendship, counsel, and laughter!"

Two years later, with some creative planning and one tight squeeze behind an immense file cabinet, there were a total of three escape routes (four, if you count hiding under the desk).

The principal has all the demands of educational leadership and management. In addition, she serves as the school's public relations expert. She represents the school to the community, parents, teachers, unions, and a host of school-related organizations. And, in her spare time, she does things like manage a budget, chaperone a dance, counsel staff members, calm a biting child, replace fuses, oversee a school improvement plan, and babysit the third grade's pet snake.

Losing the Love

It might happen gradually. Or it might happen quickly. The optimism, energy, and hope drain away under the burdens of the administrative life. The long days, evening meetings, weekend responsibilities, accountability, test results, paperwork (oh! the paperwork!), more meetings, and complaints—all conspire against peace and fulfillment. And in the midst of their overload, principals often stress their teachers and other staff members. In many schools, it's hard to tell who stresses whom the most—there's just a lot of tension and frenzy down every hallway.

Who Would Want This Job?

In the past several years, the National Association of Elementary School Principals (NAESP) and the National Association of Secondary School Principals (NASSP) have commissioned two studies about recruitment of principals. Not only do the studies show a strong link between effective school leadership and successful school improvement efforts. Disturbingly, the studies also confirm a shortage of qualified candidates who will take principal jobs. Some of the reasons behind the dwindling numbers of educators who want the job of principal are:

- new curriculum standards
- increased importance of testing
- difficult social issues
- minimal support for the challenges of the job
- shortage of resources to do the job
- compensation not commensurate with the job
- expanded job description
- lack of adequate professional development for administrators

According to Vincent Ferrandino, NAESP's executive director, "The role of the principal has changed dramatically. The demands that are being placed on the individual are such that very few qualified people are willing to step up to the plate any longer and take on those responsibilities" (NAESP, 2004).

W. Norton Grubb, University of California at Berkeley professor who studies educational management, says, "[The life of a school principal] is absolutely insane . . . We're living at a time when we are demanding that principals all be heroes. Well, there aren't that many heroes in this country in any line of work" (Guterman, 2007).

If I were to write the list of roles in my job description, I'd have to include: physical plant manager; educational planner; counselor for parents, teachers, and students; disciplinarian; framer of the school culture; benefits expert; negotiator; general manager; marketing representative; budget officer; instructional leader; education advocate; community liaison; human resources representative; employer; cheerleader; role model; truant officer; policy enforcer; crisis manager; friend to students, staff members, and parents; narcotics agent; public relations officer; and peacemaker.

In the past, the pool of potential administrators came from the ranks of veteran teachers. But fewer and fewer of those folks want the job—because they see the workload. The small increase in compensation is not worth the increased stress.

There is no question that principals are stressed and stretched. The job goes beyond what seems humanly possible. Many are buried in conflict resolution, troubleshooting, and paperwork— far away from the instructional leadership they envisioned. And, in this era of ever-growing accountability, principals fear losing their jobs if they don't bring their schools up to standards. So it's no wonder that the job has high turnover, and that some of the best people coming up through the schools with leadership potential want nothing to do with the job.

Lonely at the Top

The official job description and responsibilities are daunting enough. But rarely do these show anything close to the whole picture. There are things they don't teach in "principal school." In my tenure as school principal, I have personally . . .

. . . stood between a teacher and an out-of-control parent who was threatening serious physical harm;

. . . chased (and caught) teens selling drugs from the back school parking lot;

. . . driven, during the school day, to the county jail to post bail for a staff member;

. . . hosted 30 angry parents at once in my office (standing room only) and listened for an hour to their demands;

. . . rescued a student in the school yard from the jaws of a fierce neighborhood dog (after which, the dog bit me);

. . . dealt with two on-campus fires, neither of which matched any of the fire drill scenarios we practiced;

. . . talked a staff member out of chasing down her estranged husband with a gun;

. . . taken at least a dozen employees to the emergency room;

. . . overseen the installation of a rabbit farm on the kindergarten porch;

. . . accompanied a fearful staff member to the gynecologist;

. . . made a presentation at a school board meeting with a raging fever and swollen throat; and

. . . planned funerals for two school colleagues and attended the funerals of three school parents and two students.

Learn To Love Teaching Again

Most of the administrative tasks and worries—be they high-visibility or behind the scenes, in the job description or not—I've had to handle alone. Teachers work in a building packed with colleagues who face similar challenges and share similar rewards. But the administrator often has no one with whom to commiserate. Rarely is there another staff member in the building who has the same kinds of problems. And then there is the matter of confidentiality. Many of the principal's greatest stressors are things that cannot be shared. The natural isolation of the job makes a tough situation even more stressful.

Principals also report that they feel a weight of responsibility for all the staff members in their school. They have to make decisions that affect the schedules, workloads, and paychecks of their staff members. Often they must act as a buffer between employees or between a staff member and a parent or another administrator. It's hard for a principal to solicit or find support in making the hard choices and defending others. These are lonely tasks.

A Bad Rap for Principals

rap—*n* a negative quality or characteristic associated with a person or an object; a negative and often undeserved reputation or charge

Off to the principal's office with you!

If you can't behave, I'll send you to the principal's office!

Siri, stop that or I'll be inviting the principal here very soon.

Martha, the principal is watching you!

Tucker, do you want the principal to get her paddle and spank you?

Danny, are you begging for a trip to the principal's office?

One more remark like that, Janie, and you'll be explaining yourself to the principal.

Sam, please escort Max to the principal's office. And Max, Principal Malari will not be pleased about this.

I have personally heard parents or teachers say such things about me. I grit my teeth and try to assure the child that I am not the school monster out roaming the halls looking to eat or spank students. Recently, in a mall, I heard a mother say to her misbehaving son, "See that police officer there? If you don't behave, he's going to take you away to jail." I felt a rush of empathy for the policeman.

As if the overwhelming demands, hard decisions, and grueling schedule were not enough—principals have to contend with that mean ogre reputation! Teachers, other staff members, parents, and even fellow students use the principal as a threat or a "weapon" or other scary "tool" to get kids to behave. In many schools, the principal has a reputation that is fearsome. It is no wonder that this is probably the most frequently repeated principal joke:

Chuckle!

Did you hear about the mother who cheerfully called upstairs to her son, "Time to get up for school!"

"But I don't want to go to school," the son whined, putting a pillow over his head. "I hate that school! The teachers don't like me, and all the kids are terrible. They make fun of me!"

Stepping into her son's room and opening the blinds, she replied, "I understand, Son. But you still have to go to school. You're the principal."

Step Out of the Office (Advice to Principals)

Clearly, teachers are in danger of burnout from unrelieved stress, and so is the principal. Here are some important facts (I can supply you with research, but you only need experience and a chat with a few teachers to know they are true):

- Teachers have less stress when they know their administrators are "in their corner."
- A principal is often a major source of stress for his or her teachers.

A positive partnership is the very best weapon against the effects of stress in the school. In such a partnership, the principal and staff work toward the same goals to nurture one another in a lower-stress environment. As the leader, you can tackle this task with two actions—which are strikingly intertwined with one another:

- Take clear, specific steps to manage and reduce your own stress.
- Take clear, specific steps to create a school climate and relationships that reduce the stress for your teachers.

It is out of my own experience as an administrator that I tell you the above actions are inextricably connected. Success (or lack thereof) at one affects success (or lack thereof) at the others. If you do a good job of reducing your own stress, you will cause less stress for your staff and be able to help reduce the stress they have. When you build the kinds of relationships and promote the kinds of strategies that lead to a supportive climate for your staff, you will in turn have less stress. And remember that students and their achievement will be affected by the anxieties of the adults. Minimizing stress for yourself and your teachers will improve learning conditions for the students.

1. Manage and Reduce Your Own Stress

Most of the advice in this book is as useful for principals as it is for teachers. Be aware of the signs and effects of stress and burnout, and review the previous chapters with yourself in mind. But there are burdens unique to administrators. Here are some stress-busting suggestions given by administrators especially for other administrators:

- **Find something to laugh about several times a day.** Much of your job involves dealing with crises and solving serious problems. Laughter automatically reverses physiological stress responses and encourages positive attitudes. It makes you feel more up to the challenges.

I will not be stressed about . . .
   . . . the threatening dogs on the playground.
   . . . students calling me "The Terminator."
   . . . the 23 teachers who are out with the flu.
   . . . tonight's school board review of my performance.
   . . . the teacher who sends me the same student twice an hour.

- **Listen to music in your office.** Choose something that is pleasing or soothing to you. Many principals recommend classical music. I find that it's even calming for the students who get sent to your office. Let them sit for a few minutes, just breathing and listening to the music. The anxiety level can be lowered before you start the discussion of whatever behavior brought the student to your side.

- **Spend time with students.** They are great stress relievers. Have lunch with them, chat, or take a walk down the hall or outside. Get into the classroom and help students learn something new.

- **Keep a good book handy.** Grab a few minutes a day to read the next chapter in a suspenseful story or the next good joke or the next fascinating fact.

- **Take a few short breaks every day.** Try deep breathing, relaxation, or meditation techniques.

- **Delegate!** Share the workload where you can, and let go of tasks that others can do. Trust that they can do these tasks as well as you could do them yourself.

- **Share leadership and decision making.** Realize that you don't have to do everything alone. First of all, you will have a wider pool of good ideas for handling tough situations—and thereby may come up with better solutions. Second, this approach will cut down on some of the isolation and loneliness of your job.

- **Don't procrastinate.** Take on the hard or unpleasant stuff without avoidance. Work hard on good time management.

- **Get away.** Arrange with your board or superintendent for permission to work at home one day a quarter.

- **Leave your work at school some of the time.** Do your best to leave your work at school and really spend a weekend or evening with your family or friends. And when you are with them, BE with them—and drop the school worries.

- **Exercise regularly.** The busy all-day, evening, and weekend demands on a principal make this hard. But it is critical to managing your stress.

- **Get out of your office.** Don't become isolated. Talk with teachers and all other staff members, and connect with students.

- **Nurture relationships with your staff members.** If you are able to keep these relationships honest, trusting, and respectful—you will minimize your stress (and theirs).

- **Nurture relationships with other administrators.** Support one another and share ideas. Also make plans to enjoy these colleagues in nonwork situations. Join a volleyball league or start a dance class together.

- **Make your office a pleasant place for yourself and others who visit.** Insist on good lighting. Add green plants. Get some fresh air into the office. Keep it uncluttered. Have a comfortable place for visitors to sit.

- **Have a life outside school.** Spend time with nonschool friends doing nonschool activities.

- **Stop periodically to reflect.** Ask yourself how you are doing on this mission to reduce your stress. See the self-reflection checklist, "Stress Relief for Administrators," found in the Tools section at the end of this chapter.

Teacher-to-Administrator Tip

"I'm not looking for a buddy. I've worked for many administrators during my career. I find it easiest to work with those that are friendly, approachable, and have an intact sense of humor. I've known some who are unapproachable, unpredictable, and too rigid with rules. That type of administrator adds stress to the working environment."

— *Experienced elementary teacher, Florida*

Learn To Love Teaching Again

2. Reduce Stress for Your Teachers

Jan Richards, education professor at the National University in Ontario, California, interviewed K-8 teachers in their first five years of teaching to identify principal behaviors that they felt most encouraged them (2005). The behaviors receiving highest rankings fell into the category of emotional support (May/Jun 2007). Teachers defined "emotional support" in this way: the principal was encouraging, available, and understanding—resulting in teachers feeling empowered and confident. Teachers whose principals were not emotionally supportive felt angry, negative, frustrated, and less confident in their abilities as educators.

From the results of these interviews, Dr. Richards created a list of 22 positive principal behaviors and attitudes and used them to survey an additional 100 teachers. A few years later, she used this list again to survey a group of 75 teachers who had taught six to ten years and another group of 75 teachers with 11 or more years' experience. All three groups rated the same five principal behaviors (shown below) as most valued (Jan/Feb 2007).

1. The principal respects and values teachers as professionals.
2. The principal supports teachers in matters of student discipline.
3. The principal has an open-door policy.
4. The principal is fair, honest, and trustworthy.
5. The principal supports teachers in dealing with parents.

Richard Ingersoll, professor in the Graduate School of Education at the University of Pennsylvania has studied the reasons for teacher turnover. His results have shown that the level of administrative support for teachers in a school is a major factor in whether teachers stay in the profession (2001).

John B. Craig explored the relationship between the emotional intelligence of principals and teacher job satisfaction. (Emotionally intelligent principals are defined as those who are attuned to their own emotions, attuned to others' emotions, adept at managing their emotions and emotions of others, and skilled at building positive relationships.) Craig found that teachers expressed greater contentment and job satisfaction in settings where the principals exhibited high emotional intelligence (2008).

Such studies as these, along with common sense and the tales of many teachers, tell the story about how

It's our principal's suggestion for stress relief.

principals have the power to make a difference in teacher morale and job satisfaction. Ineffective leadership lowers morale; raises anxiety; leads to disillusionment; and leaves teachers feeling insecure, belittled, or not trusted. When teachers work with a competent leader who values and supports them, they are more enthusiastic and positive about their jobs. They are far less likely to suffer from debilitating job stress.

HOW A PRINCIPAL CAN HELP REDUCE TEACHER STRESS

Take advantage of this influence that lies in your hands, and take steps to reduce distress, boost morale, and help your teachers love their jobs and do a better job. Include the following ideas in your own repertoire of positive behaviors.

- **Note the characteristics of "emotionally intelligent" principals** (two paragraphs above). Develop and nurture these characteristics in yourself.

- **Value your teachers as professionals.** Treat them as knowledgeable educators, prepared for their jobs. Find many chances to let each one know he or she is valued by you. Avoid any behaviors that communicate superiority or condescension.

- **Support your teachers**—consistently and visibly. Support them in their dealings with students and parents.

- **Guide your school to a clear discipline policy,** give teachers training to effectively manage their classrooms, and support them in matters of student discipline.

- **Be honest, fair, and trustworthy.** See to it that, if asked, your teachers would use these words to describe you.

- **Show interest in your teachers as individual persons.** This goes beyond playing a game of golf now and then or attending a staff book club. Know their names, their jobs, something about their families and their day-to-day responsibilities. (I am shocked to meet teachers who say their principal doesn't know the names of many staff members. This happens all too often.)

- **Develop and maintain a safe, disciplined learning environment.** This will support staff efforts toward student learning.

- **Follow through.** When teachers see a principal with a clear plan, leading in a clear direction, their stress will subside and their trust will rise.

- **Set and communicate clear parameters.** People usually function best when they understand their boundaries, even if they have disagreements with them. Don't confuse teachers by having fuzzy or wandering boundaries.

　　　　Learn To Love Teaching Again

- **Be flexible.** Avoid a "one-size-fits-all" approach to leadership. When a principal responds to all situations the same way, stress levels rise. A teacher may need supportive understanding one day and a dose of reality the next. One teacher may need the principal to stand beside her during a parent confrontation. Another teacher may need the principal to stand between her and the parent.

- **Don't micromanage.** If teachers sense that you need to control every detail of school life, they will feel that their competency is undermined.

- **Keep teachers informed.** Set a good system for letting all your staff members know—with plenty of advance warning, policies, plans, changes, schedules, and expectations. There are few things more stressful that not knowing what is going on.

- **Be visible.** Get out there and relate to staff members and students. (The name plate on the door is not enough.) When a principal is visible and takes the time to establish supportive relationships, everyone in the school feels more secure. And the principal feels more connected.

- **Be present.** Keep your door open. Don't hide from any of your staff members. If you are not actually present—physically and emotionally, staff members will feel deserted. Just seeing the principal walking the hallways, greeting students and teachers, promotes an atmosphere of calm and confidence.

- **Set a model for calm problem solving and optimism.** When a crisis or issue arises, don't rant or panic or otherwise add to the frenzy that already exists inside some of your staff. Show that you believe problems can be solved.

- **Keep confidences.** Never, ever gossip about any staff member or pass on personal or professional information.

- **Make the teachers' lounge an oasis.** Take a hand in making this a pleasant, peaceful place. And, if you can, provide a calm, quiet place other than the teachers' lounge to which teachers can escape during the school day.

- **Admit to the reality of stress in the school.** Plan (and implement) specific programs for reducing and managing stress. Make this a part of your professional development plan.

- **Admit to the presence of problems.** Plan (and implement) specific strategies for improving communication and for solving problems.

- **Find ways to support and help your teachers.** Take over a class now and then to give a teacher a much-needed break. Supply ideas, resources, materials, and references with teachers. Share effective strategies. For some other ways to support your teachers, use the ideas in the Tools section at the end of this chapter.

HOW A PRINCIPAL CAN CREATE A POSITIVE EMOTIONAL CLIMATE

Is it true that the principal has put a Valium salt lick in the faculty lounge?

No, but I've used the new karaoke machine that she bought for the teachers' workroom!

Teachers are less stressed when they work in a positive environment. A principal has the power to affect the emotional climate positively or negatively. The principal who effectively manages the emotional climate of his or her school . . .

. . . **believes.** The principal acknowledges that stress is always present in one form or another in school, but believes that stress can be managed.

. . . **plans.** The principal has a plan to meet staff stress head-on, and the plan involves many strategies (from instigating laughter in the faculty lounge or monthly social get-togethers to school-sponsored exercise programs and specific professional development related to stress).

. . . **shows by example.** The principal incorporates examples of stress-reducing habits into his day. The teachers see the principal taking a lap around the track at lunchtime or sitting in on the before-school chess club for a quick game.

. . . **controls the environment.** Noise and confusion begets noise and confusion. The effective administrator takes steps to control the pandemonium that can be found in common areas such as the cafeteria and hallways.

. . . **ensures safety.** Stress will automatically be high for a teacher that feels threatened or afraid. The same holds true for students. The principal must be proactive in controlling factors such as bullying, hazing, physical violence, and abusive language—or any other form of intimidation.

. . . **communicates clear expectations.** People feel safer, more secure and less stressed when they understand the expectations. When a principal keeps teachers guessing about what is coming next or about what will be required or approved, everyone is left on edge.

. . . **shares leadership.** Lack of control over one's work environment is a recipe for stress. The principal delegates leadership, whenever possible, increasing staff ownership.

Learn To Love Teaching Again

. . . consciously avoids being a stressor. Principals can wreak havoc on an entire school. Be they subtle or overt, many behaviors confuse, frighten, or otherwise break the trust of teachers, parents, or students. The effective principal intentionally screens her own demeanor and methods of operating. Her behaviors do not include fear tactics, judgment, sarcasm, pitting or playing people against each other, humiliation, intimidation, punishment, emotional manipulation, playing favorites, disrespect, threats, palpable disapproval, demeaning, shaming, or withdrawal.

HOW A PRINCIPAL CAN BUILD TRUSTING RELATIONSHIPS

Northwest Regional Educational Laboratory examined research on the issue of trust in schools within the context of school improvement. Implicit in their findings were several recommendations for ways principals could contribute to trusting relationships with their teachers. These tips, adapted from their booklet *Building Trusting Relationships for School Improvement: Implications for Principals and Teachers* (2003), encourage the following behaviors in principals:

- **Demonstrate integrity.** Be honest in all contacts and interactions with teachers. Honesty is not something that can be faked, nor can it be practiced only some of the time. The principal has the primary responsibility for creating trusting relationships, and there is little chance of doing so if you do not demonstrate integrity.

- **Care and connect.** Take a personal interest in all members of your school community and take specific actions to let them know you care. Genuine care and concern for others leads to trust.

- **Be available.** Make it easy for teachers to find you and get the help they need. Encourage open communication and model it yourself.

- **Model effective communication.** Trust can exist only within a climate of open communication.

- **Be comfortable with dissent.** The valuing of differing opinions and views is an integral part of honest, open communication. Build a climate in which teachers can disagree with you and with each other without fear of any sort of reprisal.

- **Include teachers in decision making.** Ask for input and insights from teachers, and value that input.

- **Support innovation.** Welcome experimentation. Trust and encourage teachers to take chances and try new ideas.

- **Help to reduce teachers' sense of vulnerability.** Members of the teaching profession today bear plenty of scrutiny and criticism. Be a buffer for your teachers by valuing them. When teachers are constantly on the alert for potential reprimands or feel as though every move is being watched for mistakes, trust cannot grow.

- **Provide teachers with basic resources.** Support your teachers by seeing that they have the resources they need. Teachers who trust their principals know that they can make requests, and that if resources are not provided in a timely manner, there could be a reason beyond the administrator's control.

- **Be willing to take action when teachers are ineffective.** Everyone knows when a teacher is ineffective, inept, or just downright mean to students. A principal will build trust when he takes action in this situation—when he is strong enough to be a leader and correct the problem.

HOW A PRINCIPAL CAN LOWER THE STRESS OF TEACHER EVALUATION

In each of my first few years as a principal, my superintendent, the school board, my teachers, all other staff members, and my students' parents all took part in my evaluation. I was constantly under scrutiny. There were days I longed to strap on a pair of roller skates and serve burgers and shakes to people waiting in their cars! I'd like to forget these experiences, but I revisit them often—for one reason: I want to remember what it feels like to be under that kind of scrutiny. "Why on earth?" you ask! Here's why: among my many responsibilities is that of teacher evaluation. And for most teachers (if not all), the process of job evaluation is a major stressor. I can do this more compassionately and effectively if I remember what it is like to be the "evaluatee"!

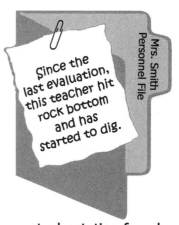

Mrs. Smith
Personnel File

Since the last evaluation, this teacher hit rock bottom and has started to dig.

– actual notation found on a teacher evaluation

The best advice I can offer to principals is this: show up often in classrooms. Get to know your teachers well. Get to know their classes, their challenges, their teaching styles, and their strengths. Stop by to read to students, help out with a project, learn some new software, or join in a math scavenger hunt.

Teacher evaluation should not be a once-a-year, or even once-a-quarter, formal, planned visit. This doesn't mean that you will never sit in on a whole lesson.

But too often, this process is relegated to a sterile, infrequent 15-minute visit followed by some paper form where the principal circles numbers or completes a checklist. This is not the best way to find out about a teacher's skills and effectiveness. Sustained contact, frequent visits, and a supportive relationship are the habits that will help you learn the real story. Some call this practice "the principal walkies." The principal is present, available, visible, and participatory—not a stationary, detached, critical observer.

What do you observe when you walk into a classroom? Observe the learners. Peek over the shoulders of busy students or listen in on group discussions. As a principal observer, you can tell so much about the efficacy of the teacher by the activity of the students. Are the students engaged? Are they focusing on the assigned task? Was there a feeling of comfort and safety in the room? Are there smiles and laugher? Are students working collaboratively, helping one another? Do they have appropriate materials? Is there evidence of creativity?

There are many benefits to this practice:

- Teachers get used to seeing your face at the door and in the classroom. They know you are there to participate—in a partnership. You take on more of a supportive, collegial role.

- The principal appears to be a partner rather than a critic. Teachers begin to see that you want to really know them and their teaching style.

- This frequent contact helps to build the trusting relationship between teacher and principal. The evaluation process, then, can be seen as affirmation of strengths and guidance toward future goals.

- When you do have sit-down, evaluative discussions, you have specific, concrete examples at your fingertips. Your feedback can be very helpful because you actually know what has been going on in the classroom.

- When evaluation is an ongoing process, rather than a short visit, you will be more accurate at identifying effective and ineffective teaching.

- You get to know teachers and their classes in a new way. You can better advocate for someone you know. I remember times when irate parents stopped by my office to complain about what the teacher was doing in the classroom (based on the *completely* unbiased reports of the student, if you will forgive a bit of sarcasm). In such cases, I would say something like, "Hmmm, Mr. Conrad, I was just in that classroom this morning, and I can assure you that your little Francine was not being picked on by her teacher. Francine was busy working with a group of friends on a story web in reading class. She was smiling and contributing to the project; in fact, I eavesdropped a bit and heard her suggest a really great idea that all the other children loved!"

- You are uniquely poised to handle problems. With trust already in place, it will be a much smoother process to tackle serious difficulties that a teacher may have in teaching or managing students. There is a much better chance that the teacher can hear the problems, accept suggestions, and make improvements.

Chuckle!

Boy: Our principal is sure dumb!
Girl: Do you know who I am?
Boy: No.
Girl: I am the principal's daughter!
Boy: Do you know who I am?
Girl: No.
Boy: Thank goodness!

Getting Beyond the Door (Advice to Teachers)

One day as I juggled phone calls, meeting agendas, and paperwork (dividing piles of paper into two piles: "Fun Stuff" and "Stuff I Don't Want to Do"), three kindergarten students, holding hands, squeezed through my doorway. The child in the middle, her huge eyes watery and her skin pale, trembled.

"How can I help you?" I inquired.

One of the bookend students said, "Teacher told us to bring Roseanna down here. Teacher said Roseanna was bad and she had to come see the prince-bubble."

Clamping down my lips to keep from laughing, I managed to push out, "So, Roseanna, what happened?"

The little girl looked at the floor and whispered, "I don't know." The two accompanying young military-guards-in-training gave Roseanna one last long look, let go of her hands, relocked their hands in the kindergarten death grip, and made their way back to class. Roseanna and I stood looking at one another. Clearly the teacher was at the end of his rope with Roseanna. But what was I supposed to do with the child? Whatever the infraction, it had happened at least ten minutes earlier—well outside the statue of limitations of a kindergartner's memory. All Roseanna knew was that she was threatened with coming to my office, and that was a scary thing. She had learned a lesson quickly: not to like the prince-bubble or the prince-bubble's office. (Thank goodness for my fish tank, worm farm, a wind-up monkey that somersaults right off the edge of the desk, and stuffed animal collection.)

If you're a teacher reading this chapter, I hope you're getting the message that principals, too, have plenty of stress. This means that your principal should empathize with your struggle to hang onto the love of your job! Discipline is just one of the potential stressors you and the principal share. Since you do share so many, the task of avoiding burnout and stress is best tackled through joint efforts of the leader and teachers. If your principal has an open-door policy (or even a partially-open-door policy), do your best to have the courage to cross the threshold. Most principals really do want to have a healthy, working partnership with their teachers. Here are 12 things that you can do to contribute to that partnership:

1. Encourage your principal to address the problem of stress at your school. Suggest this as a professional development goal, and participate in efforts to find solutions.

2. Whether or not you agree with or support everything your principal believes or does, treat him with respect. Do not join the gossip mill or get into the habit of bad-mouthing the principal.

3. Do your best to debunk for your students the myth of the "monster" in the principal's office. Help them see that the principal is one of their teachers, too. Invite the principal to participate in interesting activities in your classroom. Promote warmth, trust, and respect for your principal.

4. Do not use your principal as the first line of defense in discipline matters. Establish strong classroom management procedures so that you can handle your own discipline. When you constantly send students to the principal's office, you undermine your own authority by letting your students think you have no control, and you strain your relationship with the

> ### Teacher-to-Teacher Tip
>
> *"You usually don't get to pick your principal. So be direct and ask the principal to explain his or her administrative style and preferred means of communication."*
> – Becky, elementary teacher, Arizona

principal. Determine what the problem is, get some advice for handling it, and try to work it out yourself. Talk to the principal about it. Reserve that trip to the office for situations that are extraordinarily difficult or dangerous. Remember the boy in the story with the sheep and the wolf. Go ahead and cry wolf, but do it when you really need the help.

5. Find out what communication method is most comfortable for your principal. Would she prefer questions in writing or by e-mail? Does she respond best if you memo her prior to your visit, giving her a heads-up on the topic? Is it best to make an appointment or to catch her on the fly?

6. If your principal comes in early or stays late to get some work done, respect that time. Always inquire whether visiting at that time is appropriate. Oftentimes principals cannot get paperwork done during school hours and need some quiet time to meet deadlines.

7. When you have a moment to chat with your principal, do not assume there is time for the *War and Peace* version of your concern. Think of it as a visit to the doctor, who wants to treat you, but also has a waiting room full of patients to see. Be thorough, yet concise, in your explanation.

8. If you are approaching the principal with a problem or you have a concern that something is not working, bring a possible solution. The principal may not choose to go with your idea, but she will appreciate the fact that you thought things through and don't just expect her to solve all your problems.

9. Understand that you probably do not have the big picture on all issues at your school. The resolution to a problem may seem obvious to you, but the principal has to consider many things before making even the simplest decision: laws, school policies, current and future budgets, current and projected enrollment figures, the physical plant, reaction of the school board, input from the superintendent, how the decision will affect the teacher and students across the hall, commitments made to other teachers, information about a child's background you may not know, and impact on the community (just to name a few).

10. Assume that the principal is your advocate. Until experience proves otherwise, give the principal the benefit of this doubt. Don't be a part of creating a "them against us" mentality regarding your administration.

11. When the principal visits for a teacher evaluation, resist the urge to have a contrived dog-and-pony show performance. (Take it from me, a seasoned principal: these can be spotted within ten seconds and they always look contrived.) Welcome the chance to show off your honest efforts and to demonstrate instruction infused with your personality, gifts, and talents. Be yourself and extend collegiate warmth to your principal's presence. This will assure that when it comes time for constructive guidance, the principal will be able to give you valuable and sincere input.

12. Don't make judgments about the principal's activities. No matter when you see the school principal, she most likely IS doing **something**. What looks random to an observer is no doubt purposeful to the administrator. If he is roaming the hallway, your principal may be checking to see if the new cleaning crew is doing their job. If she is standing out on the front sidewalk before school, she might be checking to see if Alexandria's father is under the influence of alcohol as he drops her off at school. If he brings his lunch to the staff lounge, he may be sending a statement to chronic gossipers to "cease and desist."

A Relationship of Mutual Trust

Chuckle!

Mr. Kurson, the new school principal, was astounded to find the door to the supply closet wide open. He was more shocked to see teachers bustling in and out, carrying piles of textbooks and other instructional materials. At his former school, supplies were kept under lock and key, and doled out only after triplicate copies of the appropriate forms had been signed and approved. Mr. Kurson took the custodian aside.

"Do you think this is wise," the principal whispered loudly, "to trust the teachers with open access to the supplies?"

After studying Mr. Kurson for a moment, the custodian replied, "We trust them with the children, don't we?"

Remember that game where you fall backwards, trusting that the partner standing behind will catch you? Even if you've done it before, there is usually trepidation when you take the fall. Questions like these flash through your mind: *What if my partner thinks it's funny to see me hit the ground? What if my partner isn't quite ready at the moment I fall? What if my partner really does not like me as much as I think she does? What if she is not strong enough to hold me?*

It's always risky to trust someone. As a principal, you could assume that your teachers will balk at their responsibilities, react angrily to a policy, or be resistant to new ideas—and protect yourself behind a "me against them" shield. As a teacher, you could assume that the principal expects perfection, feels superior, or will constantly judge you—and protect yourself behind an "us against her" shield. Such stances will increase stress for all parties and will diminish chances of a successful learning environment for students. Trust is always far more nurturing and productive than suspicion or fear.

In a 2009 study, researchers Robert Moody and James Barrett studied stress patterns of teachers and administrators (2009). Their research concluded that:

- Administrators are highly stressed.
- Administrators cause stress for teachers.
- Administrators know their teachers are stressed.
- Teaching is stressful.
- Teachers are aware of their stress (even if they don't cope with it well).
- Teacher and administrator stress affects the students and their achievement.

Though disturbing, these conclusions give us all a thumbnail sketch of the issue and show the interconnectedness of the lives of teachers and administrators. Given that both jobs are stressful, there is hope for mutual understanding and support within a school staff. And of prime importance is the acknowledgement that the students and their achievement are a part of the equation. So the urgency to address stress in a principal-teacher partnership applies not only to the welfare of the adults, but to the very basis of our reason for being educators—to help children learn.

A trusting relationship between a teacher and a principal cannot be one-sided. Both must work to prove reliability and to earn respect. Yes, the onus is on the school's leader, as he is the one in the more powerful position, and thus, the one to set the tone. But it behooves each teacher to make efforts to contribute. It is not the principal's responsibility alone to establish the trusting relationship. Both need to know that when they fall, someone will be there to catch them—and when they succeed, someone will be there to cheer.

We asked elementary, middle-school, and high-school teachers to describe characteristics of teachers with whom it is easiest to build respectful, trusting relationships (the kinds of teachers that they like to hire). In turn, we asked elementary, middle-school, and high-school teachers to identify characteristics of effective principals that they appreciate. What follows is a sampling of their answers.

What Teachers Say

My principal always practices what he preaches. When he presents information to us during in-service sessions, the principal demonstrates a good instructional model, which we could then take back to our classrooms.

– Elizabeth Link, middle-school teacher, Ohio

I am never forced to teach the same way my peers teach. The principal gives us leeway and professional respect, which allows us to develop our own styles and create unique classroom experiences.

– Leah Lederer, elementary school teacher, Idaho

My former principal always took the time to praise us when she saw something she liked.

– Walker Nemat, middle-school teacher, Delaware

Our principal puts a huge emphasis on professional development. It is clear that he works hard to make in-service days interesting and related to the instructional focus. He also encourages us to be innovative within our own classrooms. And then he gives us time at staff meetings to talk about what did and did not work.

– Sarah Minot, high-school teacher, California

The teachers receive constant feedback from the principal. During our evaluations, he does not just give advice. Because he has spent time each week poking around in our classrooms, he knows what is going on and he always makes time to give us a thumbs-up or offer constructive criticism. Teachers are able to improve all year long, and there are no surprises at evaluation time.

— Patricia Bryan, high-school teacher, Hawaii

We are always encouraged to improve ourselves and to continue to learn. The principal puts literature about workshops and seminars in our boxes and gives us professional articles to read before each teacher meeting. I like that the principal cares about my professional growth.

— Jeffrey Laurens, middle-school teacher, Louisiana

My principal set up a peer coaching program, which not only helps the new teachers, but always teaches something new to us veterans as well.

— Matt Toole, high-school teacher, West Virginia

Teacher-to-Teacher Tip

"It is a MUST to have a healthy, open, and trusting relationship with your administrator. This is your best source for advice and support in any situation."
— Stephanie Smith, elementary teacher, Texas

What Principals Say

I love to work with teachers who are passionate about learning—who, with their enthusiasm will be excited about delivering instruction and will therefore excite the students about receiving instruction.

— Rich McCauley, high-school principal, New Jersey

I look for a teacher who is naturally comfortable with kids, who respects and honors their individuality—someone to whom kids are instinctively drawn. It is a hard-to-name quality. But if a teacher possesses it, she is a natural Pied Piper to her students, and instruction becomes that much more effective.

— Geoff Boswell, middle-school principal, Kentucky

Compassion is at the top of my list. A teacher needs to be able to understand and empathize with his students. You cannot just teach curriculum anymore without recognizing the learning, emotional, and physical challenges many of our students bring to the classroom.

— Bill Hodgeman, elementary school principal, Illinois

The ideal teacher shows a passion for education. I am passionate about my students and my job, and I look for that same positive energy from my staff.

— Robin Duncan, high-school principal, New Mexico

The teacher should have a sense of humor. He should be willing to laugh at himself and to inject a little bit of fun into instruction. A teacher who takes himself too seriously quickly loses any connection to his students. A sense of humor also comes in handy when dealing with potentially difficult situations, such as working with colleagues and parents.

— Candace Smith, high-school principal, Massachusetts

A good teacher must be a good team player.

— Ranya Taleb, middle-school principal, Georgia

I want to work with teachers who have great flexibility—who can roll with the punches. In education, we never know what each day will bring. A teacher can react stressfully to each unexpected curve thrown her way; or she can assess the situation, deal with it to the best of her ability, and move on.

— Kaye Dawkins, elementary school principal, Vermont

I want teachers who understand that change is a challenge, not an imposition.

— Robert King, middle-school principal, Oregon

MEMO: from Principal McSpectre

TO: all staff

RE: My Open Door Policy
Your principal welcomes you to bring all concerns directly to her immediately.

Office Hours: OPEN all the time!

~~M - W: 5:15 am – 5:17 am~~
~~Th-: noon to 12:04 pm~~
~~Closed Fridays~~

Falling in Love Again

A respectful, trusting relationship between the teachers and the leader in a school may be just about the best stress-buster of all. Do not underestimate the importance and power of such a partnership. In a school with this mutually supportive climate, you can almost hear the "whoosh" of tension leaving the building. It is only in an atmosphere where the principal feels he is working with a cooperative team of teachers who respect and trust him that his passion for the job can truly flourish. It is an atmosphere where teachers feel valued, supported, trusted, and safe enough to love teaching again.

Me Moment

Here is a true pampering tactic for the weary principal (or teacher). Pick up a cucumber on the way home from school and use it to soothe your burning eyes and aching head. Slice the cucumber, keep two slices, and chill the rest. Lie back on a couch, bed, or recliner, and cover each eye with a slice. Breathe deeply, and relax until the coolness fades. Keep the moment going by replacing the cucumber eye pads with cool slices.

Take it even further with a cleansing and refreshing cucumber facial mask. Just blend a few leaves of fresh mint, add half of a cucumber (peeled and seeded), and purée these in a blender. Beat an egg white and fold it into the puréed cucumber mixture. Apply this mask evenly to your face and leave it on for 15 to 20 minutes. (If the doorbell rings, don't answer it.) Then rinse your face with cool water and pat it dry.

Whichever tactic you use, eat the other half of the cucumber, as it is known to have properties good for the intestinal tract and to be beneficial for rheumatic conditions. Just don't eat the last cucumber that your spouse planned on using for the dinner salad. (The stress of the ensuing tension will counteract the relaxing properties of your cucumber facial.)

Chapter 8 **Tools**

I'm self-reflecting.

Stress Relief for Administrators
A Self-Reflection

✔	**Stress-relieving Habit**

_____ I listen to calming or upbeat music on the way to school and in my office.

_____ I spend time with students daily.

_____ I find good ideas to help my teachers.

_____ I am involved in some activity that helps me grow in my profession.

_____ I am always reading a good, relaxing book.

_____ I actually do delegate—many times a week.

_____ I get outside a few times a week to work or play.

_____ I have good time-management habits.

_____ I have realistic expectations.

_____ I don't put off unpleasant, burdensome, or difficult tasks.

_____ I break big jobs into manageable tasks.

_____ I identify the positive characteristics of any situation.

_____ I communicate regularly with all staff members.

_____ I ask for feedback from my staff and genuinely listen to their concerns.

_____ I have regular relaxing habits—such as meditation, reading, gardening.

_____ I take regular breaks to get out of my office.

_____ I don't run away from problems.

_____ I do something every day to relax or nurture myself.

_____ I take note every day of what I like about my job.

_____ I spend time with friends outside of work.

_____ I visit with, share with, and learn from other administrator colleagues.

_____ I am fairly good at leaving my stress at work.

Relax and Rejuvenate Your Staff

1.
Fun Event Plan

Administrators and teachers put their names in a hat. Draw two names from a hat to envision and plan a "fun event." This event can include whole families or be adults only! Planners select a time and post a flier. (No one is pressured to attend!) This helps to build relationships and deepen bonds by giving staff members time to get together in a nonstress, nonwork environment.

2.
Walking-in-Your-Shoes Switch

Switch positions for the day! Put the administrators' and teachers' names in a basket. (Split the grade levels into two baskets, so teachers will either move at least two grades up or down). Have each person select a name from the basket and switch places with that person for a full or half day. This has several effects: You learn about other workers' jobs; you find that life is not necessarily easier in someone else's shoes; you appreciate your own position; and you appreciate what others do.

3.
Weekly Workout Buddies

Teachers meet in the school's gym, either before school or after school, for a "teacher 30-minute workout." If the gym is in use, then move some desks to the side in a large classroom. Windows should be covered for privacy. There's no need to get a trainer; just roll in the TV with everyone's favorite upbeat exercise DVD. As we all know, exercise is the best stress reliever. Teachers who work out three times a week not only feel better mentally, but also notice physical results quickly.

4.
Play Together

Working out together is one way to share the stress-relieving benefits of exercise. Many kinds of sports activities can do the same. Play volleyball, kickball, or basketball together. Have some events that fit all ages and levels of fitness. Creative relay races, Ping Pong games, or badminton tournaments can all be adapted to a varied group. Plan a physical activity several times a year. Or even better, set up a schedule of regular times to play together.

5.
Intentionally Relax Together

At the least, plan a brief relaxing activity to start each meeting or other time the staff gathers together. Use a deep-breathing or stretching activity, or borrow a simple yoga technique. Even better—find a way to schedule a yoga class that is available after school for all staff—at least once a week. Make sure YOU participate.

Student Stress Relievers

Tips for Cutting Classroom Stress

1. Teach time-management skills to your students.

Students have plenty of stress, too. You can help them avoid some of it by providing good time-management and organizational tools for students. Give them and show them how to use such things as calendars, timetables, schedules, and assignment notebooks. Teach them study techniques. Show them how to break tasks into smaller, manageable chunks. PRACTICE time management in the classroom.

2. Help them prepare for tests.

Tests are WAY stressful for students! Give them good study guides for tests. Review with them. Teach them good test-taking and test-prep skills.

3. Build a relaxing environment.

Make sure your classroom is a place where students feel safe and calm. Play soothing music. Pay attention to scents and colors that help to de-stress. Allow time for transitions. Don't yell or threaten. Have things well planned so that students don't pick up frenzy from you.

4. MOVE!

Do something physical several times a day. Get students out of their seats. Change locations. Plan learning activities that require them to move. Stand up and stretch. Take a walk outside. Don't ever keep students sitting still all day. (This won't work anyway!)

5. Take time to relax. Teach them techniques.

Do deep-breathing or stretching techniques as a class. Build your own repertoire of tricks that get the whole class to consciously unwind. Plan time for games and puzzles such as crossword puzzles, card games, memory games, Sudoku puzzles, Rubik's Cube, darts (the Velcro kind), and other classroom-appropriate games.

6. LAUGH!

Include lots of humor in your learning activities and classroom life. Laughter is an automatic stress reliever.

7. TALK!

Give students time to talk. Make discussion a part of your learning events. Trying to keep quiet all the time is very stressful for students. Social interaction is critical to good learning and healthy development.

Share the Hugs

Ideas for Keeping a Positive, Nurturing Environment

Try these ideas. Then add your own to the list.

"I Notice You" Notes

Write a positive note to a few staff members every day. If possible, make each note pertinent to something you have observed or some encouragement you know the person needs that day. This helps the staff member feel "seen" and appreciated by you—and can make a great difference in his or her day!

Surprise Treats

Even adults love treats. Make sure you put some in your employees' mailboxes periodically. Show that you really know and care about individuals by personalizing the treats. (For example: If someone loves chocolate—make theirs chocolate. If someone is diabetic or dieting, make theirs nonsugary. Know your staff members! And, by the way, use healthy treats as often as possible. You can also bring a treat to the faculty lounge or custodial lounge now and then.

Monthly Potluck Lunches

Plan a monthly potluck lunch. Plan to provide a main dish and post a sign-up sheet in the lounge for other items. Select a theme and decorate the lounge to make it fun and inviting. When people love certain dishes, collect recipes and get a volunteer to put them into a "Staff Favorites Recipe Book." You can even sell these to raise funds for new equipment or some other need!

"We Support You" Bear

Get a wonderful new, huggable stuffed bear. Pay attention to the moods and stresses of the day. When a staff member has a bad day (has a confrontation with a parent or student, has to report a child abuse issue, feels sad about a student's situation, and so on), the bear appears in his or her room. Nothing needs to be said. The bear is there to show support from everyone. When others see the bear in that person's room, then they can offer their support or just give a pat on the back. The bear moves to the next recipient as needed. Try to see that the bear makes it all around the school building by the end of the year. (Sanitize the bear as necessary.)

Staff Meetings that Build Relationships

A single arrow is easily broken, but not ten in a bundle.
-Japanese proverb

Surprise and de-stress your staff! Make each staff meeting a place where something happens that builds community and lightens burdens. Try some of these ideas. Once you start this habit, you'll think of other techniques.

How well do we really know each other?

Each staff member writes three things about themselves on an index card. (Two are real facts and one is a false statement.) Each person reads a card out loud. The group tries to guess which statement is false.

What do we have in common?

Split into groups of three or four and brainstorm characteristics that all the members share. (Do not list anything that has to do with teaching.) Focus on talents, hobbies, families, passions, and common interests. After a set amount of time, the groups will reunite to share their lists, paying particular attention to the commonalities in each.

How can we help teammates avoid problems/crises?

Before the meeting, choose small items that can be used to represent problems or crises that may occur within the school community. Mark Start and Finish lines on opposite sides of the room and place the items on the floor. Divide into three groups and blindfold a member from each group. The teams will then attempt to talk their blindfolded member across the room from Start to Finish. Each object kicked or stepped on counts as one point against the team; the team with the fewest points wins. After the game, talk about the objects and what they represent. Brainstorm ideas for avoiding these problems in the school.

Our school needs me because . . .

Often teachers and administrators do not toot their own horns about their talents, efforts, or contributions to the school. In this activity, teachers have two minutes to "sell" themselves to the group. Give a couple of staff members the chance to do this at each meeting. If "selling themselves" seems too uncomfortable, switch the activity to "Our School Needs YOU Because . . . ." One staff member prepares a sales pitch about another staff member!

Building a School Together

Break into groups of four or five people. Give a stack of newspapers and a roll of masking tape to each group. The task is to build a model school, using only the supplies provided. Set a time limit for planning and another for construction. During the construction phase, NO ONE CAN TALK! After the time is up, discuss what was learned from the process.

Whose Life is It Anyway?

Provide paper and a pen for each staff member. Set a time limit. Each person is asked to write an account of a true (or mostly true) personal experience. (Note: the crazier the story—the better!) All papers are folded, labeled, and placed in a basket. A facilitator draws four stories at random and reads the names of the writers aloud. Then the stories are mixed up and read to the group. The object is to guess which story matches up with which person.

Warm-Up Games

Prepare tables with board games, short puzzles, or card games. Choose games with rounds that can be completed quickly. When staff members arrive, set them in groups to play the games or finish the puzzles. This gives everyone a chance to unwind, talk, and laugh—without the pressure of anything work related!

Warm-Up Jokes

Successful meetings end with hearty laughter! Encourage staff members to contribute favorite jokes, and save their contributions in a box or basket. Have a different staff member choose and read a joke to end each meeting.

* Make sure YOU (the administrator) participate in every activity!

Make the Teachers' Lounge an Oasis

Change your teachers' lounge into a "stress-free" zone. Use ideas such as these to make the transformation:

Teachers' Lounge
Stress-free
Gossip-free
Positive-Words-and-Thoughts-only
ZONE

1. On the door, post a sign something like the one shown here.

2. Discuss with your staff the importance of using positive words and positive thoughts. Research shows that negative words and negative thoughts take away energy. Positivity energizes and contributes to health.

3. Do your best to make the lounge a gossip-free zone. Model this yourself.

4. The lounge should be a peaceful area not a work area. Move all work equipment into another area.

5. Paint the lounge a warm color. Take a staff vote to choose the perfect color. Blues and greens are relaxing.

6. Take out the worn furniture and replace with comfortable chairs and couches. If your lounge is small, use smaller chairs (and no couch).

7. Ask or beg your parent-teacher organization for a wall-mounted flat-screen television.

8. Mount pieces of art on the walls (no school posters) to create a homelike atmosphere.

9. Decorate any eating area with a warm tablecloth and flower arrangement. Make it relaxing and elegant.

10. Introduce a pleasant smell. Lavender is relaxing. Peppermint is invigorating. Or, try the scented air-fresheners in a vanilla or ocean scent.

11. Have a CD player available for some relaxing music.

12. If there is enough room, you can add any of these stress-relieving activities: a card table and chairs with a 500-piece jigsaw puzzle, a foosball or air-hockey table, or a knitting (needlepoint/crochet) area.

Resources

CHAPTER 1 RESOURCES _____

Works Cited

p. 10   Smith, A. et al., (2000). *The scale of occupational stress: further analysis of the impact of demographic factors and type of job* (2000). Centre for Occupational and Health Psychology, 2000. Sudbury, UK: HSE Books.

p. 12   Brantley, J. (2003). *Calming your anxious mind.* Oakland: New Harbinger Publications.

p. 12   Chichester, B. & Garfinkel, P. (1997). *Stress blasters.* Emmaus, PA: Rodale Press.

p. 12   Davidson, J. (2003). *The anxiety book.* New York, NY: Riverhead Books.

p. 19   Creagan, E. T. (2009). Positive thinking: Practice this stress management skill. *Mayo Clinic,* April, 2009. http://www.mayoclinic.com/health/positive-thinking/SR00009.

p. 21   Rotherman, A. (2004). Opportunity and responsibility for national board certified teachers. *Progressive Policy Institute*, March 2004. http://www.ppionlin.org/.

p. 23   Wong, H. K. & Wong, R. T. (1991). *The first days of school: How to be an effective teacher.* Sunnyvale, CA: Harry K. Wong Publications.

p. 23   National Education Association (2003). *Status of the American public school teacher 2000-2001.* Washington, D.C.: NEA.

p. 23   Harrell, K. (2003). *Attitude is everything: 10 life-changing steps to turning attitude into action.* New York, NY: HarperCollins.

p. 23   Davis, M., Eshelman, E. R., & McKay, M. (2000). *The relaxation and stress reduction workbook.* Oakland, CA: New Harbinger Publications.

p. 23   Canter, L. (1994). *The high-performing teacher: Avoiding burnout and increasing your motivation.* Santa Monica, CA: Lee Canter & Associates.

Other Recommended Resources

Cosgrove, J. (2001). *Breakdown: The facts about teacher stress.* London, UK: Routeledge.

Queen, J. A. & Queen, P. S. (2003). *The frazzled teacher's wellness plan.* Thousand Oaks, CA: Corwin Press.

Schindelheim, F. (2004). *Relieving classroom stress: A teacher's survival guide.* AuthorHouse (Online Self-Publishing Service).

Singer, J. N. (2009). *The teacher's ultimate stress mastery guide: 77 proven prescriptions to build your resilience.* Thousand Oaks, CA: Corwin Press.

Web Information to Investigate

Websites and the information on them change frequently. Always check a web address and examine the content before using the information or before recommending the site to anyone else.

Top 10 most stressful professions; Work stresses and colleague irritation.
http://www.jobbankusa.com/news/business_human_resources/top_10_most_stressful_professions.html.

Study links preschool teachers' stress to student expulsions.
http://articles.latimes.com/2008/jan/11/local/me-expulsions11.

Coping with stress in the special education classroom: Can individual teachers more effectively manage stress? http://www.ericdigests.org/1998-2/coping.html.

CHAPTER 2 RESOURCES

Works Cited

p. 36   Fuchs, L.S., & Fuchs, D. (1986). Effects of systematic formative evaluation: A meta-analysis. *Exceptional Children, 53,* 199-208.

p. 43   21st Century Fluency Project (2009). Understanding the digital generation. *The Committed Sardine.* http:// www.committedsardine.com/perspectives/UDG_Perspective.pdf.

Other Recommended Resources

Collins, A., & Halverson, R. (2009). *Rethinking education in the age of technology: The digital revolution and schooling in America.* New York, NY: Teachers College Press.

Doidge, N. (2008). *The brain that changes itself.* New York, NY: Penguin.

Johnson, S. (2006). *Everything bad is good for you: How today's popular culture is actually making us smarter.* (2006). New York, NY: Riverhead Trade.

Prensky, M. (2010). *Teaching digital natives: Partnering for real learning.* Thousand Oaks, CA: Corwin Press.

Prensky, M. (2005). *Don't bother me mom—I'm learning: How computer and video games are preparing kids for learning.* New York, NY: Paragon House.

Prensky, M. (2001). *Digital game-based learning.* New York, NY: McGraw-Hill.

Rosen, L. D. (2010). *Rewired: Understanding the I-generation and the way they learn.* Hampshire, UK: Palgrave Macmillan.

Small, G., & Vorgon, G. *iBrain (2008).* New York, NY: William Morrow.

Tapscott, D. (2010). *Born Digital: Understanding the First Generation of Digital Natives.* New York, NY: Basic Books.

Tapscott, D. (2008). *Grown up digital: How the net generation is changing your world.* Columbus, OH: McGraw-Hill.

Web Information to Investigate

Websites and the information on them change frequently. Always check a web address and examine the content before using the information or before recommending the site to anyone else.

Blogging basics: Creating student journals on the web.
http://www.educationworld.com/a_tech/techtorial/techtorial037print.shtml.

SPeNSE: Study of personnel needs in special education: Final report of the paperwork substudy. March, 2003. http://www.spense.org/Results.html.

Get your students blogging. http://www.21classes.com.

21st century fluency project. http://www.21stcenturyfluency.com/.

Rubrics for teachers. http://www.rubrics4teachers.com.

Sites to see: Podcasting. http://www.educationworld.com/a_tech/sites/sites074.shtml

CHAPTER 3 RESOURCES

Works Cited

p. 86   Epstein, J. (2008). Improving Family and Community Involvement in Secondary Schools. *The Education Digest, 73(6),* 9-12.

p. 86   Mattingly, D. J., Prislin, R., & McKenzie, T. L. (2002). Evaluating evaluations: The case of parent involvement programs. *Review of Educational Research, 72(4),* 549-576.

Other Recommended Resources

Applebaum, M. (2009). *How to handle hard-to-handle parents.* Westerville, OH: National Middle School Association.

Berger, E. H. (2007). *Parents as partners in education.* Upper Saddle River, NJ: Prentice Hall.

Bruzzese, J. (2009). *A parent's guide to the middle school years.* Westerville, OH: National Middle School Association.

Puckett, D. (2010). *Tips for surviving and thriving through the middle school years: A guide for parents and teachers.* Nashville, TN: Incentive Publications.

Vopat, J. (1998). *More than bake sales.* Portland, ME: Stenhouse Publishers.

Web Information to Investigate

Websites and the information on them change frequently. Always check a web address and examine the content before using the information or before recommending the site to anyone else.

Edutopia. http://www.edutopia.org.

National Coalition for Parent Involvement in Education. http://www.ncpie.org.

National Parent Teacher Association. http://www.pta.org.

Parent newsletter templates. http://www.education-world.com/a_admin/newsletter/templates/index.shtml.

Parent involvement. http://www.partnershipforlearning.org/category.asp?CategoryID=23.

Parent involvement activities in school improvement plans. http://educationnorthwest.org/resource/254.

Resources for parents. www.onetoughjob.org.

School, community, and family partnerships. http://knowledgeloom.org/sfcp/index.jsp.

School newsletter template.
http://office.microsoft.com/en-us/templates/TC010182551033.aspx?WT.mc_id=42.

CHAPTER 4 RESOURCES

Works Cited

p. 105 Ginott, H.G. (1993). *Teacher and child*. New York, NY: Collier Books MacMillan Publishing Company.

p. 107 Ginott, H. G. (1993).

p. 114 Merton, R. K. (1968). *Social theory and social structure*. New York, NY: Free Press, p. 477.

p. 114–115 Rosenthal, R. & Jacobson, L. (1968, updated 1992). *Pygmalion in the classroom: Teacher expectation and pupils' intellectual development*. Carmarthen, UK: Crown House Publishing.

Other Recommended Resources

Berckemeyer, J. (2009). *Managing the madness*. Westerville, OH: National Middle School Association.

Cushman, K. & Delpit, L. (2005). *Fires in the bathroom: Advice for teachers from high school students*. New York, NY: New Press.

Cushman, K. & Rogers, L. (2009) *Fires in the middle school bathroom: Advice for teachers from middle schoolers*. New York, NY: New Press.

Ginott, H.G., Ginott, A., & Goddard, H. W. (2003). *Between parent and child*. New York, NY: Three Rivers Press.

Marzano, R. J., Marzano, J. S., & Pickering, D. J. (2003) *Classroom management that works: Research-based strategies for every teacher*. Alexandria, VA: Association for Supervision and Curriculum Development.

Thompson, J. G. (2010). *Discipline survival guide for the secondary teacher*. San Francisco, CA: Jossey-Bass.

Web Information to Investigate

Websites and the information on them change frequently. Always check a web address and examine the content before using the information or before recommending the site to anyone else.

Classroom management. http://www.nea.org/tools/ClassroomManagement.html.

CHAPTER 5 RESOURCES

Works Cited

p. 139–140 Teacher mentoring program gets rave reviews and results. *Press Release: Office of the Governor, State of Alabama, September 8, 2008.* http://www.governorpress.alabama.gov/pr/pr-2008-09-08-01-mentoringprogramreviews-video. asp.

p. 140 Does mentoring reduce turnover and improve skills of new employees: Evidence from teachers in New York City. *National Bureau of Economic Research Working Paper No.13868.* http://www.nber.org/digest/aug08/w13868.html.

Other Recommended Resources

Newman, S. (2005). *The book of no: 250 ways to say it.* Columbus, OH: McGraw Hill.

Ninday, D., et al. (2009). *Mentoring beginning teachers (second edition).* Portland, ME: Stenhouse Publishers.

Web Information to Investigate

Websites and the information on them change frequently. Always check a web address and examine the content before using the information or before recommending the site to anyone else.

Resources for mentoring. http://www.teachermentors.com.

Some teacher mentoring resources. http://www.middleweb.com/mentoring.html.

CHAPTER 6 RESOURCES

Works Cited

pp. 160–169 U.S. Government (2004). Building the legacy: IDEA 2004. *The individuals with disabilities act.* 2004. http://idea.ed.gov.

p. 162 U.S. Department of Education (2009). Protecting students with disabilities: Frequently asked questions about Section 504 and the education of children with disabilities. (Section 504 of the Rehabilitation Act of 1973). *Office for Civil Rights.* http://www.ed.gov/about/offices/list/ocr/504faq.html.

p. 168 U.S. Department of Education (2010). *Family educational rights and privacy act (FERPA).* http://www2.ed.gov/policy/gen/guid/fpco/ferpa/index.html.

p. 168 ASK Family Resource Center (2008). 6 principles of IDEA (handout). http://www.askresource.org/publications.html#idea.

pp. 174, 175 Rose, C. (1987). *Accelerated learning.* Accelerated Learning by Colin Rose. New York, NY: Dell Publishing Company, 1987.

Other Recommended Resources

Quinn, P. O. (2000). *50 activities and games for kids with ADHD.* Washington, D. C.: Magination Press.

Learn To Love Teaching Again

Web Information to Investigate:

Websites and the information on them change frequently. Always check a web address and examine the content before using the information or before recommending the site to anyone else.

Assistance to states for the education of children with disabilities and preschool grants for children with disabilities: final rule. http://idea.ed.gov/download/finalregulations.pdf.

Title IX, part E uniform provisions, subpart 1—private schools. www.ed.gov/policy/elsec/guid/equitableserguidance.doc.

FERPA Section-by-Section Analysis. Special Education & Rehabilitative Services. http://www.ed.gov/policy/gen/guid/fpco/pdf/ht12-17-08-att.pdf.

National Dissemination Center for Children with Disabilities. http://www.nichcy.org.

Teaching students with autism. http://www.ericdigests.org/2000-3/autism.htm.

Autism in the classroom: Practical techniques of teaching. http://autistic-students.suite101.com/article.cfm/autism_in_the_classroom.

Teaching students who are deaf-blind. http://www.netac.rit.edu/downloads/TPSHT_Deaf_Blind.pdf.

New teaching methods for deaf children. http://www.amitynewsletter.org/index.php?storyID=192.

Methods for teaching deaf children to read. http://www.deafchildrenandsigning.com/methods-for-teaching-deaf-children-to-read.html.

Teacher tips for children with emotional disturbances. http://www.twu.edu/inspire/Fact_Sheets/emotional.htm.

Teaching students with emotional & behavioral disorders. http://www.geocities.com/whitt2_1999/sped6706ch4.html?20052.

Strategies for teaching students with hearing impairments. http://www.as.wvu.edu/~scidis/hearing.html.

Teaching hearing-impaired children in mainstream classrooms. http://www.associatedcontent.com/article/628673/teaching_hearingimpaired_children_in.html.

A gentle teaching approach for mentally retarded students. http://specialed.about.com/od/devdelay/mentally_disabled.html.

Severe and/or multiple disabilities. http://www.nichcy.org/Disabilities/Specific/Pages/SevereandorMultipleDisabilities.aspx.

Multiple disabilities: Characteristics and background information. http://specialed.about.com/od/multipledisabilities/a/multiple.html.

Strategies for teaching students with motor/orthopedic impairments. http://www.as.wvu.edu/~scidis/motor.html.

Other health impairment. http://arksped.k12.ar.us/documents/policy/rulesandregulations/H1.pdf.

Strategies for dealing with ADD in the classroom. http://www.kidsource.com/feingold/add.strategies.html.

Strategies for teaching youth with ADD and ADHD. http://www.ldonline.org/article/1370.

Smart tools: What is LD? http://www.smartschools.ph/SmartSchools/SmartTools/TeachingStudentsWithLD.htm.

Learning disabilities: Signs, symptoms, and strategies.
http://www.ldanatl.org/aboutld/teachers/understanding/ld.asp.

Types of learning disabilities. http://www.ldanatl.org/aboutld/teachers/understanding/types.asp.

Teaching methods for dyslexic children. http://www.dyslexia-teacher.com/t6.html.

Teaching students with dyslexia in the regular classroom.
http://findarticles.com/p/articles/mi_qa3614/is_199610/ai_n8753702.

Accommodations and modifications for students with handwriting problems and/or dysgraphia.
http://www.resourceroom.net/readspell/dysgraphia.asp.

Strategies for teaching students with communication disorders.
ttp://www.as.wvu.edu/~scidis/text/comm.html.

Understanding and teaching students with traumatic brain injury. http://www.fldoe.org/ese/pdf/trauma.pdf.

Teaching students with traumatic brain injury. http://www.jjc.cc.il.us/StAR/PDFs/brainInjury.pdf.

Strategies for teaching students with vision impairments. http://www.as.wvu.edu/~scidis/vision.html.

Educating students with visual impairments. http://www.hoagiesgifted.org/eric/e653.html.

Learning style survey. http://www.longleaf.net/learningstyle.html.

What is your learning style? http://www.ldpride.net/learning-style-test.html.

Do you know your middle schooler's learning style?
http://www.scholastic.com/familymatters/parentguides/middleschool/quiz_learningstyles/index.htm.

Personal learning styles inventory. http://www.howtolearn.com/lsioptin_student.html.

CHAPTER 7 RESOURCES

Works Cited

p. 197   Signs of the Times (2003). Deep sea marathon runner.
hww.signsofthetimes.org.au/archives/2003/october/ourtimes.shtm

p. 204   U.S. Government (2001). PL 107-110: The no child left behind act of 2001. *U.S. Department of Education.* http://www2.ed.gov/policy/elsec/leg/esea02/index.html

p. 204   Fertig, B. (2010). Teachers' union sues to halt release of teacher evaluations. *WNYC News, October 10, 2010.* http://www.wnyc.org/articles/wnyc-news/2010/oct/20/union-sues-stop-release-teacher-evaluations.

p. 204   Felch, J., Song, J., & Smith, D. (2010). Who's teaching L.A.'s kids? *Los Angeles Times, August 14, 2010.* http://www.latimes.com/news/local/la-me-teachers-value-20100815,0,2695044.story.

p. 204   Lawin, T. (2010). School chief dismisses 241 teachers in Washington. *New York Times, July 23, 2010.* http://www.nytimes.com/2010/07/24/education/24teachers.html.

Other Recommended Resources

Caine, R. M., et al. (2009). *12 Brain/mind learning principles in action: Developing executive functions of the human brain.* Thousand Oaks: CA: Corwin Press.

Campbell, K. et al. (2009). *The Nuts and Bolts of Active Learning.* Nashville, TN: Incentive Publications.

Cushman, K. (2010). *Fires in the mind: What kids can tell us about motivation and mastery.* San Francisco, CA: Jossey-Bass.

Hale, J. A. (2007). *A guide to curriculum mapping.* Thousand Oaks: CA: Corwin Press.

Pogrow, S. (2010). *Teaching content outrageously. How to captivate all students and accelerate learning.* San Francisco, CA: Jossey-Bass.

Silver, D (2005). *Drumming to the beat of different marchers.* Nashville, TN: Incentive Publications.

Springer, M. (2010). *Brain-based teaching in a digital age.* Alexandria, VA: Association for Supervision and Curriculum Development.

Wiggins, G. & McTighe, J. (2005). *Understanding by design, expanded 2nd edition.* New York, NY: Prentice Hall.

Web Information to Investigate

Websites and the information on them change frequently. Always check a web address and examine the content before using the information or before recommending the site to anyone else.

Jeopardy generator. http://www.coderedsupport.com/jeopardy.

Who wants to be a millionaire generator. http://www.coderedsupport.com/millionaire.

Maze generator. http://www.billsgames.com/mazegenerator.

Bingo generator. http://www.teach-nology.com/web_tools/materials/bingo.

Crossword generator. http://puzzlemaker.discoveryeducation.com/CrissCrossSetupForm.asp.

Sudoku generator. http://www.edhelper.com/sudoku.htm.

Powerpoint presentations in all subjects. http://www.pppst.com/index.html.

Virtual field trips: http://www.theteachersguide.com/virtualtours.html.

CHAPTER 8 RESOURCES_____

Works Cited

p. 218   NAESP (1998). Is there a shortage of qualified candidates for openings in the principalship? *National Association of Elementary School Principals.* http://www.naesp.org/misc/shortage.htm.

p. 218   Guterman, J. (2007). Where have all the principals gone?: The acute school-leader shortage. *Edutopia.* http://www.edutopia.org/principal-shortage?page=1.

p. 224   Richards, J. (May/Jun 2007). Emotional intelligence: Key to leadership success. *Principal Magazine. Web Exclusive 86 (5).* Accessed from http://www.naesp.org/ContentLoad.do?contentId=2236.

Richards, J. (2005). Principal Actions Key to Retaining Teachers. *Education World.* http://www.educationworld.com/a_issues/chat/chat158.shtml.

Richards, J. (Jan/Feb, 2007). How effective principals encourage their teachers. *Principal Magazine, 86 (3),* p. 48-50.

p. 224   Ingersoll, J. Teacher turnover and teacher shortages: An organizational analysis. *American Educational Research Journal, Fall 2001, 38 (3),* p. 499–534.

p. 224   John B Craig, J. B. (2008). The relationship between the emotional intelligence of the principal and teacher job satisfaction. Dissertations available from ProQuest, January 1, 2008. Paper AAI3310476. http://repository.upenn.edu/dissertations/AAI3310476.

p. 228   Northwest Regional Educational Laboratory (2003). *Building trusting relationships for school improvement: Implications for principals and teachers.* Portland, OR: NWREL.

p. 234   Moody, R. & Barrett, J. (2009). Stress levels of school administrators an teachers in November and January. *Empirical Research, 7 (2),* April 27, 2009.

Other Recommended Resources

Farber, K. (2010). *Why great teachers quit: And how we might stop the exodus.* Thousand Oaks, CA: Corwin Press.

Queen, J. A., & Queen, P. S. (2004). *The frazzled principal's wellness plan.* Thousand Oaks, CA: Corwin Press.

Web Information to Investigate

Websites and the information on them change frequently. Always check a web address and examine the content before using the information or before recommending the site to anyone else.

A principal's guide to stress relief. National Association of Elementary School Principals, *Leadership Compass 5 (2)* Fall, 2007. Retrieved from: http://www.naesp.org/leadership-compass-archives-0.

A survival guide for frazzled principals. *National Association of Elementary School* Principals. The 24-hour principal. November/December 2006. Retrieved from: http://www.naesp.org/24-hour-principal-novdec-2006-0.

Learn To Love Teaching Again